The Musician's Guide to Licensing Music

HOW TO GET YOUR MUSIC INTO FILM, TV,
ADVERTISING, DIGITAL MEDIA, AND BEYOND

DARREN WILSEY

with Daylle Deanna Schwartz

BILLBOARD BOOKS / *New York*

Copyright © 2010 by Darren Wilsey and Daylle Deanna Schwartz

Published in the United States by Billboard Books, an imprint of the Crown Publishing Group,
a division of Random House, Inc., New York.
www.crownpublishing.com

BILLBOARD is a registered trademark of Nielsen Business Media, Inc.

Library of Congress Cataloging-in-Publication Data

Wilsey, Darren.
  The musician's guide to licensing music: how to get your music into film, TV, advertising,
digital media, and beyond / Darren Wilsey with Daylle Deanna Schwartz.
    p. cm.
  Includes index.
  ISBN 978-0-8230-1487-3 (pbk.: alk. paper)
  1. Music trade–Vocational guidance. 2. Copyright–Music. 3. Copyright licenses.
I. Schwartz, Daylle Deanna. II. Title.
  ML3795.W496 2010
  346.7304'82–dc22
                          2009033870

Printed in the U.S.A.

Cover design by Kara Plikaitis

Text design by Nicole LaRoche

10   9   8   7   6   5   4   3   2   1

First Edition

This book is dedicated in loving memory of my
best friend and music mentor while growing up,

ROBERT "MUGSY" McMULLEN
(1964–2007),

and to my father,

TIMOTHY WILSEY
(April 6, 1951–April 6, 2009).

Contents

Introduction

The music industry has undergone dramatic changes in just a few years, especially for independent musicians. Getting signed to a record deal offers less potential to earn a living than ever. Talented musicians now seek other avenues for generating income streams. The most appealing one is getting music licensed, which can create a much better income than a record deal or touring. A record deal can offer a small advance and the artist may never see another dime. Touring can incur more expenses than an artist earns for a performance. So, music licensing appeals to most musicians. It provides up-and-coming artists (major label or independent) with solid opportunities.

Having worked as a TV and film composer, I've sat beside many editors, producers, and directors over the years and witnessed firsthand the various factors that influenced their decisions with regard to music selection. At times, their final choices were surprising, but never anything less than insightful.

There's no clear formula to getting music licensed since the process is highly subjective. The best thing I learned is what to avoid! I became a lot more proactive, learning the rules of the game and, to protect myself, becoming fluent with terminology related to placing songs on TV. I've dealt with scam artists and some fairly well-established companies that ripped me off or owe me a substantial sum of money for marketing my music. It's surprisingly difficult to track your music and know where or how it's being used. For example, I had no idea my song was featured on *Queer As Folk* until fans of the show e-mailed me, wondering where to purchase the song. At first I had no idea what they were talking about! It's a really small world, and my feeling is that those who are deceitful won't last long. There is (at most) one degree of separation in this facet of our business.

A common piece of advice that's frequently offered to songwriters is to "write what you know." This mantra also served as my guide and method for writing this book. Over the years I have worn many hats in the music business. Doing so opened my eyes to a fuller picture and helped me develop a better appreciation for the ways artists and various players in the industry interact and work together for the sake of doing business. Like many of you, I'd describe myself as being a musician first and foremost. However, this book isn't intended as an "us against them" manifesto or obsessed with conquering the "evil empire" known as the music industry. The truth, at least from my own experiences, is that to enjoy the satisfaction of having some degree of success, you eventually will need to embrace an "us *and* them" collaborative mentality.

Sure, it's possible to occasionally encounter people who'll try to take advantage of you, under the presumption that as an artist you're perhaps too desperate or uninformed to know any better or put up much of a protest. But it's not fair or true to assume that this is a given. I've known more than one artist who, for whatever reason, almost seem to enjoy portraying or succumbing to the role of victim within the context of an agreement they entered. After reviewing a copy of these agreements at their request, I found the terms of the agreement appeared to be more than fair.

Within the music marketplace, everyone—from artists to executives—has his own set of goals and legitimate concerns. What's important is to not only understand your own point of view, but where those with whom you're doing business are coming from as well. This is one of the perspectives I'd like to bring into the conversation as it pertains to music licensing. Taking the time to give some thoughtful and careful consideration to the other side's interests is worth the effort; people will often want to work with you when they realize you've taken their issues into account.

As a professional musician, you'll be selling a product, service, or both, and the ability to generate sales is what affords you the luxury of staying in business. For the purpose of this book, the main focus will be a business and marketplace that stems from the sale of granting permission to use audio content through licensing deals. This book also explores the possibility of creating opportunities for your work now, with the goal of being paid for it (and other opportunities that may result from your actions) later.

III

The Business of Music Licensing

Licensing music is the future of the music business and the future is now! The process always involves contracts and terminology that traditionally have been misunderstood by the people who stand to gain or lose the most—the artists. That's why it's important to grasp the details of how music licensing works. More and more songwriters are trying to license their music, which makes it much more competitive. Those with the most knowledge definitely have the best shot at getting the deals, as long as they also have high-quality music to offer. Let's start with the basics of licensing, to give you a sense of the world in which you'll be operating.

What Is Music Licensing?

For the most part, *music licensing* means that the owner of a song gives permission for part or all of this song to be used in a TV show, movie, commercial, or other format where music is played along with visuals. The process involves clearing rights to use a musical composition that either already exists or will be written and recorded for the opportunity at hand. It's common to have songs licensed with lyrics that support the story, or reinforce an idea, emotion, event, or action. In television, songs are most often licensed for "one time use" as part of a single-song licensing agreement. In such a case, the licensed song will appear in a single episode.

The person or party who authorizes permission to use a song based on those terms and conditions outlined within the final draft of the agreement is called the *licensor*. Other references to licensor could also include "owner," "artist," "representative," or "publisher." The person or party who seeks or is given permission to use a song is called the *licensee*. Other references to the notion of licensee may include "company," "director," "network," "producer," "filmmaker," or "studio."

The dollar amount that's agreed on for a given licensing fee can vary considerably—two different song licenses for the same episode or movie can command two completely different licensing fees. Each licensing opportunity, whether it's for television, film, advertising, video games, brand entertainment, or any other venue, has its own royalty structure and type of uses. There is no fixed payment standard. The project's budget largely determines the musician's compensation, although it helps to have strong negotiating skills as well.

When you get a record deal, the label will often control your music, which can limit how many income streams you can create. If you're independent and you paid for the recordings and/or equipment used to make a recording, you own the master recordings and publishing rights, and therefore the legal right and authority to license, lease, lend, or transfer these rights. When an entity interested in licensing your music learns that you own and control all of the various rights to your recordings (see Chapter 3 for a detailed discussion of rights), you become more appealing from their vantage point, especially if a deadline is tight. It creates the potential to greatly simplify the negotiation process from a licensing party's perspective, partly based on an assumption that clearance will be less of a hassle. If the situation starts to become a hassle, it cancels out this advantage.

Licensing agreements are usually nonexclusive in nature, so entering one doesn't restrict or limit the song's owners and publishers (who may be one and the same) from pursuing other licensing agreements in the future. Therefore, one good song can generate many licensing deals. A song licensing agreement doesn't involve the transfer of the ownership and copyright of the song itself to a licensing party. Instead, the license grants legal permission, referred to as *clearance*, to use and include some portion of a song within the context of another party's creative project. The terms of licensing can vary greatly from deal to deal.

It's possible, though less frequent, to encounter licensing offers that mandate one or more terms of exclusivity or limitation. One likely scenario is if a song is licensed for use in association with a product, brand, or advertisement campaign. The company may insist that the song can't be licensed for use in association with a similar product or promotion, especially that of a competitor, for a specified amount of time. These exclusive limitations often expire after a period of somewhere between one and seven years. Since entering this type of licensing deal limits the range of opportunities that can be pursued in the near future, the proposed fees will usually reflect this restriction, and will likely be significantly higher as a result. Licensing fees for these situations can range from $10,000 to $100,000 and up.

Benefits of Getting Music Licensed

While establishing contacts and landing music placements may take some time and effort, in the end, it can be very worth your while. Whether you're an artist whose ultimate goal is to advance your career by doing more live performances and selling CDs, or you're a songwriter who mainly wants to focus on creating music that can be licensed, if you're talented and understand the business, it can be very lucrative on many levels.

Up-and-coming artists, whether on major labels or independent ones, usually seek three things to advance their musical careers: more income; exposure; and credits for their press kit, which they can use to attract more income, exposure, and credits. Getting music licensed offers the potential for all three! There are many solid opportunities that go way beyond the fees you get from having your music in a film, TV show, commercial, or video. All of them can be very beneficial to building a solid career in music.

Money

It's always good to find as many revenue streams as possible to earn an income from your musical talent. Music licensing can be a big one! Financial gain can come from more than just one source. There are licensing fees, broadcast royalties, and in some cases, soundtrack album royalties, merchandise, and sheet music. One song licensed to a TV show can create an income stream from ASCAP (The American Society of Composers, Authors, and Publishers), BMI (Broadcast Music, Inc.), or SESAC (Society of European Stage Authors & Composers) royalties that can last for years if the show gets rerun or syndicated both here and overseas. Chapter 6 elaborates on all the different ways that money can be earned from licensing music.

Exposure

Meaningful national exposure has the potential to be even more valuable than up-front royalties because it can generate different income streams and career opportunities down the road. Having a song in a popular network show like *Grey's Anatomy*, or a pop culture hit like *The Hills*, can literally break an act. Many unsigned recording artists have become well known after one of their songs was heard in a TV commercial. Signed recording artists can energize their careers, like Moby did, by having songs in popular television commercials.

Getting your song onto a movie soundtrack can drive many fans to your site and to digital stores. Many unknown artists have had their careers launched when music lovers heard a song in a film, on a TV show, or woven into a TV commercial. Even if they don't know a song's title or its artist's name, potential fans will search the Internet and track the music down to buy it if they like what they heard. Artists say their sales on iTunes can soar from one song placement. Through increased visibility, licensing creates value that goes way beyond the licensing fees and royalties.

Publicity Value

Even if you don't get paid a lot or your music is used in a low-visibility project, your credibility expands when your songs are licensed by another entity. Bragging rights can be beneficial for marketing and getting press attention. When an unknown artist has songs licensed, especially in popular TV shows, films, video games, or advertising, it adds authority to an otherwise generic press kit.

Licensing Songs versus Composing Scores

People often confuse licensing songs with composing music scores. The traditional roles in film, TV, theater, and advertising that distinguish *songs* and *scores* as distinct categories may appear to be straightforward. However, the fine line between them continues to blur; songs can be composed for a specific project, and a film score recording can be licensed for use in a new and entirely different movie. Labeling a certain situation as being licensing versus composing is a matter of context rather than musical style.

Commissioned Scores

A *score* is most commonly a collection of instrumental compositions used in film and television. Unlike most commercial-sounding pop songs, a score (also referred to as *underscore*) is often based on orchestral instrumentation and takes advantage of all of the arrangement options this offers. But unlike classical music or more serious and academically inspired concert music, modern film scores frequently blend these traditional idioms with elements of pop, rock, electronic, or jazz music, and may include a splash of sound design layering for effect. The merging of these otherwise opposing musical flavors renders a sound that's synergistic, and is often described as having cinematic qualities. This sonic chemistry allows the music to support visual imagery.

A film or television score serves to accentuate moments of high drama, suspense, comedic relief, or romance. A composer often oversees the writing and recording of the score while the entire creative process is guided by varying amounts of input and suggestions from a director, producer, music supervisor, or all of the above. The amount of input, guidance, and involvement that's either offered or insisted upon varies considerably from project to project. Unlike a song licensing deal, the situation described here is for an employment arrangement, and requires a very different type of contract that clearly states when this employment begins and ends. It also clarifies the delivery deadlines, payment schedules, and the work-for-hire status (see Chapter 5) of the employment.

Providing a score can involve either terms of employment defined as being "work for hire" and transfer of copyright, or terms that are nonexclusive and similar to rights granted through the use of a blanket licensing agreement (which offers unrestricted access to a fixed amount of audio content for a specified amount of time). Large-scale films and some television shows have sizable production budgets and may opt to commission the score with the understanding that the publishing will be owned by the film studio, production company, or investors. This approach requires setting aside a percentage of the project's net funding into a music budget that is robust enough to cover:

- All recording and production costs associated with the score soundtrack for hiring studio musicians, sound stage rental, audio engineers, and technicians.

- A separate composer fee that's paid to the composer for performing specific creative services as part of the employment duty. As such, the terms of this employment are clearly defined and understood as being work for hire. This important clarification is what allows the employer, rather than the person who created the music, to obtain ownership of the copyright.

On the surface, these terms may sound unfair, but the composers who are willing to accept these jobs are paid quite handsomely for the sacrifice of giving up further rights to their work. That's why this type of arrangement usually just applies to big-budget productions. Yet the fastest growing categories in film and television production are low-budget, medium-budget, and independent productions. This includes the bulk of most reality TV shows, pilots, indie films, educational and historical documentaries, infomercials, and local and regional television commercials. Add to this an expanding number of outlets for both professional and amateur quality audiovisual content produced for online streaming, sale or distribution webcasts, Web series, and many others. Expansion in these production sectors is the result of:

- a dramatic reduction in production costs that were previously entry-level barriers
- an ongoing demand for new content fueled by emerging marketplaces and methods of distribution, sales, and broadcast

A lower budget production will probably not seek to commission an original score and obtain ownership rights. Under these circumstances, if a composer is hired, any fees that are paid will be considerably lower than the big-budget and high-profile work-for-hire gigs discussed earlier. How much less, you wonder? Remove a few zeros and divide by three!

Often, as a matter of necessity or the job requirement, by accepting a gig, the composer will likely assume some, if not all, of the burden related to score production costs. For filmmakers, using virtual instruments, notation and video editing software, various gadgets, and clever mixing tricks can dramatically reduce score production costs. When done properly, the resulting score excerpts can fool the majority of listeners into believing it sounds "real." While nothing can match the richness and beauty of a passionate and highly skilled human performance, sadly, in many instances, deadline- or budget-inspired approximations are often accepted as good enough.

The upside to this labor-intensive gig is that the composer will more than likely retain full ownership of whatever music and recordings get created in the process. The composer fee and accompanying composer agreement, in essence, grants the production company the same nonexclusive rights with regard to the score that would be expected in the case of a single-song licensing contract. In a sense, the composer fees in these situations amount to a blanket licensing fee covering the use of an entire score.

Commissioned Songs

Just as scores can be commissioned, so can songs. A specialized request of this nature can happen if there's a definitive need for a song that has a specific stylistic attribute or lyrical content and it isn't readily available anywhere else. The songs are usually prominently featured during opening or closing title credits or during a pivotal or high-profile moment. It's always the best situation to have someone specifically ask you to produce a custom-tailored song and even more ideal when this request is accompanied by a reassurance that the song you write, record, and deliver will almost certainly be used.

In addition to licensing fees for a commissioned song, there might also be a small production budget for working within a tight deadline or other inconvenient circumstances. If you receive a request of this nature today, chances are that the final mix will have to be delivered by tomorrow afternoon or soon after. The short deadlines that are common in these situations can significantly up the ante. Keep in mind that specialty requests may entail writing and producing a song that includes one or more uncommon or unusual elements. By accepting the offer, the burden of supplying them becomes yours.

A few years ago, I was asked to write a song for a commercial that had a 1980s new wave vibe. I was provided with some lyrics that couldn't be changed. It was a challenge. I had to find a great male vocalist who was also capable of correctly translating the lyrics into Spanish and singing them like a bona fide rock star. Furthermore, this person had to live in my neck of the woods in order to make the recording. Satisfying all of these requirements within the span of a day turned out to be a formidable challenge, but miraculously I was able to pull it together. If you want to get considered for these kinds of requests, you need to have a lot of contacts and resources for finding the right people and elements to make it work in a very short amount of time.

Recycled Score

There's also a growing trend toward licensing scores for reality TV shows, sports programming, documentaries, and video games. This involves the use of a preexisting recording that's usually a genre-specific instrumental underscore, which has become available for licensing, although it wasn't written or composed for the project at hand. The source might be a track from music library CDs or music that is now being marketed for new licensing opportunities, in spite of its having been initially written for another project, as long as it was done with nonexclusive terms.

The application of some thoughtful sound editing can create the impression that it's original. The licensing fees associated with clearing the rights to a score track may turn out to be less expensive than commissioning something original or providing an alternative when time constraints don't make hiring a composer a realistic option.

Soundtrack Albums

A film's *soundtrack* is the collective sum of all music cues that appear in the film or television show itself. Musically speaking, the soundtrack is everything that gets heard by the audience in a movie theater or on a TV or home entertainment system. A *soundtrack album* is a collection of songs that may or may not have appeared in the film's soundtrack. It's music associated with the film that's been packaged and sold in album form for the purpose of promoting it. Many of us have dealt with the frustrating experience of purchasing a soundtrack album, only to discover that a favorite song that was featured in the movie is nowhere to be found on the soundtrack album. But it's not uncommon to have songs included that weren't in the film. It usually means that the company releasing the soundtrack couldn't get the license to use the song or the parties who controlled it wanted too much money. If a deal can't be agreed on for a song to be in a soundtrack, it's replaced by another that fits.

Overseeing the release and distribution of a soundtrack album is an entirely separate process from that of obtaining master license clearances for recordings that appear in the film itself. Obtaining the necessary clearances for use in the film or TV series may require dealing with a long list of record companies, artists, and publishers. However, the process of releasing a soundtrack album usually involves one record company that oversees the album's release, marketing and promotion, administration, mechanical licenses, advances, and royalty payments for each song appearing on the soundtrack album.

Music Libraries and Production Music

Production music refers to genre-specific music collections that haven't been written for any particular program or film. It's usually provided by music libraries, which some may regard as being the musical equivalent of a stock photo library. People who need music content can pay for the right to use that music for their specific projects. It can be used one song at a time or in bulk. Libraries have become more popular and increased in number as budgets get tighter. They provide access to a larger variety of music for less money. Producers use library music when they need fillers and small pieces of music for a limited cost.

> *Production music is almost always used as background music (underscore), behind someone talking; big melodies and loud solos aren't used much, as they tend to interfere with dialogue. For example, ESPN uses tons of production music as background for all of its sports highlight shows, and it's mixed way in the background so you can clearly hear the "vocal talent."*
>
> STEVE SECHI, Composer, Producer, and
> Co-owner of two music libraries

The steps required for obtaining a well-known song for a film, video, or TV show can be a complicated process and is often both time-consuming and expensive. Music libraries can be much simpler, faster, and cheaper to get music from. The more frequent use of library music in part stems from the music library company's ability to offer a relatively affordable one-stop licensing option (more in Chapter 2), where both synchronization and master rights get cleared in tandem. Furthermore, entire CD sets or collections can be licensed in tandem under the terms of a blanket license agreement (more in Chapter 4).

Some directors attach a certain degree of stigma to production music, believing it to be generic sounding. But in recent years, the bar seems to have been raised much higher for the material music libraries provide.

Music libraries send out collections of music on CDs to those who might be able to use it. Many tend to specialize in one type of music. It could be Latin, hip-hop, drum & bass, romantic cues, or music appropriate for televised sporting events. While music libraries have mainly carried instrumentals, more and more are taking on full songs. It pays much less than licensing a song on your own but if you have music that gets used over and over in many productions on TV, your ASCAP, BMI, or SESAC royalties (more in Chapter 6) can provide a very nice regular income stream. If you love creating music and have your own home recording equipment, you might want to do some specifically to submit to music libraries.

> *I think that music libraries are a fantastic way to get your music in front of the right people. The quality of most libraries is much higher than people would expect and many supervisors, editors, and agency creatives turn to libraries when they need fast solutions, which is just about every day. But it's important that the deal that artists strike with the library company not infringe on other potential opportunities. My advice is to retain ownership of both the writer's and publisher's share of your music until a deal comes along that truly makes sense to give up those rights. Most song libraries [a collection of songs, featuring vocals, that are pitched for licensing opportunities] won't ask for ownership, but stock libraries [genre-specific collections of background instrumental music] always will. There are benefits to both; it just depends on how much you believe a song is worth.*
>
> ALEX MOULTON, Founder and creative
> force behind Expansion Team

Demand for Independent Music

The demand for musical content keeps increasing. But with this demand comes a decrease in the budgets to pay for music. That opens the doors wider for independent artists who want to license their music. Why would an entertainment project license independent music over that of a major-label artist? Two major factors drive more and more music supervisors and producers to search for good independent music for their projects: *money* and *time*. Major-label demands and red tape can make licensing from an independent artist much more palatable.

It may seem more likely that those who need music would want major-label artists who have recognizable names and music. But it's not easy to deal with the labels, which, in the end, determine whether to grant a master license based on what is being offered as the fee. The tricky part is that there are no standard rates, so a record company is not obligated to say yes to what they may deem to be a lowball offer. If a record company is accustomed to being offered fees in the range of $25,000 to $30,000 from production studios to license a master recording, agreeing to an indie filmmaker's offer of $1,000 would drive down that music's market value considerably in the future, once the word gets out. So they'd rather get nothing than take less than what they think they should get. That leaves the door open for independent music!

A major-label artist may nurture a relationship with a music supervisor and convince him to use one of her songs, only to see the deal thwarted when the label insists on much more money than the film's budget allows. Meanwhile the artist, who would have been happy with the fee offered, ends up with nothing, as the music supervisor looks elsewhere for music that's within his budget. Major-label artists can feel powerless about how their music is used, or not used at all, because of major-label fee policies.

On the flip side, independent artists are happy to license their music for less, since it still can be very profitable. Just as major labels need much larger sales than an independent label does, they also price their music much higher for licensing. So indie music can seem very appealing to someone who needs musical content and is on a tight budget. These days, most productions are looking to save money so independent music makes a better fit for any budget. In fact, most soundtracks for network television series and films released theatrically usually consist of a mixture of independent artists, major-label artists, and perhaps a bit of library music or original scoring scattered in between.

Music, which is usually put in near the end of production, is often needed fast. A project can take months or even years to complete filming. But, when it's done, the production company may have little time to add music. Large record companies are known to respond slowly to requests and if they discover upon review that a fee being offered is below the average of past requests, the production company may not even hear back from them! Requests for major-label music need to go through a lot of red tape to get clearance for a song's use. This could be a deal breaker for a project that needs music immediately. Since most independents own rights to their songs, they can work very fast and don't need to get a bunch of people to sign off on the agreement. If someone contacted you about licensing one of your songs, wouldn't you rush to accommodate them? That attracts more opportunities to get music licensed.

Indie artists can also bring a "coolness" factor to a project. If there's a lot of buzz around an artist online or through an independent tour, a music supervisor may pick up on that and see it as valuable for his project. So don't underestimate the worth of independent music for licensing. Opportunities are there for those who pursue them with high-quality music.

||||||||||||||||||||||||||||||||||||||||||||||||||||||||||||||||||||||||||||||||||||||||||||||||||||||||||||||||||

CHAPTER 2

Music Licensing Players

In order to get your music licensed, it's important to understand the roles of both sides of the licensing picture:

- The players who need musical content and provide opportunities to get your music licensed. They place music in a large assortment of projects, in different capacities that are discussed below.
- Those who represent people who create music and work to find licensing opportunities. If you're either uncomfortable or lack the resources to self-market effectively, there are people who might do it for you. I say might, because finding representation can be as hard as finding a record deal. No one has to work with you.

If your music is good, it can attract people who can facilitate the licensing process. This chapter explores the roles of each player and what options are available for working with professionals and services that offer additional pathways for getting music licensed. I'll discuss the roles and services typically provided by each of these players and also offer suggestions for spotting red flags to avoid.

Music Supervisors

Music supervisors play a pivotal role in the world of music licensing. When a project has one or more of them handling the music for it, they serve as intermediaries between those who supply music (e.g., bands, publishers, marketing services, attorneys) and those seeking to license it (e.g., filmmakers, directors, producers, production companies). Music supervisors oversee all aspects of acquiring music and making sure that all the legal components of licensing are in place. In addition to choosing music, a music supervisor wears many hats. He is the creative person who seeks and chooses the best music for a project, the administrator who handles all the paperwork, the safeguard for making sure all aspects of a song are clear, and the number juggler who tends to budgets that need stretching. The process includes:

- Making appropriate suggestions for all scenes that have been identified by a director and producer as needing music.
- Attending "spotting sessions" to map out the scenes that need music, for how long, and what type.
- Forwarding paperwork to entitled parties; collecting and filing signed copies.
- Addressing correspondence related to announcing music requests, screening submissions, and forwarding suitable matches to the director or editor.
- Making sure that all music is cleared, which means that whoever controls the copyright has given permission for the song's use and every part of the song has been checked to make sure that it's legal to include.

In short, music supervisors are responsible for locating, negotiating, clearing, doing the administration for, and delivering ready-to-go music that satisfies the musical requirements at hand. Music supervisors maintain collections of music that they put together from submissions and music they discover. Some will be on CDs, while some may consist of bookmarked links to individual artists' sites. If they get a CD or link to tracks they like but it's not right for a current project, they'll often add it to their collection. When supervising a project, most will first see if they have a track readily available, or have worked with someone who may have the right piece of music, before they further seek out music that fits their needs. "Quick" is an operative word for music licensing. When a project is on a tight deadline, music supervisors want music that they know is already cleared, preferably from people who they know can deliver it.

For a specific request for a song by a popular band or a classic hit, the music supervisor forwards a licensing request form to all of the entitled parties, including any publisher, record label, songwriters, or legal representative involved in licensing the song. These forms are not actual licenses, but rather, a precursory introduction and request to pursue entering a licensing agreement. A request form typically includes a basic overview of the project identifying its director, studio, airdate, network affiliation, theatrical release date, territories, and the distribution company. It also provides details about the intended use of the song, and the exact duration of its use in the soundtrack.

It's common to use only a portion of a song. But, if one is used for the opening of a film or TV show or as the end title credits are shown, a song might play out for its full duration (referred to as *feature use*). It may also be used in the background, such as playing on the radio as people have a conversation. For a song that normally includes vocals, a music supervisor may seek licensing for an instrumental version if one exists. It's her job to find this out.

Music supervisors must work within their budgets, and this obviously influences their licensing fees. Once a fee is offered, it can be accepted, rejected, or negotiated back and forth, up to a point. The parties are never obligated to accept an offer, and all must agree to the terms of the deal at hand for the song to remain in the final edit of the project for commercial release.

When there's a need for music, music supervisors often first turn to publishers, music production companies, boutique marketers, or licensing services with whom they already have done business successfully—they gravitate toward those that have a proven track record for delivering appropriate submissions that are both available and affordable (or at least negotiable). This can potentially save a lot of time. Music supervisors know that submissions forwarded from these companies are already precleared, since they have agreements in place with the songwriters and labels they represent. If these primary go-to music sources can't provide a solution, other options are explored. That's when you might have a chance to submit your music for their project.

Clearing Songs

A music supervisor must make sure that there's clearance for all the music she uses. This means getting the rights to use each piece of music in a project. The persons controlling the copyright can issue a license. Music supervisors are aware that squeaky-clean preclearance isn't necessarily guaranteed when dealing directly with a musician who might not understand all of the legal intricacies. This makes them hesitant to work with people they don't know well, which is understandable, considering the potential for headaches, liability, litigation, and huge expenses that could result from including a song that's not fully cleared and needs to be removed after being placed in a project.

> We had an artist that we had been working with for about a year. We got them two placements in the same week. We were told, and had paperwork verifying, that we were able to use 100 percent of the publishing and 100 percent of the master recording rights. And right at the last minute, after we had already signed the license and the song was already in the show, the music supervisor came back to us and said, "Hey, we looked at the song on the ASCAP database, and we see that there is a major publisher attached to the song. What's the deal with that?" So we went back to the writer, who told us that his cowriter had sold his publishing to a major publisher a couple of months before, but no one had notified us to tell us this was now the case. So we had to very quickly scramble and ask his new publisher not to create a fuss, and fortunately they were okay with it.
>
> KEATLY HALDEMAN, CEO, pigFACTORY

If a song needs to be replaced at the last minute due to improper clearance, the music supervisor has the challenge of locating and clearing a suitable substitute fast. This may seem simple on the surface, but at the very least, it may require rendering a new master edit, readjusting and producing a new sound mix, and disregarding or discontinuing the use of copies of the project that are already in circulation. At its worst, this could become a nightmare scenario. Independent filmmakers who are careless with these details sometimes pay a hefty price. One company lost its distribution deal because, upon further scrutiny, it became apparent that music featured in the film wasn't properly cleared. That's why clearing the music properly is as important as finding the perfect tracks.

Music·Editors

Music requests, submissions, screenings, and all the rest happen as the result of mapping out the spots in a project where the need for music still exists. The editor may place one or more pieces of music into the cut, that unlike temp music (see page 107), was done knowing that this music was also available, affordable, and is what immediately came to mind when first assembling the edit. This may all have happened before the first spotting session took place. Although it may sound like cutting out the music supervisor, this is a common occurrence and is most often interpreted by both as a courtesy that saves the music supervisor time since some projects require clearing many pieces of music without a moment to spare.

Most professional video editors have their own collections, too, that they can pull from right away. If you have an opportunity to get to know a music editor, it helps to develop even a casual relationship. If he likes your music a lot, it can go into his collection and might be forwarded to the music supervisor as well.

Music Production Houses

People at music production companies create music used in advertising and other media outlets. Often they're hired by advertising agencies to put the music together for a commercial. Like music supervisors, they often work with the same people consistently but they are open to finding new sources of good music. These producers tend to need more instrumental music but the trend has been going more to licensing songs. Once you develop a relationship with one of them, they may call on you regularly for music. A company may house only one producer, or be comprised of teams with several. In addition, most have a list of freelancers who are on call for specialty gigs or are well qualified for producing music in specific musical genres.

AMP (Association of Music Producers; www.ampnow.com) represents many of the music houses that do a majority of music for advertising houses. Their website has a page with contact info for all their members; URLs are included if the production house has one. Many will talk to you if you call and would listen to music you send for consideration for future needs.

Getting Representation versus Self-Representation

For music creators who lack time or other resources to self-market music effectively for licensing opportunities or are uncomfortable doing it, there are professionals and services that can do it for you. These players represent additional pathways for getting music licensed. *You* control both the master and synchronization rights (see Chapter 3) until you formally sell or assign these rights to another party who agrees to pursue, negotiate, and/or enter deals on your behalf. Opting for this type of arrangement can bring good results if you're represented by a person or company that's already familiar with the subtleties, jargon, and type of arrangements that accompany the provisions in most licensing deals. Someone who is in the business of marketing music should have industry contacts and a system for conducting business already in place and be professionally equipped to handle any issues and responsibilities that are a normal part of doing business. Pitching music is a full-time job!

While you can license on your own, the process of successfully finding and securing music placements can be very challenging. Time is a constraint for everyone. Although it's possible to pitch your own music, doing it effectively in the long run can be inefficient. The hours spent marketing is time not spent developing your art. Both are full-time jobs. My best results came from forming a network where the work and benefits are shared among many team players. People who need music prefer to get it from reputable people than from an unknown artist. A representative provides peace of mind since they only pitch music that's cleared. Solid representation can get your music moved up the screening priority stack. When there's an established relationship between the party making the request and your representative, your music will at least get heard. If a request generates hundreds of submissions, not all get listened to. Since time is a factor, music that fits the bill and gets heard first often snares the offer.

When is the right time to seek representation? A good piece of advice that I heard was, "Do as much on your own as you can, while you can." I'm a strong proponent of this approach. Do it yourself until the time required for addressing an endless to-do list becomes self-defeating, leaving insufficient time for creating your music and refining your craft. The more you accomplish on your own, the more you can offer a potential representative. The more licensing credits or contacts you have, the more likely someone will want to work with you. No one has to represent you. Competition is stiff. While the quality of the music is the biggest factor, the legwork you put in before approaching someone can only improve your chance of getting someone good.

If you're new to the business and handle the contracts and negotiations without the benefit of professional representation, your correspondence and discussions with them may turn a licensee off. Because they're so busy, there can quickly come a point when dealing with you directly is burdensome or a hassle. This creates the potential to both jeopardize the opportunity at hand and ruin future prospects. Whoever oversees the licensing process and handles your correspondence and negotiations needs to conduct business in a way that's professional and levelheaded. Other requirements include good communication skills, a knack for business negotiation, and the ability to read cues given by others. Call it mastery of the art of the deal, shrewd business instinct, or a talent for calling bluffs. If these skills are not your forte, keep your eye out for representation once you have some credits.

When a contract is signed and approved, the one who negotiates the terms of the deal on your behalf is in effect your spokesperson. His manner and presentation skills can have a huge impact on the outcome of a given situation, good or bad. Should the negotiating party create an impression of being unreasonably difficult, unethical, or dishonest, it's ultimately to your detriment. Pay attention to how you like dealing with him. If he turns you off, it may be a sign to look further.

I want anyone who represents me to be organized and professional. For example, when representatives forward payments, they should be accompanied by any important documentation, such as copies of TV or film cue sheets (see Chapter 6) or a contract, which are frequently omitted. When I send them checks, such as royalties for deals they brokered, I return the favor by including copies of any relevant documents.

It's important to try and find representation with stamina—people who are in it for the long haul. A career in music can be like riding a seesaw. There may be periods of radar silence and then quickly and often unexpectedly the quiet is interrupted by an urgent request for music immediately. Trust in your representative is imperative.

It can be very exciting, especially early in your career, if someone expresses interest in your music and offers to help market it. Knowing that a potential representative is willing to commit time and work to further your career can be so intoxicating that it blindsides you to some red flags that might be more easily spotted by those with more business experience. Without question, the right representation can do wonders for an artist's career; doors open that may not otherwise. But, the key is finding the *right* person or company to market your music. Temper your excitement and pay attention! Some music producers exaggerate their credits, industry contacts, or experience. Upstart music publishing companies with little experience licensing music and the related administration are happier to offer deals. They might make you pay up-front service fees and also sign exclusive publishing deals prior to them getting any music placed.

If an individual or company offering you representation and marketing services approaches you but you're unfamiliar with them, do your homework! Research and get referrals from other songwriters they've worked with. Camaraderie exists between most artists so if a representative burns one, they'll usually share that experience to make sure that it doesn't happen to others. With that said, keep in mind that someone new to the business might still be able to help further your career. In fact, she can be more effective since she must work harder to prove herself.

If you give someone without much of a track record a chance, the terms of your arrangement should be both provisional and flexible. For example, rights and entitlements are transferred only if the representative successfully brokers a satisfying deal. Many arrangements these days reflect a performance-based paradigm where commissions get paid and rights are assigned only as a consequence of results. Furthermore, the contractual arrangements should make it easy for either party to opt out of an agreement if it doesn't work out as planned. An attorney should draw this up.

Intermediary professionals include managers, agents, attorneys, song pitchers, music supervisors, record company A&R (artists and repertoire), publicists, wire services, marketers, publishers, consultants, and membership-based classified services. If they're talented and dedicated, any of these representatives should be able to get past the so-called gatekeepers in the music industry.

Working with a Representative

Soliciting the time, service, career advice, and resources of a legitimate third party for the purpose of marketing and promoting your music comes with a price tag. Most commonly, it's in the form of up-front service fees or commissions that will be deducted on future earnings that the service provider gets you. The exact dollar amount and percentage breakdowns can vary considerably. From your point of view, the best situation isn't necessarily the representation that charges the smallest commissions. It's most important to work with someone who believes in your talent and can give you some priority. Some companies may offer lower commission rates, but in doing so, may be forced to represent a lot more artists and spread themselves too thin. While commission rates vary and can be whatever you agree to, typical rates are:

- An agent's commission rate is usually between 15 and 20 percent per one-year term. In some cases, these commissions can apply to all forms of annual income, regardless of whether the agent did something to generate it.
- A membership marketing service commonly charges a monthly or annual membership fee and the artist retains all licensing fees and broadcast royalties.
- A pitching and marketing service generally charges no up-front service fees but retains up to 50 percent of any licensing deals they broker; however, they take little or nothing from your future publishing royalties.
- A copublishing deal charges no up-front fees but retains up to 50 percent of *both* licensing and future publishing royalties.

Some artists get indignant about giving away much of their song royalties. They fervently cling to all their rights and refuse to sign with a representative who wants what they deem as too much. I want you to recognize how much work is required to effectively perform these services so you can understand why these professionals are also entitled to benefit financially from the successful placement of your music. Many songwriters hold all their rights tightly, end up with their rights intact, but don't make a dime. What's the point of that? This is very important to remember:

One-hundred percent of nothing is still nothing.
You have to give to get.

If you guard your songs too carefully against anyone taking a cut, you also may shut yourself out of creating an income situation. Ask yourself, "Is not placing any songs worth keeping all of the money?" Few people help you make money for free. You need to be prepared to give up a percentage of the money your music earns if you want a representative to shop your music to people who might pay to use it. This is the reality of the business world, whether in music or other fields.

Music Publishers

Music publishers make their living by marketing songs. Getting a good one can be as hard as trying to get a major-label record deal. So what exactly does a publisher do for a musician? The extent and scope of services that are provided can vary depending on the terms of the deal they make with a songwriter. In short, a music publisher handles most or all of the business that revolves around songwriting for the songwriters signed to them—both marketing them for income-earning opportunities and handling all the administration involved in monitoring, collecting, and handling essential paperwork. A decent one will do at least some, and possibly all, of the following:

- Pursues synchronization (and possibly master) deals for the use of songs on TV and in film
- Pitches songs for use in advertisements, games, and mobile media
- Negotiates the terms of contracts and licensing deals, and negotiates and collects licensing fees
- Places songs with other artists who are in need of original material
- Addresses paperwork and administration for licensing deals they brokered on behalf of the artist
- Showcases the talent they represent by forwarding CDs, bios, and press
- Provides the artist with feedback and suggestions as new material is brought to their attention

- Notifies the artist about opportunities that are at hand, or in the pipeline
- Forwards music requests that have specific directions and asks the artist for any suggestions
- May provide networking opportunities and introductions to other musicians, music producers, or other industry contacts
- Files title registrations with performing rights organizations
- When applicable, files copyright registrations
- Provides or ensures that administration services will be properly handled when securing international licensing deals and/or collecting royalties worldwide
- Assists artists with tangential business affairs that otherwise tend to deter creative output

Music publishers go after deals that generate revenue for both the publishing company and the writers and copyrights under representation. This especially applies to smaller publishers that are new to the business and working with a relatively small pool of songs and artists. Well-established publishing companies have back catalogs that may already generate a steady stream of royalties, giving them some cushion during any lulls in the marketplace. Smaller publishing companies probably don't have this kind of luxury. For them, striking deals is a matter of necessity to remain in business. Before you sign with a publisher, ask:

- What other artists do they represent? Request a compilation CD. Listen carefully. If you're impressed with the overall quality of the songs, performance, production, and presentation, it's an indication that the publisher is legit or an up-and-comer since they have high standards.
- What are their most recent TV and film song placements?
- Is the deal being offered to you exclusive or nonexclusive?
- Will they pay you an advance?

A lot of people say, "You never want to sign your publishing away." That's not always true! Publishing companies are not the big bad entities some people make them out to be. They are there to create wealth and a value in a copyright. When you sign a publishing deal, you're essentially becoming partners with that publishing company. So make sure to choose yours correctly! The publishing company should be very excited about your music, have a marketing plan for what they are going to do with it, and clearly show that they plan to work hard. Stay away from a company that's just lukewarm, or a big company, unless they offer a huge advance. It's just being smart and savvy with what you do with your copyright. Make sure the people are the right partners, because you're essentially getting married to them and you want it to be a healthy, happy marriage.

KEATLY HALDEMAN, CEO, pigFACTORY

Major Music Publishers

The major music publishers are:

- Universal Music Publishing Group/BMG
- EMI Music Publishing
- Warner/Chappell Music Publishing
- SONY/ATV Music Publishing

Getting a music publishing deal with one of these companies can be very advantageous. Having one tends to come with respectable, if not impressive, advances. A long series of corporate mergers, catalog purchases, and new partnerships over the years has created direct links between these music publishers and film studios, record labels, and other forms of media, which are all owned by the same parent company. For example, the SONY Corporation not only has a music publishing company and several record labels (Columbia, Epic, etc.), but there's also SONY Pictures, and its electronics manufacturing and retail division (cameras, camcorders, etc.). Besides its record label, Universal also has its hands in both music publishing and film production.

Transactions and business deals that used to involve distinct companies and separate facets of the entertainment industry can now in theory all happen under the umbrella of a self-contained massive parent company. When a major music publisher represents your songs, fees paid for licensing tend to be larger. Their rosters are full of major-label artists and well-known songs, which command bigger bucks and are requested by licensees instead of pitched. But they will sign a songwriter who isn't with a major label if he's had some success and they see a decent market for his songs.

While a music publishing deal can be very lucrative, there are also some drawbacks. The priority and attention that's available for any given song may be short-lived, and with time, you may get lost in the shuffle due to the enormous number of song titles also represented. Another issue can be the larger fees they demand. Your publisher might refuse an amount that you'd jump at. So your songs might sit instead of getting deals. These deals tend to be exclusive. This means the publisher acquires ownership of the copyright. This isn't necessarily a bad thing, as long as there's an ongoing commitment to market your songs. However, once a song slips off the radar in the massive music catalog, it has a tendency to remain in a dormant state. Then you're stuck in a deal that does you no good.

Boutique Publishing and Marketing Companies

Smaller, hands-on, boutique publishing and marketing companies offer a strong alternative to the large corporations. They tend to represent much smaller catalogs and, as a result, conduct business with more efficiency. These companies mostly work with independent artists whose songs and recordings have a level of quality that can compete in the marketplace. These companies also tend to be less discerning about what opportunities are worth pursuing. They're often hungry for success and driven by a quest to establish a name for themselves in the industry. Any opportunity that offers a chance for forward momentum is fair game.

Some song placement opportunities may not be worth the effort from the vantage point of a larger and more expensive music publisher. But it can be a decent payday for a smaller one doing business with far less overhead and able to offer more flexibility when it comes to fee negotiations. While no one deal will afford them the luxury of an early retirement, success within their business model is placing songs with slow and steady consistency. Over time, lots of small deals begin to appear as impressive. In some cases, so much so that major record labels and publishers have turned to these marketers for help under the terms of a partnership, copublisher, subpublisher, or administration agreement.

Boutique music publishers, on the whole, tend to be independent-artist friendly, and are often willing to consider the prospect of working with an unknown artist based on the merits of the song quality. Looks, media hype, or press may not matter. Because their talent pool is smaller, you'll receive more personal attention, priority, guidance, and career feedback when necessary. On the downside, they rarely pay advances on signing a songwriter. They also may focus their marketing efforts on licensing music for lower budget productions. But, those do lead to better placements in the future.

Not All Publishers Are Alike

In the past few years, more and more people who call themselves publishers have come onto the scene. I'm not convinced that everyone using this job title assumes all of the roles of a traditional music publisher. Some mainly focus on collecting publishing royalties for placing a song. I don't have a problem with this in itself. However, if five years down the road the ball gets dropped because someone is asleep at the administration wheel, it can end up being to everyone's disadvantage. While it may not be intentional, an inexperienced or inept publisher may simply fail to understand some important but obscure facets of music publishing, like handling foreign administration or issues that stem from soundtrack albums, or following up on deferred payments that are now due. This is why it's crucial that you do research on anyone who wants to represent you.

It's important to appreciate that, at least in the beginning, for a publishing agreement to work to its full potential there must be a long-term commitment for the ongoing administration that can follow. There can be a long trail of royalties down the road, but you might never see it if your publisher isn't vigilant. That's why you should hesitate to sign with someone who obviously seems most concerned with making a fast buck. In the traditional sense, a good publisher is an artist's best friend and the two rely on each other. If you find the right partnership, you should enjoy a very productive and symbiotic situation. But ad hoc publishers often don't follow through, especially when pitching songs is a new game to them. They might not even have an office, and could be unwilling to meet with you in person. Songwriters who are desperate to work with a publisher almost always regret signing with these types later. You've been warned!

Publishing Administrators

The distinctions between the roles and titles of a *publisher* versus an *administrator* are sometimes confused, and understandably so. This is because while the publishers discussed above handle the marketing of songs, they also do the administration. Publishing administrators limit the scope of their services to reviewing deals, filing registrations, addressing paperwork, forwarding notices, collecting fees, and so on. If, for whatever reason, the burden of effectively performing these necessary responsibilities becomes too much for you to handle and you don't have representation by a publisher, you can turn to an administrator for help.

> *Often it is very difficult, overwhelming, and confusing for songwriters to manage the flow of royalties, administration, and copyright management of their music when they are busy trying to be creative. However, it is extremely important for any composer to understand the "business" side of music so that they can make the right deals and get the most, both financially and opportunity-wise, out of their music career. The role of an administrator is to help with the financial part of that equation by looking after song copyrights and maximizing the collection of royalties coming from these copyrights. An administrator works directly with performing rights organizations on a business level and is able to develop key relationships that enable quicker and more efficient service than perhaps a composer could do individually. Being that every performing rights society deals with so much volume, they appreciate having fewer contacts to interact with as it makes their work processes more efficient. An administrator may represent a number of composers' copyrights and can therefore communicate on behalf of many of them at the same time, thereby eliminating the need for the PRO to answer queries from each individual composer.*
>
> MEGAN HALDEMAN, Copyright Management/
> Royalty Accounting, pigFACTORY

A publishing administrator can be especially helpful if you license music in foreign countries (more in Chapter 17). Royalties work differently in each country and a good administrator knows where to look for money you may have earned.

A publishing administrator provides a service and gets paid based upon fees or commissions. They have no ownership. Think of an administrator as being an extra set of hands.

Lawyers

If you're presented with a licensing deal, or any deal that involves your music, you probably won't quite understand the terms of the agreement. Don't try to figure it out on your own or turn to a lawyer friend who is new or unfamiliar with the entertainment industry. I strongly advise that you seek the guidance of an entertainment lawyer. Upon reviewing the contract, she can answer most of your questions directly and enlighten you about unfamiliar terms that can be confusing.

A lawyer can spot possible red flags and suggest specific revisions and omissions when necessary. Your lawyer should be the one who interacts with the person offering a licensing deal and questions points in the contract, asks for clarification about details that aren't clear, and/or offers alternative terms for how your music will be used and how much money you get.

> *Serious artists need to have quality advice and counsel. They are not usually equipped to know all of the best practices of doing business. That's not a criticism, and while there are certainly exceptions to the rule, it's usually a fact at least at the outset of a career.*
>
> ROBERT ROSENBLATT, Esq.

Good attorneys will do more than just review contracts. They often play a pivotal role in securing licensing and other career or exposure opportunities. Some pitch songs to music supervisors and work with composers in an agent type of capacity. The majority of positive experiences in my own career as a songwriter have been associated with deals and opportunities that were facilitated or negotiated by an attorney—many more than the number brokered by managers, agents, and other pitching services. Two attorneys I've worked with have been responsible for securing scoring gigs, TV placements, film placements, soundtrack placements, album placements, and more. When attorneys work within the context of artist representation, their presence has a certain appeal for all parties involved with a negotiation.

If you're offered a licensing deal, you want to accept or decline an offer with the confidence that your final decision was based on knowing the legal points were understood and in your best interest. Should a particular deal come to fruition, the company licensing your music feels better knowing that you were properly advised. The presence of an attorney can often streamline the process of contract negotiations. Most companies prefer dealing with the efficient communications that often result from dealing directly with an attorney instead of the songwriter. Music industry opportunities are embedded with many potential liabilities, such as copyright infringement, payment schedules, publishing rights, and exclusivity. Because of this, some deals completely depend on the participation of an attorney who can negotiate the contract and finalize the deal.

The role of an attorney often morphs into secondary roles and responsibilities that are otherwise addressed by managers, agents, mediators, or A&R people. It's not uncommon for a manager to have a background in law or vice versa. From my own experience, I've found that attorneys are probably the players in the industry who are least likely to waste their time (and subsequently mine) by presenting long-shot or pie-in-the-sky opportunities. When they call, odds are that a legitimate offer is on the table.

> When a band or artist sends me music hoping to solicit my representation, I look for original sound, solid song construction, clear expression of ideas, a businesslike approach, and a respectful attitude. I'd pass on content that doesn't contribute in some positive way or on someone who thinks she or he is doing me a favor by letting me listen to his or her music—what I call "entitled artist syndrome."
>
> PEGGY O'BRIEN, Esq., Sound Advisors, Inc.

Sometimes I need to correspond directly with a licensee to address technical questions firsthand. I like that attorneys trust me in these situations. Most other professional intermediaries seem to worry that the songwriter might try to cut them out of a deal if she has direct contact with the licensee. In contrast, attorneys tend to not think this way. The problem is that an environment of mistrust or secrecy often creates a good deal of inefficiency for you. When an attorney is able get beyond this point and see the bigger picture, it makes working with him more appealing.

A classic problem that arises when a songwriter does not have direct communication with a licensee can occur when you work with an advertising agency to produce an original song for a commercial. Let's say a soda company hires an ad firm to produce the TV commercial. As the ad agency's project creative director goes about bringing the soda company's campaign vision to life, she must find an appropriate piece of music that can be licensed or created within the campaign's budget. If she can't find a preexisting song that works for the soda company's specifications, she may call someone at a licensing company known for representing some up-and-coming music producers who create good, relatively affordable music. The licensing rep finds a music producer. By then the details for the music request may have changed into something considerably different from what the soda company wants. Ideally, the music producer should speak directly with the composer, but it rarely works this way since one or more of the intermediaries may consider direct contact as a potential threat. Fortunately, many attorneys don't buy into this network of communication roadblocks because they respect trust.

One-Stop Licensing Services

Over the past ten years, a number of companies that are building their business around pitching songs for TV and film placements have emerged. The encouraging news, at least so far, is that expanding markets are a reflection of demand. So who is doing the pitching? At first, it was mostly publishers and lawyers. But pitching music requires no license or certification, so anyone with a few solid contacts on the inside and marketable audio content that has been precleared is technically eligible to start pounding the pavement.

Marketing services spend a good deal of time researching leads that come from word-of-mouth referrals, classified ads, and specialty publications that contain descriptions of either in-progress or upcoming film or video projects. They also respond to specific music requests, forward information on prospective licensing parties with suitable music request suggestions, and handle all the paperwork that follows. Since they make money when you do, it's in their best interest to find projects that might be able to use your music. "Industry only" or "entertainment profession" wire services announce job opportunities in the pipeline for actors and film crew, and include song and music request opportunities. Subscription eligibility may require that you verify your credentials through a referral to ensure you are indeed what you claim to be: a "legit" agent, publisher, or record label.

> We look for something that stands out sonically and/or lyrically and that can fill a void in our diverse roster.
>
> MICHELLE BAYER, Artist Representation and
> Pitching Songs, Shelly Bay Music

These marketers are in demand because they offer filmmakers and production companies great convenience. Reputable marketers dramatically streamline the licensing process because most offer "one-stop music licensing," which allows them to grant clearance for both the synchronization and master licenses (more in Chapter 3) in tandem. Indie artists usually make up the bulk of their catalog content and, in many cases, the music they market boasts songwriting and production whose quality is indiscernible from what's being pitched by major labels. Marketing materials often display "100 percent synch and master," which has helped make one-stop music licensing more hassle free.

These marketers already have agreements in place with the owners of the songs and recordings being represented, which means they've been granted permission to pursue licensing opportunities freely and negotiate deals on behalf of all parties. Their commission is often a 50/50 split on any licensing deals that result from their effort. Although these marketers are often not publishers in the traditional sense, their deal may involve publishing rights pertaining to placements they're responsible for securing. For this privilege, they assume the responsibility of handling all necessary paperwork for these licensing deals, providing clients with copies of the contracts, and distributing payments once available.

> Our agreements are the same for all. They are fair and nonexclusive, which allows for all of our artists to sign up with various record labels and publishing companies. We only take a percentage on the songs we place.
>
> PATRICK ARN, President, Gotham Records/
> Gotham Music Placement

When doing business with marketers, you must proceed with caution. Some companies charge artists a service or membership fee, which is completely legitimate if that's all it is. But then, they also try to "double dip" by collecting on the licensing fees and publishing royalties for placements that might happen as the result of using the service. Most legitimate companies will do one or the other, are nonexclusive, and only take their share of the licensing fee. Be careful about signing away too many rights. Any publishing money that comes in should be yours. A good lawyer who knows about licensing will be able to advise you.

‖‖

CHAPTER 3

Music Licensing Agreements

As I said earlier, licenses are agreements that give permission to use music. Each type of license is for a specific use. Depending on your needs, you can enter into a variety of agreements. This chapter will discuss the most common ones.

Two are required for including copyrighted music in TV and film—the *master license* and *synchronization license*. Traditionally speaking, a master license is typically administered by a record company. A synchronization license is typically administered by a publisher (or whoever owns the copyright). However, this is not always the case and several variations for who administers each license are possible. Within the past ten years, there's been a growing trend for copyright owners and/or their representation to offer a potential licensee the ability to gain clearances for both licenses in tandem. Having this ability simplifies the licensing process and is one reason why it has become much more common to hear indie music and score in films.

The vast majority of music licensing situations involves clearing two licenses and each can be with a different party. It's commonly understood that songs or musical compositions—both lyrics and music—are eligible for copyright protection. However, a separate copyright protection applies to the *recording* of the song or composition in question. The term *master recording* refers to a *specific recording* of a song, and for licensing purposes, it applies to the specific recording that will appear in the film or TV show that requests its use. Although, historically, record companies have been in charge of negotiating the terms of a master licensing agreement for most commercially released master recordings, they often do not own the copyright of the song itself. Licensing the song or composition often requires negotiating with the song's publisher, songwriters, or beneficiary. The fact that a given song usually has two distinct copyrights explains why two separate licenses exist for audiovisual media. The U.S. Copyright Office's Form PA (Performing Arts Works) is used to register song copyrights and Form SR (Sound Recordings) is used for recording copyrights.

MUSIC LICENSING AGREEMENTS

Terms Roundup

FAQ	KEY QUESTIONS	JARGON TERMS	EXPLANATION IN LAYMAN TERMS	EXAMPLES
WHO?	Who enters a licensing agreement?	Licensor and Licensee	Licensor is the person, company, or representative who authorizes/ grants a license. Licensee is the party requesting licensing approval for use of a song and specific recording.	Licensors: bands, publishers, record companies, attorneys, authorized pitching services, etc. Licensees: filmmakers, TV networks, video production companies, advertising agencies, etc.
WHAT?	What is being licensed?	Composition and Master	Two licenses are filed, one clears the rights for use of the song; the other clears the rights to use a specific recording of that song.	Synchronization License: clears rights to the song. Master License: clears rights to a specific recording of the song being licensed.
WHERE?	Where is the license valid?	Territory	A specific location or venue, region of the world, and possibly beyond.	"Sundance Film Festival," "North America," "The Universe," etc.
WHEN?	When does the license begin and end?	Term	The length of time between when the license begins and ends.	"One Year," "Three Years," "In Perpetuity"
WHY?	Why do they want to use my song?	Use, Usage, Duration	Details related to how the song is used, for how long, and in what context.	Usage descriptors include: theme song, feature, and background instrumental, end title credits, etc.
HOW?	How will my song be used in film/video?	Grant of Rights, Media, Use, Other Options	Outlines details related to how the song shall be copied and distributed within the context of the video, and the options sought in relation to how the video gets released, and possibly used in other contexts.	Right to copy, record, exhibit video including the song. Right to transfer license. Rights related to media types and methods of release (television, theatrical, DVD, PSP, UMD, "Out-of-Context Promo," and "making-of" options).

Master License

A *master license* grants the right to someone who needs musical content to use a preexisting sound recording of a musical composition in a media project. The person who owns the master recording issues it. Record labels typically try to get control of the master when they sign an artist. If that happens, the label is the one to give the master license. Prior to the proliferation of high-tech home recording equipment that can deliver major label–quality audio, record companies absorbed the sometimes substantial costs typically associated with producing, manufacturing, and distributing albums featuring songs recorded by artists signed to their label. In return for doing this, the record company owned the copyright associated with any recordings produced within a timetable outlined as part of the artist's recording contract. Nowadays, that's changing.

If you paid for the recording and/or equipment used to make the recording, unless otherwise specified, you own the master of your song. A master license is issued for one song at a time. No matter how many songs someone may want to license off of your album, they must proceed one song at a time. Successfully licensing a song or instrumental composition for inclusion in a film or TV show requires the ability to quickly and completely grant clearance rights in relation to the sound recording of a song or composition.

A master license addresses clearance issues in relation to a particular recording of a song. It grants the person or company requesting this clearance, such as the TV network, production company, or film director, the right to embed this specific recording as part of the film soundtrack or TV show for a specified duration. Permission is granted in exchange for what's usually a one-time payment known as a *master licensing fee*. Once you enter an agreement, the video, film, movie, or DVD can be freely manufactured, duplicated, exhibited, marketed, sold, and distributed without the need or obligation for additional compensation from the licensee to the licensor in relation to this specific use.

Using the song anywhere else within the production technically requires a revised master licensing agreement and/or additional payment if such additional uses were not included in the original agreement or the licensor granted a blanket license (more in Chapter 4) that has since expired and now requires a renewal. In some cases, additional payments can be negotiated that are the result of mechanical royalties (more in Chapter 6) if there are DVD sales. The likelihood of successfully negotiating these add-on provisions often comes down to either the clout of the artist, his lawyer, or a film's music budget, or lack of one. Here's a sample of how a master license can read:

SAMPLE PROVISION: Rights Granted Through a Master License
Licensor hereby grants to Producer the right to publicly and/or privately, throughout the universe, use the Masters, embodied in the Film, by any and all methods of exhibiting the Film, and in any and all media, whether known or hereafter devised, including, without limitation, the following:

- Theatrical exhibition to audiences in motion picture theaters and other places of public entertainment, including, without limitation, the right to televise the film into such theaters and other public places;
- Free television exhibition, whether by network, non-network, local, or syndicated broadcast;
- Pay television, subscription television, CATV, cable television, or any and all other closed circuit broadcasts into home or hotel-motel television; and
- In any transportation facility.

For the purpose of clarity, consider a situation where the same song ends up being recorded by two different bands at different times and in different locations. This situation represents three copyrights. The first copyright involves whoever wrote the song and/or oversees publishing administration. The two remaining copyrights pertain to each distinct and unique recording. Until the copyright is sold, purchased, leased, or transferred, these recordings technically belong to whoever paid for their creation. When multiple recordings exist, a filmmaker must only be concerned with clearing a master license for whichever recording they plan to include in the film. The distinction in terms of fees that may be suggested by various master owners isn't trivial.

Regardless of whatever recording ends up being selected, the song remains the same. This is why the same publisher handles licensing issues related to the song itself.

Master licensing fees for a recording by a well-known performer can vary quite dramatically. A huge factor that influences the price of a particular master licensing fee is directly related to the artists featured on the recording. As you'd expect, the popularity of the song or the artist largely determines what they can ask for. Other factors that may influence cost include the usage and duration. A record company is in no way obligated to match or reduce its own licensing fee if the person or company controlling the copyright offers a lower rate for the synchronization license.

As a general rule, clearing the rights to a recording that features an iconic band or performing artist can get very expensive, ranging anywhere from several thousand dollars to a million and upward, especially if it's to be used as part of a national or international advertising campaign. To protect the value of its catalog, a record company will often maintain a nonnegotiable baseline for its most highly prized recordings so licensees without deep pockets have little chance to license them. A $50,000 master licensing fee for the use of a particular recording could easily exceed an independent film's entire budget. I've also heard about instances where record companies intentionally limit the number of licenses annually granted for a particular recording to protect its value.

For first-time filmmakers who tirelessly pour their hearts and souls into a film project on a shoestring budget, licensing fees present a tough issue. There are no standardized fees. That's why they appreciate being able to work with indie artists to get good music quickly at a fee that fits their budgets — obtaining both licenses from the same person.

Synchronization License

The rights associated with a sound recording are often dealt with separately and independently from the other category of TV/film music clearance — the right to synchronize a song or a piece of music with a visual image.

For this right, the person who wants to use your music must get a *synchronization license*, referred to as a synch license for short. It grants clearance and permission to synchronize and embed a song or musical composition with a visual image—moving pictures—for a specified time duration. While a synch license is most commonly used for licensing music for film or television shows, it is required whenever music is used together with visuals. It is usually granted by the persons or company that either wrote the music and/or owns the copyright. This might be the composers, songwriters, lyricists, producers, or publishers.

Master License versus Synch License

A master license encompasses the recorded material and the synch license covers the actual song itself. A master license is issued by the owner of the master recording—this could be the record label or the individual musician. The master licensor grants the right to use the sound from the original recording. A synch license is issued by the music publisher and gives the person or company requesting a license the right to rerecord a song for use in synch with their visual project. Whoever controls each component of the song is the party that issues the appropriate license.

To use a song in a film, TV show, or other visual medium, permission comes either directly from the songwriter(s) or a publisher/representative who has been assigned the authorization to represent its copyright in a licensing agreement. In addition to clearing the rights to use the song, the right to use a specific master recording of the song requires its own separate clearance. For example, if a filmmaker wants to use a Beatles' song you covered and recorded on your own, he must come to you for the master license, as you own this recording. The record label that owns the original Beatles recording has no claim on it. But the person or company who owns the copyright to that composition must also issue a license. That's why if you own everything, it's much easier and faster.

I'm often asked, "What exactly is the composition?" As it applies to music licensing, it isn't what you hear on a CD. The concept of *composition* refers to the actual song itself. When you listen to a CD, you're hearing a master recording of the composition. The body of a musical composition can be expressed or demonstrated in a number of ways — with printed scores, handwritten manuscripts, lead sheets, sheet music, lyric sheets, chord charts, and performance — even without a recording. Each of these representations proves that a song actually exists, regardless of whether it has been recorded. It's possible that, due to technological limitation or a lack of access to recording equipment, the composition's creator could not make a recording. In such a case, the primary tools for preserving the integrity of a composition would most likely have been a pen and manuscript paper.

Keep in mind that there could potentially be numerous recordings of one particular song/composition in existence. That song doesn't change. The same person will always issue the synch license. But, a separate master license is needed to clear each specific master recording that's used. Clearing the rights to use one particular master recording of a song *does not* provide or include clearance for any other master recordings of this song that might also exist. If the recording cleared is performed by Band A, that's the one that must be used in the project. If there's another version of the song recorded by Band B, this is a different recording of the song, and requires its own master recording license.

License fees vary from project to project and are determined based on a variety of factors, such as how the music will be used, for how long and how many times it will be used, and where the project will be shown. Fees are quite often negotiable, especially for students and independent filmmakers.

Sample License

Here's a sample of a license that consolidates the process of clearing the master and synchronization rights for the use of a song into a single agreement. This hybrid synch/master license is a type frequently encountered for a single-song, single-use, one-stop music licensing agreement. Merging both contracts offers convenience in situations where one party controls both the synchronization and master rights. I left my name in to show you some of the details.

MASTER AND COMPOSITION USE LICENSE

Licensing Company
123 Music X Street, Music City, CA 12345
Phone: (XXX) XXX-XXXX I FAX: (XXX) XXX-XXXX
E-mail: music@XXXXX.com

Re: "NAME OF SONG" performed by NAME OF ARTIST / "NAME OF TV SHOW, YR 1–6" EP: 204

Dear NAME:

This confirms the terms of the agreement between Darren Wilsey (d/b/a Darren Wilsey Music) on the one hand ("Licensor") and NAME OF PRODUCTION COMPANY ("Licensee") in care of NAME OF REP for the license granted by Licensor for the use of the following master recording (the "Recording") and musical composition (the "Composition") in "NAME OF TV SHOW, YR 1–6" EP: 204.

1. TERMS:
RECORDING: NAME OF SONG
COMPOSITION: NAME OF SONG
ARTIST(S): NAME OF ARTIST
RECORD COMPANY(S): Metrophonic Records, Inc.
WRITERS(S): Darren Wilsey / (*Performing Rights Organization*)
PUBLISHER(S): Sonic Disobedience / (*Performing Rights Organization*)
TERM: Perpetuity
TERRITORY: The World

    a) **LICENSE TERMS** (including in-context advertising and promotional rights): World Perpetuity, Expansion of current licenses to all media, now known and hereafter devised excluding theatrical.
    b) **LICENSE DATE:** September 2008
    c) **COVERS 1 USES(S):** Background instrumental. Duration 0:10
    d) **TOTAL MASTER LICENSE FEE: $5,000.00**, payable to Metrophonic Records, Inc.
    e) **TOTAL COMPOSITION LICENSE FEE: $5,000.00**, payable to Sonic Disobedience

2. ADDITIONAL PROVISIONS
    i) First release: September 8, 2002
    ii) License covers a 100% interest in the total copyright of the recording

and a 100% interest in the total copyright of the composition in the subject territory.

iii) This license shall be assignable to other parties.

iv) End title credits for the Composition and the Recording will appear substantially in the following form:

NAME OF SONG

Performed by NAME OF ARTIST

Written by Darren Wilsey / (Performing Rights Organization)

Courtesy of Sonic Disobedience

v) Cue Sheet Credit: Publisher: Sonic Disobedience

vi) PRO Affiliation: _____ [Please make any necessary changes to Cue Sheet credit]

vii) Licensor warrants and represents that it owns or controls the respective percentages of the copyright in and to the Composition and the Recording as set forth in paragraph 1 for the Territory and that it owns or controls all rights necessary to enter into and fully perform the terms hereof. Additionally, Licensor warrants and represents that neither the Composition nor the Recording incorporate "samples" (unless otherwise set forth in paragraph 1) and that use of the Composition and the Recording pursuant to the terms herein will not infringe upon or violate the copyright of any person or entity.

Best regards,

Darren Wilsey

D/b/a Sonic Disobedience

TIN (Tax Identification Number): XX-XXXXXXX

ADDRESS

PHONE NUMBER

AGREED AND ACCEPTED:

Signature

Date

Contact Name: Darren Wilsey

Licensor

Broad Rights/All-In Licensing Agreements

Use of the term *all-in* refers to licensing agreements that offer the licensor a one-time-only licensing fee in exchange for acquiring what has grown into a vast expansion of media rights covered by these agreements. From a filmmaker's vantage point, the all-in agreement affords the broadest rights for using music that can be freely duplicated, exhibited, marketed, sold, publicized, and distributed in any format without the need or obligation for additional payment beyond the one-time, flat-rate licensing fee agreed to. As a result, all-in agreements tend to be accompanied by slightly higher licensing fees. However, accepting this one-time payment in exchange for granting a broad scope of media rights, unless otherwise specified, often amounts to forfeiting future payments from potential mechanical royalties generated by the sales of the movie in DVD format or episodes sold as downloads online. A sample contractual provision that grants a licensee broad media rights as part of an all-in song licensing agreement is:

MEDIA: Broad rights in any and all media and means now known and hereafter devised (including, without limitation, theatrical, nontheatrical, all forms of television [including, without limitation, pay-per-view and video-on-demand], a full videogram buyout [including, without limitation, videocassette, DVD, PSP, and UMD], the Internet, and other linear transmissions to home and personal monitors). Includes in-context promos and clips.

A simpler way to state the all-inclusive nature of an agreement is to include a broad statement such as:

License Fee: $3,000 "all-in."

Including:

- Theatrical and nontheatrical release
- All forms of television (including, but not limited to, pay-per-view and video-on-demand)

- A full videogram buyout (including, without limitation, videocassettes, DVD, PSP, and UMD)
- Internet and other linear transmissions to home and personal monitors
- In-context promos and clips

All-in deals, which have become increasingly common, run the gamut of media rights sought and granted. The licensing party often requests "broad rights in any and all media and means," including both media that's currently in existence or any other type that might become available in the future. The vastly expanded coverage that's now afforded by a one-time payment represents a complete contrast to song licensing deals from the past. Why the change?

All-in deals can avert costly problems later. Many classic TV shows from the 1970s, '80s, and early '90s were produced during an era when the idea of packaging each season as DVD box sets to be sold by retailers internationally wasn't part of the picture. Producers acquired any music licensed for these older but still popular TV series through deals that kept licensing fees to a minimum. The primary method used was to only option television rights in the song licensing agreements. Years later the limited scope of those options that were initially granted became an issue for the studios and networks who owned these shows.

Back when those shows were created there were no DVDs so the production companies didn't seek those rights. As DVDs got popular, attempts were made to expand the scope of the release options that were omitted in the original agreements. But the record companies who owned the masters and the publishers who owned the compositions declined the new fees offered to them, and frequently responded with counteroffers. They made licensing fee adjustments that were allegedly, shall we say, far more robust. It made a good case for getting all-in deals!

Soundtrack Album License

If your song is chosen to be on a soundtrack album, it can mean more money and exposure for your music. In order to use a song on a soundtrack album, the production company needs to negotiate with the record label that released the sound recording and the publisher who controls the copyright, or you if you're independent. The master and synch licenses do not give permission for this use (mechanically making copies of a movie or recording and selling copies). Enter into the conversation another type of licensing deal: the mechanical license (more in Chapter 6). Selling copies requires that the owner of the sound recording issue a mechanical license and royalties are paid for every record sold.

For songs that have already been recorded, and not for the movie per se, managing to get all of the entitled parties to agree to whatever terms, conditions, and dollar amount fees are being offered as part of a mechanical licensing agreement/soundtrack album deal can be a tall order. Any up-front monies offered in these situations amount to advances against future sales only. As with any licensing agreement, should negotiations reach one or more insurmountable roadblocks between parties, either conceptual or financial, the deal can get scrapped and the song/recording in question must be omitted from the project. This is why there are often so many songs on a soundtrack album that aren't in the film while songs in the film are omitted from its playlist.

Be aware that if references to soundtrack albums are made within the context of a synch/master agreement, they often serve little purpose other than to provide a courtesy reminder that the licensing agreement has nothing to do with a soundtrack license. If a soundtrack album does come to fruition, any related details will be discussed at that time, and will merit a completely separate agreement. Examples of provisions regarding soundtrack albums that are included in a synch/master agreement are:

- "Soundtrack Album: to be discussed upon distribution deal"
- "Producer may acquire from publisher the rights to use the composition on a soundtrack album in association with film for distribution and sale throughout the territory at a later date, and under a separate agreement. The applicable rates and terms of a soundtrack album license will be negotiated then."
- "In the event that a third-party record label should release a soundtrack album in conjunction with the picture, licensor agrees to the inclusion of the composition for the minimum

statutory mechanical rate in effect, as of the date hereof. Licensee and third-party label shall not be obligated to include the composition on any such soundtrack release. Additionally, licensor agrees to allow a third-party record label the use of the master recording on the soundtrack, subject to negotiations in good faith. Licensee and third-party label shall not be obligated to include the master recording on any such soundtrack release. Licensee shall use the best efforts with third-party label to include the composition and master recording on any such soundtrack release."

- "Company agrees to provide artist with the opportunity to be included on the soundtrack album. For purposes of clarification, although no advance is required for inclusion in the soundtrack album prior to release, inclusion on any soundtrack album shall not be regarded as a gratis royalty-free clearance. It is understood that a master royalty and mechanical royalty will be paid for sales, from initial release of the soundtrack album. Said royalties will be payable under separate licenses, negotiated in good faith at a later time."

In most instances, soundtrack album provisions rarely promise or guarantee that the song being licensed must also be included on the soundtrack album, should one happen. Furthermore, nothing restricts the licensing party or third party overseeing the release of the soundtrack album from including songs on the soundtrack album that were not licensed for use in the film.

I came up with a strategy to address this point and make it a little less wishy-washy. For a project that requests at least six of my compositions (songs or score), I request permission (without obligation) to release a soundtrack album having a title that links this music with its use in the film. My soundtrack doesn't need to be the "official" version, and could simply go by the title, "Music from/featured in NAME OF FILM." Some producers find this advantageous, as a form of tangential promotion for their project on my dime. For other projects, if a definitive plan for releasing a soundtrack album already exists, agreeing to this request could, though not always, create a conflict of interest. While I don't continue to pursue it if there's resistance, it never hurts to ask. My biggest belief is, *Rather than wait for somebody to hand-deliver an opportunity that may never happen, try to create it yourself!*

Festival Use License

Some licensing agreements are more limited in terms of the rights they grant. A *festival use license* grants a filmmaker permission to use your recording in a film, but only for its showing in film festivals. This right expires within a specified duration. Releasing the film in any capacity extending beyond the scope of film festivals requires a revised license and additional fees. This includes any continued use of this recording in the film itself, promoting it, or other methods of distribution and releases that might occur in the future.

Independent filmmakers planning to show their films at film festivals often prefer to negotiate a reduced fee by only asking the songwriter/composer for a festival use license. Filmmakers know that, without distribution, the life of their film may end at the conclusion of its festival run. Therefore, they don't want to pay up front for rights they might not need. Filmmakers most commonly get distribution for their films by going to film festivals. That requires having music for their project. So they opt for this lower-rate license to get to first base and then renegotiate the terms if the film gets picked up.

Once the rights to a film are either sold or licensed for theatrical, television, or DVD release, these deals provide the filmmaker with a source of revenue for covering any necessary expansions in clearance for music in the movie that until then was limited to film festival rights. This opens the door for a second installment of licensing fee payments. It's best to negotiate and make reference to conditional fee payments—a dollar amount that is part of the festival rights license—to avoid lowball offers later on. Always use an attorney with lots of experience making film music deals to help with this! A well-drafted licensing agreement will specify the duration of use, where and how often your music is used, and other details. Negotiating in advance for possible future performances in different types of media (e.g., theatrical, TV, cable, Internet) will often result in what is known as a *step deal* (more in Chapter 6).

Licensing Rights in Disguise

Sometimes licenses are granted through the use of generic-sounding documents, like "music releases," "consent forms," or "clearances." These tend to be shorter in duration but broad in scope as far the permission they grant without any need or obligation for future compensation.

Maybe you've been asked (or required) to sign a similar release form before appearing as an extra on a movie set, agreeing to have your band filmed as part of a televised concert event, permitting your picture to appear in a publication, or participating in a televised interview. Whatever the situation, the rationale and incentive for passing out these release forms is always the same: a) By signing it, you are granting permission to someone else to use something you own—your music, your image, etc. b) By singing the agreement, you "release" the party that seeks your permission from any further obligation to provide you with any compensation (monetary or otherwise) in the future. Compensation may be nothing, a one-time payment, deferred payment, or the courtesy of providing you with a copy and credit. These are sometimes what are used as makeshift music licensing deals (especially gratis use) or of live radio performances.

Should someone ask you to sign off on a release form, doing so may not strike you as being as impressive or nearly as important as being offered a music licensing deal. Just realize that on a nuts-and-bolts level, both may in fact provide someone with similar rights or legal permission to use your music. Rights granted via *consent* and *release forms* are often the equivalent of signing a *gratis use* licensing agreement.

Request Letters

Prior to signing a song licensing agreement for a motion picture, it's customary for the potential licensee to send a request letter. This letter is similar in format and content to what might be expected in a synch/master agreement, although it isn't a licensing deal just yet. This preliminary request to use the song/recording in the film confirms that it's available for use under the terms they're asking for. An important distinction is that these letters give the movie studio the right—but not the obligation—to include the song in the film. Entering the licensing deal phase happens only if the song remains in the movie after the final edit. At this point you pray to yourself, "Please don't edit out the scene that uses my song!" Here is a sample of a music request letter:

MOVIE STUDIO—MUSIC DEPARTMENT

Jane Doe
Director
Music Clearance and Licensing
Theatrical Business Affairs
VIA FACSIMILE: (XXX) XXX-XXXX

March 5, 2010
Representative's Name
MUSIC PLACEMENTS, Inc.
(Business Address)

Re: Motion Picture: NAME OF FILM
Master Recording and Composition: "SONG TITLE"

Dear Representative:

Pursuant to your approval dated March 4, 2010, this letter will confirm the quote approved to FILM PRODUCTION COMPANY, Inc. and their successors and assigns for the use of the following master recording and composition in the above-referenced motion picture.

MASTER/COMPOSITION: "Song Title"
ARTIST/COMPOSER: Name of Artist/Name of Song Writer (BMI) 100%
LABEL/PUBLISHER: Name of Label/Name of Publisher (ASCAP) 100%
LICENSE FEE: seven thousand five hundred dollars ($7,500)
USE/TIMING: one (1) background vocal; up to thirty seconds (:30) in duration
MEDIA: all media now known and hereafter devised (including, without limitation, video-on-demand), incl. in-context trailers and Internet
TERRITORY/TERM: worldwide/perpetuity

WARRANTY: OWNER represents and warrants that it owns and controls 100% of the master recording and composition for its territory listed above, and that it owns or controls all rights necessary to enter into and fully perform the terms hereof.

Additionally, in the event that the above-referenced master recording is used in the final, edited version of the motion picture and credits are provided, please review the following screen credit and include any necessary changes in the space provided.

"Song Title"
Written by Song Writer (BMI)
Performed by Artist/Band
© 2010 by (Publisher) (ASCAP)
Courtesy of MUSIC PLACEMENTS, Inc.

If the foregoing does not accurately reflect your understanding of our agreement, please notify me immediately. Otherwise, please return a countersigned copy of this letter for our files.

MOVIE STUDIO shall be under no monetary obligation in the event that the master recording is not included in the proposed project.

Thank you very much for your assistance with this matter. Please feel free to contact me by phone, fax, or e-mail with any questions or concerns.

Kind regards,

Jane Doe (signed)

CONFIRMED AND AGREED TO:

(Name of Publisher)
By: (Publisher)
An Authorized Signatory

In this case, the deal is being brokered by a fictitious song-pitching service ("MUSIC PLACEMENTS, Inc."), which explains why the letter is addressed to them. The letter is forwarded to the entitled parties of the song/record being represented. If the terms are acceptable, the letter gets initialed by the entitled parties, and is then returned back to the requestor. With any luck, the terms that are proposed and agreed upon as part of an initial request form will blossom into a full-fledged licensing agreement (hence making the fees an obligation rather than a contingency). However, at the stage of forwarding/receiving a request form, that doesn't have to be the case. For example, a request to use a song during a movie scene is initially approved by the licensor, however it never amounts to finalizing an actual licensing agreement because the scene in question ends up being cut during the final stages of editing the movie.

Missing from the letter is any mention of a soundtrack album. Although it's not necessary for this stage of the confirmation, it may be worth asking for such a reference to be included at the time of drafting a licensing deal. In other words, if the song is licensed for use in the film, every effort will be made to insure that it gets included on a soundtrack album, if and when there is one.

Performing Rights Organizations (PROs)

Performing rights organizations (PROs) are the American Society of Composers, Authors and Publishers (ASCAP); Broadcast Music, Inc. (BMI); and the Society of European Stage Authors & Composers (SESAC). Each one collects performing rights royalties on behalf of its members, who are songwriters, lyricists, composers, and music publishers of all types. They then distribute these royalties to their members. PROs license the rights to use the public performances of their members' music for network and cable TV, cable movie channels, nightclubs, stores, restaurants, and other places where there are public performances. When you license music for use on television, they collect the royalties you're entitled to.

> *All three U.S.-based PROs have different things to offer. ASCAP has a comprehensive range of opportunities for our members. In addition to educational events like the ASCAP "I Create Music" Expo and NY Sessions, we have showcasing opportunities at the Sundance Film Festival, SXSW, CMJ, and others. But most importantly, because we are a member-owned organization, ASCAP members can rest assured that ASCAP is doing its utmost to protect their intellectual property rights*

through legislation and through our licensing efforts. Being involved,
checking our website and taking advantage of opportunities presented
by ASCAP are the best ways to get the most out of membership.

RANDY GRIMMETT, Senior Vice President,
Domestic Membership, ASCAP

You don't need to be signed to a record or publishing deal to join a PRO. If your music is being broadcast on television, radio, or cable stations, or performed in venues licensed with PROs, you're entitled to royalty payments. The performing rights organizations oversee the entire process of collecting and distributing performance royalties. Any entitled party having full or partial ownership of a song's copyright, or that has been authorized or assigned the right to do so via some preexisting agreement, can register song titles. PROs only distribute royalties for broadcast performances. They have nothing to do with royalties for CDs sold and digital downloads.

Every song that's broadcast on television gets documented on a *cue sheet* (more in Chapter 6). The assortment of songwriters and publishers listed could be members of all three performing rights organizations. Each PRO only credits its own members. Other PROs listed on a given cue sheet are forwarded their own copy to scrutinize.

Should you join a PRO before your songs are getting broadcast or performed? I suggest you do. This way, when your first song gets licensed or is being broadcast, you can definitively indicate your performing rights affiliation as part of the paperwork. When this information isn't included on cue sheets or playlists that are then forwarded off to the PROs, it can cause considerable delays, oversights, or omissions. Trying to collect on past royalties owed to you that were overlooked the first time around can be a real hassle.

No one will work with you unless you have your business in order,
and one order of business is to affiliate and register your works with a
PRO. You must belong to a PRO in order to get paid for any public
performances that have been licensed to film or TV. And any licensing
company or music supervisor is going to want to know what your affili-
ation is, and what your publishing companys name is.

LINDA LORENCE CRITELLI, Vice President,
Writer/Publisher Relations, SESAC

PROs are there to help songwriters. Once you have a song that is being submitted for possible placement in television, or you want to make the effort to get it licensed, speak to a representative from your PRO. If they like your music they might be able to advise you on a direction, or put you in touch with someone who could help you. All of the PROs host various workshops and seminars, and some are specifically geared to the business of music licensing. If at all possible, attending some may be worth the effort.

CONCEPTUAL RIGHTS FOUND IN MUSIC LICENSING

TYPE	EXPLANATION
COPYRIGHT	The right to make copies and oversee the sale and distribution of an intellectual property.
GRANT OF RIGHTS	Rights that are granted/acquired in relation to what the licensing party cites as essential permissible activities; clarifies all rights that are allowable and thus can be performed with respect to licensed material (e.g., copy, record, rerecord, exhibit).
OPTIONS	Additional rights sought, though not required for a licensing deal to proceed; thus allows for the option to include these rights as part of the present agreement, or revisit in the future and as necessary.
FILM FESTIVAL RIGHTS	License that grants song clearance in and as part of a film festival exhibit only. This license has a clear expiration date, and the definition of territory may be limited to a specific venue; restrictions are placed on the scope of options authorized through this agreement, and do not extend beyond film festival use.
DVD RIGHTS	Option that allows for the manufacture, release, distribution, and sale of DVD; may include mechanical royalty provisions for licensor.
TELEVISION RIGHTS	Option to release via television broadcast.
SOUNDTRACK ALBUM RIGHTS	Provision that typically gives licensee the right, but not obligation, to include song on a soundtrack album in the future.
THEATRICAL RIGHTS	Option to exhibit and display in theaters.
TRANSFER OF RIGHTS	Licensing party's right to transfer or assign the rights granted via agreement to a third party without further obligation to licensor.

BIOGRAPHICAL RIGHTS	Licensing party's right to connect artist's song, name, image, likeness, and biography within the context of the song's use in a project (film, TV series, trailer, etc.).
MORAL RIGHTS / DROIT MORAL	A facet of copyright that protects author from any unauthorized alterations, revisions, affiliations, or manipulations that serve to distort, devalue, or defame either the work itself, or the reputation of its creator.
LIMITED MEDIA RELEASE RIGHTS	The right to implement one or more predetermined and predefined types of media as the means or method for a release, exhibition, sale distribution, or sale (e.g., TV, theatrical, videogram, Internet).
BROAD SCOPE MEDIA RIGHTS	Licensing party's broad spectrum rights in "any and all media and means"; includes media that is currently in existence or any other type devised in the future for a one-time licensing fee payment (i.e., "all-in" deal).

‖‖

CHAPTER 4

Licensing-Related Agreements and Terms

No two music licensing agreements are exactly the same. Some provisions or terms might appear in an agreement used to license music by one company and never be mentioned in an agreement offered by a different company. The terms for the same type of license may feature slight variations in the smaller print while in the broad sense, they're both used to clear the same basic rights.

The vast majority of licensing contracts share a bullet-point list of common features. You'll see the recurring use of certain terms, concepts, phrases, grant of rights, and the telltale legalese that makes all of it sound overbearing. I prefer shorter agreements that feature language that's clean, succinct, and gets to the point. But not all licensing situations can accommodate this preference, since all pertinent specifics must be included. I'll take a comprehensive contract that protects me from problems down the road to one that's brief but leaves room for plenty of potential loopholes.

Most nonexclusive music licensing agreements are one to four pages long. The lengthier ones are usually the result of someone's attorney adhering to the C.Y.A. (Cover Your Ass) philosophy. Should an agreement be offered that starts out as a one-pager, but after your attorney's review it grows to a four-page contract, it's probably best to trust his inclination for adding the provisions. Other types of music contracts come preloaded with a considerable amount of bulk and excessive wording. This is often the norm for agreements that include a transfer of copyright, terms of exclusivity, or step-by-step breakdowns of the convoluted method used for calculating and distributing royalty payments in the future, such as an exclusive publishing deal. In this chapter, I'll explore the common agreements that guide the music licensing process to help you understand what each one means, what each is needed for, and under what circumstances it would be better to use each of them, including:

- Agreements between artists and those who are in the business of representing music to pursue licensing opportunities. There are different types of representation agreements, and the prevailing business arrangements and special considerations that often apply to each are discussed below.
- Some specialized types of music licenses that offer limited or unrestricted amounts of clearance to those people who actually license music.

This overview isn't intended to replace seeking additional or necessary counsel from others who are experts in such matters and capable of providing competent services. It's always a good idea to have proper legal representation. The contractual aspects of song licensing can be tricky business at times, and on occasion can present some slippery loopholes. It's up to an attorney, not you, to recognize what needs to be reworded or taken out of an agreement. But when you understand the basics, you can discuss your options intelligently with the professional representing your interests instead of just going along with what he or she says. To the nonlawyer, this stuff may seem a bit dry, but it can make or break your licensing music income. So, please read it and familiarize yourself with it.

Nonexclusive Song Marketing Agreements

In Chapter 2, I discussed the players you might work with who can represent your music for licensing opportunities. Now I'll discuss some of the terms you may be asked to agree to if you want to work with them. First, let's look at nonexclusive marketing agreements, which won't involve the transfer of copyrights or ownership. Furthermore, the artist isn't prohibited from entering similar agreements with other companies in the same business, or that offer similar services, as long as it doesn't limit or restrict concurrent terms that are now in effect from other prior agreements. Some terms to watch for are:

- COMPANY will never own any part of your song including publishing or any other royalty.

This type of agreement allows the marketing company to collect commissions that are based upon "up-front" licensing fees only, and as such, the company is not entitled to any back-end performance royalties (more in Chapter 6) that might come about as a result of a licensing deal in the future.

- COMPANY is entitled to 50 percent of the synchronization and master licensing fees for any placement made by COMPANY only.

Marketing deals based on this business model have become less common over the past ten years, as both a matter of necessity, and in response to the laws of supply and demand. The marketplace has become flooded with available music as TV and film production budgets steadily decline. The general result of this has driven down the size of licensing fees being offered. In order for marketing services to stay in business or have an incentive to work hard on behalf of the songs they represent, many have been forced to adopt revised business models to nonexclusive copublishing agreements (more on this below).

As with virtually all agreements, there should be clear reference to payment schedules and/or accounting practices, and termination. Some samples are:

- Both parties agree to send the 50 percent money owed within thirty days after receiving the master/synch money.
- This is a nonexclusive agreement and may be terminated by either party for any reason. However, any money owed to either party must be paid regardless of termination.

It's important to remember that by entering a marketing agreement, you give another party the right and legal permission to represent your music and do business on your behalf. This obviously includes them being allowed to enter into licensing agreements, negotiate fees, complete necessary paperwork, and collect and forward payments. In most cases, all you will be expected to do is sign off on or "okay" the final draft of the licensing deal. Though less often discussed, but tacitly implied, you're not expected, encouraged, or in some cases allowed to take part in the direct negotiations with the licensing party. The middleman does not want to be cut out and it's made clear in your agreement if he or she feels this way:

- Composer may not engage in contact with Client or Advertiser as per this or any matters. All concerns are to be addressed with COMPANY.

Schedule A

Many agreements include references to the Schedule A. This is often attached as a separate form. The Schedule A lists each song included or covered by the terms of the marketing agreement, along with every song's entitled parties (songwriters and publishers) and which performing rights organization you belong to. It's possible that your name is all that ends up appearing on the list. However, in the event that the names of any other songwriters or publishers happen to find their way to the Schedule A, even if for only one song, they must also sign the agreement for it to be completely legit. Be aware of that if you collaborate on songs! Every aspect must be signed off on.

- By signing this agreement you acknowledge the above terms, you have used no samples that aren't cleared in your music, and you own all publishing and master rights to the songs listed in Schedule A. If you do not fully own all rights, those who are also owners must sign this agreement as well.

Take extra care to ensure that all of the information you have provided is correct, complete, and without omission. The information entered on the Schedule A form is what's most often referenced for the purpose of filling out and submitting cue sheets. It's also forwarded for inclusion in the end title music credits in movies or TV shows. Retroactively correcting any mistakes that are overlooked becomes a sizable headache for all so they make a big deal out of getting it right initially.

Nonexclusive Copublishing Agreements

Many of the contractual terms and services rendered in a nonexclusive copublishing agreement share similarities with a nonexclusive marketing agreement. The key distinction is that in addition to being entitled to profit from a certain percentage of the up-front synch/master licensing fees, the company giving a nonexclusive copublishing deal is also entitled to share a percentage of the back-end broadcast performance royalties (and possibly other types), and does so operating under the assigned title of "copublisher." Any royalty profit-sharing will only pertain to those licensing deals and subsequent broadcasts that occur as a direct result of deals brokered by the copublisher. The songwriter is free to make other kinds of deals that don't interfere with this one.

Using Alternate and/or Derivative Titles

Because some copublishing agreements are nonexclusive, the artist who has one is free to pursue and enter into additional nonexclusive copublishing agreements with other companies that provide the same basic services under nonexclusive terms. Should this happen, it creates a scenario where multiple companies may be actively pitching the same song at the same time, though not necessarily for the same licensing opportunities. This is akin to two or more stores selling the same product to their own regular customers.

Since each company is only entitled to profit from deals that resulted from their own direct involvement, it's important to keep this distinction crystal clear. When *one song* is the subject of *multiple licensing deals* brokered by *different copublishing companies*, it can be challenging to make sure that the correct parties involved are credited. Having multiple deals through multiple companies creates the potential for confusion, error, and oversight with regard to distributing broadcast royalties. A common solution is to allow each company to use its own unique alternate title for a given song.

- In the event of securing a licensing agreement for use of a COMPOSITION, and for the purpose of simplifying the royalty administration of the licensed COMPOSITION,

>OWNER and COMPANY will mutually agree in writing to give the COMPOSITION a new title (hereinafter referred to as "NEW TITLE").

Once a new title is established, the company will use it for pitching, licensing, paperwork, administration, registration, cue sheet entries, and credits. This acts like a unique "fingerprint" for this derivative song title, at least from the company's vantage point. Once a specific copublishing company has established a song's new title, it can't be used by anyone else. Using derivative titles makes it easier for a songwriter to work with more than one company and have each pitch the same songs.

Nonexclusive Rights of Entitlement

When a company works with you as a copublisher, it also assumes the burden of other administration responsibilities, many of which must extend beyond the scope of licensing agreements. However, for any rights entitlement to take effect, an executed licensing deal must also be in place.

- COMPANY will have the right to register this NEW TITLE with all performance societies, mechanical rights societies, third-party licensees, and the U.S. Copyright Office.
- If and when a COMPOSITION is licensed including but not limited to a synchronization use, COMPANY will administer that use of the COMPOSITION and/or NEW TITLE worldwide in perpetuity.
- COMPANY will also register the COMPOSITION and/or NEW TITLE with the appropriate performing rights society.

The underlying business model proposed above has become one of the tenets of the so-called new music industry. It illustrates a recurring theme of performance-based profit sharing and rights entitlement. The artist loses nothing by entering an agreement of this type, because in the event that the company is unable to successfully secure licensing agreements in the future, no rights are transferred and all of it is pursued at the company's expense. Because of this contingency, it's highly unlikely for an agreement of this nature to involve up-front cash royalty advances set against future earnings, since there may be no future deals.

Schedule A should include reference to all original and corresponding derivative songs that are covered by the agreement or possibly listed and addressed as its own unique form (i.e., Schedule B, C, etc.). The suggested alternate titles will require your review and approval, especially in the event that other companies are already marketing these same songs as nonexclusive copublishers. It's important to ensure that the alternates that are being suggested aren't already in use somewhere else. Trust me, this can happen and it's best not left to chance.

Nonexclusive Agreements: Exclusive Agreement Prevention?

In a nonexclusive copublishing marketing agreement, the artist is not restricted from entering deals with other nonexclusive copublishers. It is possible for an artist to work with several concurrently. However, for any given song marketed in this capacity, there is the potential to create a restriction worth mentioning. Having a nonexclusive publisher may limit, or possibly eliminate altogether, the ability to enter into an exclusive publishing deal on behalf of the songs in the future. This is because there may be terms and requirements that are stipulated in an exclusive deal which can't be fully performed or satisfied if there are prior conditions currently in effect from past licensing agreements that were brokered by the nonexclusive copublishers on your behalf with various third parties.

A termination clause featured in a nonexclusive marketing agreement may allow either artist or copublisher to end the terms of service. But doing so only serves to cease future marketing and *does not* nullify any of the terms that were agreed upon or rights that were granted as part of past licensing agreements. This technically prevents a would-be exclusive publisher from ever having complete control of the compositions that had prior agreements.

> A *common practice for publishers or song licensing companies, and sometimes TV and film production companies, is to use single-song publishing contracts, where, basically, if they get a placement for an artist, then they own the publishing exclusively. Some people think companies that ask for this type of agreement are sharks, but it depends on your point of view. You should always be careful*

if somebody is going to want to own your copyright, but it's not necessarily a negative situation. Just weigh your options carefully. One of our artists was involved in a situation like this and it worked very well for her. When we signed her, she had two songs under a deal with a film production company that allowed the company to place the songs in their films and pay her a synch fee, and now they own the copyright to those songs. It sounds harsh, but, they have already placed at least one of those songs in yet another film. I think they will continue to place those songs in future films so it's not a bad situation for her. Plus, since she's a very prolific writer and able to record her own material, giving them two of her songs isn't such a big deal. She can always write and record more.

KEATLY HALDEMAN, CEO, pigFACTORY

Exclusive Music Publishing Agreements

The most significant feature of an exclusive publishing deal is that it involves the transfer of copyright ownership from songwriters to publishers. Copyright law allows that the creator/owner of an original song has the ability to lend, lease, license, loan, or transfer rights and privileges to another person or party. In the case of an exclusive music publishing agreement, the transfer includes all rights and privileges with regard to authorizations, administration, the ability to enter third-party agreements, licensing deals, marketing, promotion, and the manner and methods that are used when pursuing opportunities for the songs in the future.

Simply put, you may have written the song but it now belongs to someone else. Exclusive song publishing deals will, at the very least, acquire the rights to the composition, although it's possible that some agreements will include terms that also acquire ownership rights of the master recording. This gives the publisher the exclusive right to market the song(s) in a one-stop licensing capacity in the future.

Music publishing is where music licensing starts. You cannot license a song without licensing the rights to a song first and in order for that to happen, one needs a music publisher because we have relationships with licensors, are aware of opportunities. In addition,

*music publishers know what song to pitch, and the market with
respect to fees, not to mention the legal expertise to draft licenses, and
have the manpower and know-how to monitor use and payment.*
> DAVE PETTIGREW, Senior Vice President, Strategic Marketing,
> and Head of Advertising and Games, Warner/Chappell Music

Is an exclusive deal right for you? The thought of "getting signed" for
something after working for possibly years on your music can be intoxicating. The benefits of being signed are different for each individual. It's a
balance between your own area of artistic expertise and the types of services
and opportunities the company you sign with is best equipped to handle.
An exclusive copublishing deal offer can represent a definitive first step on
what you hope will be a road to bigger and better things. Besides, just about
everyone who has made it to some extent in the biz has more than likely
entered into one or more of these agreements at some point in the process,
right? So how bad can any of it be? The potential for a contractual agreement that binds two parties exclusively can end up escalating your career or
feel like a big disappointment. Which way this goes is influenced by a variety
of factors.

The level of expectation you have in your vision of success when you enter
into an exclusive agreement and the presumptions you make about what it
can do for your career are big influences on how you feel about the company
you work with. Those initial beliefs create a benchmark that you'll use in the
future to evaluate whether you have success or failure in connection with
getting your songs marketed. Are your standards, expectations, and goals reasonable, realistic, and attainable? Or are they the type that would be difficult
for any publisher to deliver under the same circumstances?

Most artists think their music is special. Feeling that way can lead to the
erroneous assumption that all you need is to have someone to represent
your music and then everyone will want it. Unfortunately, that's not how it
works. Getting a deal comes with no guarantees for any song placements.
Of course, the publisher will try to get licensing deals. But even if you're
signed, the deals may not happen. These expectations lead to creating some
lofty goals, such as licensing your songs for inclusion in upcoming television
shows or pitching your songs to a well-known artist, with the hope that they
record their own version for inclusion on their upcoming record, resulting

in the song becoming a Number One hit! When that doesn't happen, you end up on the disappointment side. And, you're locked into a deal that isn't satisfying.

> *I've seen songwriters who are desperate to get their music licensed agree to the relinquishment of a piece of their copyright ownership and control when nothing is promised, or delivered. The songwriter is betting on the competence and support of the publisher whether or not the publisher delivers a synchronization or a useful one.*
>
> PETER M. THALL, Esq.

The publisher's clout, commitment, and ability to deliver the goods are the biggest influences on whether you're going to be happy with an exclusive copublishing deal. Having tremendous success with getting your music licensed in top films, TV shows, commercials, etc. is possible, but the likelihood for your dreams to come to fruition depends on the publisher's connections, prior business relations, industry clout, and credibility. Be sure to ask a prospective publisher what their goals are in relation to marketing your music. Talk to other songwriters who have agreements with them and see how they feel. The answers they provide will help you assess if this deal is the right one for you. You don't want to sign an exclusive deal with a company that can't deliver what you want from them.

Even under the best of circumstances, the fickle nature of timing and luck can have a considerable influence on how a situation actually plays out. You might have some great songs, according to both you and the publisher. But they may be a bit out of step with the current notion of mainstream accessibility. You may just miss a trend or window that seems to love your music. Publishers, like the rest of us, aren't psychics and can't predict what will work tomorrow as they sign you today. Another distinction of exclusive publishing deals is that the vast majority will involve either an up-front cash advance against future earnings or a lump-sum payment that's a buyout fee payable upon entering the agreement (more in Chapter 6).

Dead Battery Exclusive Publishing Deals
Let's assume that five years ago you accepted an offer to publish ten of your songs exclusively with a company. You remember that at the meeting when

the deal was signed there was a feeling of excitement and enthusiasm, openly expressed by everyone. You signed the contract, got a check, shook hands, and left the meeting with a smile and anticipation of good things on the horizon.

Now fast-forward to the present. Five years have since passed and it appears that nothing ever materialized as a result of the publishing deal. There could be any number of reasons for this, and not necessarily due to a lack of effort by the publisher. But whatever the reason, at this point, it's easy to convince yourself that those songs are no longer a priority to the publisher. They're probably not in circulation or being marketed. Because of the exclusivity, you're not in a position to go out and market the songs yourself. So, are you a prolific songwriter? If the answer is yes, the situation may not have much impact on you, because you have written many more songs that are as good or better since. However, if you're not prolific, and perhaps not even a songwriter and those ten songs were your "babies," this becomes a very disappointing scenario.

If you want to get those songs out, you can try to contact the publisher and ask for permission to market these songs in a copublishing capacity. If the songs are indeed sitting on a shelf collecting dust, they may have no issue with your suggestion. However, as an exclusive publisher, they could decline your offer, and for the moment, there isn't much you can do about it. You could also inquire about getting the songs back, which means returning the copyrights to you. In your mind, the cost for doing so might be the same dollar amount as the advance you were originally paid. But the publisher isn't obligated to accept your offer or this price. It's possible that they'll only agree to a much higher price, citing the "expenses and losses that have been suffered as a result of the ongoing promotional cost." This type of situation can happen when an exclusive publishing deal falls short of meeting the artist's initial expectations.

Before you accept an exclusive publishing deal, figure out the cost of recording and producing your music, including hiring musicians, a producer, and a recording engineer, or paying for studio rental time. It literally affects the value of the recording, if not the song. Once you have a sense of the dollar amount, and on a per-song basis, it's easier to decide if an exclusive publishing deal makes sense, especially if the advance being offered doesn't allow you to at least break even. It's bad enough if you can't do anything with the songs, but it's worse if you're out of pocket on the cost of recording them!

COMMON BUSINESS ARRANGEMENTS

Songs Under Agreements

TYPE	RESTRICTIONS	TRANSFER OF COPYRIGHT	PAYS ROYALTY ADVANCES OR UP-FRONT PAYMENTS	NOTES AND EXPLANATIONS
COMMISSION-BASED SONG MARKETING SERVICE	No	No	No	Company is entitled to retain a percentage commission on any "up-front" licensing fees with regard to any deals company secures on behalf of artist.
FLAT-RATE MARKETING SERVICE	No	No	No	Company charges a monthly or annual flat rate for providing marketing service; artist retains all licensing fees and performance royalties that may occur as a result.
NONEXCLUSIVE COPUBLISHING	No	No	No* *with rare exception	Company is entitled to retain a commission on up-front licensing fees, in addition to back-end performance royalties as an assigned copublisher; only applies to the licensing agreements they secure on behalf of artist.
EXCLUSIVE COPUBLISHING	Possibly	N/A Mutual consent required for any transfer to occur	No	Example: two parties who both share writing credits 50/50 and publisher rights 50/50 for a song. Entering a deal on behalf of this song requires mutual consent.
EXCLUSIVE PUBLISHER	Yes	Yes	Yes	Copyright ownership of the composition is transferred to publisher, who acquires legal and exclusive control of the song. However, annual royalty statements are distributed to songwriter for deals that are secured by publisher in the future.
PUBLISHING RIGHTS BUYOUT AGREEMENT	Yes	Yes	Yes	All rights to a song/recording are purchased for an agreed-upon flat-rate fee. Purchaser is not obligated to pay future royalties. However, songwriter may retain the right to collect "writer's share" performance royalties that come about in the future, distributed by their performing rights organization.

Blanket Licenses

For a filmmaker who likes the idea of buying in bulk, the notion of acquiring music content through the use of a *blanket license* will be appealing. A blanket license allows for the temporary unrestricted use of music that's been prepackaged as part of a genre-specific CD set or library collection that is available for use in a *single* film or video project, or for a specific number of episodes/programs that will be created within a specified time period.

The audio content covered by the terms of a blanket license can be delivered on CDs, DVDs, and more recently, external hard drive(s). If digital delivery is also available, the tracks can be downloaded online from a licensing party's network server. Blanket license agreements often require that discs or hard drives be returned to the licensing party upon expiration of the license, or when a production comes to an end.

Options Clauses

Options have to do with the scope and types of release rights that are included in a licensing agreement. These can appear in the form of contractual add-ons, giving the option to include them as part of the agreement now in hand, assuming that the price tag quoted for acquiring them is right. Or, they can just as easily be ignored or omitted should it make the net fee too expensive; or they can be revisited at a later time. Options are not always mandatory for whatever business agenda is at hand for the licensing party.

An additional incentive for agreements that feature options is that the practice of carving out what isn't absolutely necessary, at least at present, tends to foster a business dynamic that accommodates more flexibility and room for fee negotiation. By setting certain rights to the side, and for now calling them options, it may leave the licensor with little choice but to adopt a "sliding scale" in terms of defining an appropriate fee under these otherwise restricted circumstances. The incentive behind the options business model is based on the presumption that, the fewer rights that are being granted, the lower the clearance costs. On the surface, this seems reasonable, and is a common business practice. However, the licensor isn't obligated to accept an offer, in spite of whatever rights have been carved out for this agreement. One simple reason for declining an offer is that the rights currently sought aren't available at this time or otherwise.

Options that are commonly included or carved out of a music licensing agreement for such purposes include televisions rights, cable rights, Internet rights, pay-per-view rights, film festival rights, DVD and distribution rights, theatrical rights in one or more territories, soundtrack album rights, merchandising rights, advertising rights, and a growing list of emerging rights that apply to new or future digital media applications. The rights that are currently sought may include various combinations of any of the above or only one. As you can probably imagine, this has the potential to cover a wide spectrum of rights, and because of the variety, it's rare to encounter any two companies using the exact same music licensing agreement.

Traditionally, licensing fees have been directly related to the number of options a licensing party intends to use as part of releasing, distributing, or publicizing their content. For example, if a series has been produced, at least initially, for the sole purpose of airing on television and there's a budget to license X number of songs per episode, the producers may argue that they should be entitled to adjusted rates since the show won't be shown in theaters or released on DVD, so they're only concerned with clearance as it relates to television broadcast.

Eliminating nonessential options from an agreement, such as theatrical release, DVD sales, pay-per-view, etc., often makes a case for negotiating lower synch/master fees. This was a common feature of licensing agreements through the late 1990s. No one could imagine that one day there would be a market for "Seasons 1, 2, and 3" DVD box sets or on-demand television. Nor could they foresee that people would have the ability to surf through channels and revisit old TV shows while flying on airplanes or have shows made available in foreign movie theaters. Since so much technology is so recent, there were no provisions for downloading an entire series on an iPod. So options keep increasing as content becomes more widely available in more places. This is one reason it's important to have a good entertainment attorney who understands when to give up options and when to insist on more money for them.

|||||||||||||||||||||||||||||||||||||||||||||||||||||||||||||||||||||||||||||||||||||||||||||||||||||||||||||||||||||||||||||||

CHAPTER 5

Protecting Your Music

It may seem obvious that you must do everything you can to protect your music, yet many musicians fail to do so. You also must make sure that all agreements with people you work with are written down and spelled out. This chapter is devoted to explaining some of the legal issues you should understand. As I've said before, this knowledge isn't meant to be a substitute for having an attorney review anything you plan to sign. But it's important to familiarize yourself with the basics of what your attorney recommends.

Band Agreements

Band agreements are always recommended to avoid problems down the road once you start making money. Are you doing a lot more than everyone else and feel you should get a bigger cut once money starts coming in? Spell it out in writing. Often one person writes the songs but the whole band contributes to the arrangements when they're recorded and each member signs the copyright form. That's fine if you don't mind sharing in what could be a lot of royalties for songs you basically wrote. Think down the line before sharing everything. Sometimes sharing keeps up the group's morale. But, if you start to resent getting just a small amount of royalties for songs you wrote most of, it will ultimately cause problems.

Royalties don't have to be shared equally. If you want to give some credit to other members of the band but not an equal split, put it in writing. Otherwise, everyone whose name is on the copyright form is entitled to an equal amount. A good lawyer can advise you about how to do the splits. Here is a sample agreement with some explanations:

SAMPLE BAND AGREEMENT

AGREEMENT dated as of the _____ day or _____, 20___ among (Musician 1), (Musician 2), (Musician 3), etc.

WHEREAS, Musician 1, Musician 2, and Musician 3 seek to enter into an agreement regarding the formation of a band named (NAME OF GROUP).

NOW THEREFORE, in recognition of their mutual interest in playing together as a group and achieving recognition and remuneration for live performances, the Parties hereby agree as follows:

RIGHTS AND RESPONSIBILITIES

1. To share all expenses and compensation for live performances equally (one-third to each).
2. Any decision to admit additional members to Band must be unanimous.
3. Musicians may be hired from time to time for specific performances, but any payment to such musician(s) will be discussed and agreed unanimously.
4. Any decision regarding hiring or entering into agreement with managers, lawyers, etc., shall be made jointly.
5. Musician 1 and Musician 2 are the co-writers of the (NAME OF GROUP) songs to date, and as such, have the sole right to enter into any publishing agreement regarding the songs.
6. Negotiations with potential record labels or others interested in promoting the band shall be conducted jointly.

ALTERNATE DISPUTE RESOLUTION

Any controversy or claims arising out of or relating to the Agreement shall be settled by arbitration. The arbitration will be conducted in accordance with the rules of the American Arbitration Association, conducted in New York City, with one arbitrator mutually selected by the Parties.

GOVERNING LAW

This contract shall be governed by the laws of the State of New York, excluding its conflict of laws rules.

ENTIRE AGREEMENT

This Agreement contains the entire understanding among Parties. No modifications or waivers hereunder shall be valid unless the same shall be in writing and signed by the Parties.

IN WITNESS WHEREOF the Parties have executed this Agreement as of the day and year written about.

_____ Musician A

_____ Musician B

_____ Musician C

Notes on Sample Band Agreement

"To share all expenses and compensation for live performances equally (one-third to each)."

Let's assume there will be three band members entering into this hypothetical agreement. The first three provisions deal with gigs, along with the possibility of needing some additional backup musicians once in a while. All three members agree to share expenses accrued with regard to live performances. Notice that there's no reference to recording costs. This is an important oversight. It seems reasonable to assume that if all three band members share expenses related to studio and recording time, each is entitled to one-third ownership of any master recordings that come as a result, regardless of who writes the songs.

Unless clarified as being the case, the percentage ownership of the masters is an assumption, and as such, brings along with it the potential for hard feelings and disagreements down the road. Remember that in licensing deals, song ownership and recording ownership are each addressed separately. Both licenses do not necessarily involve all band members or the same combinations. Clearly addressing this detail beforehand will make any licensing offers in the future much more fluent and keep band politics in check.

RIGHTS TO BAND NAME The other omission in this agreement, and one that's a common point of contention, is ownership or rights to a band name. This will be an issue in the event that one member decides to quit the band, citing "irreconcilable creative differences" as the justification. All the band members need to discuss how this can be properly handled. Whatever solution you reach should be included in the agreement. The following are some hypothetical clauses that address the issue of band name (only one would apply for a given band agreement):

> "In the event of retirement, termination, or death of a band member, the remaining Parties shall have the right to continue the business of the Band under the same name, either by themselves or in association with a replacement."

> "In the event of retirement, termination, or death of any band member entering into Agreement, all remaining Parties agree to cease doing business of the Band under its current name (NAME OF GROUP)."

> "In the event of retirement, expulsion, termination, or death of Musician B, the remaining Parties agree to fully relinquish any rights and entitlement to continue doing business of the Band under the same name, and as indicated in the Agreement."

> "The band name (NAME OF GROUP) is owned and controlled exclusively by Musician C, and a registered U.S. Trademark."

The Protection of Copyright

No music business book is complete without discussing the significance of copyright. Copyright is a fundamental legal right bestowed upon the originator of an intellectual property that gives him or her the exclusive rights to determine how many copies are made, distributed, or sold. Simply put, a copyright for your song gives you the right to copy it, or not to copy it. This is a right that's not trivial, particularly if you write music, screenplays, or create art for a living.

Copyright protection is given to original works. However, while you can copyright a song, you can't copyright an idea. Your songs must be put into a tangible form. If you sing a song over and over to an audience, it's not protected. If you sing into a tape recorder, you have a copy of the song, so copyright laws cover it. Whether you write it down on paper or record the song, as long as it's in a tangible format, you own that song and the rights to copy it or give others permission to use it, on your terms.

The entire entertainment business hinges upon the existence and enforcement of copyright, which gives you the right to own an original creation, and subsequently license and profit from it. Without copyright protection, the monetary value associated with art is uncertain at best. Copyright protection entitles songwriters to receive monetary payment for the use of their original music in film and TV. The law requires one to obtain legal permission from the copyright owner to use or include any such musical content as part of another original work, and must be addressed *prior* to any public exhibition, sale, staged or theatrical performance, broadcast transmission, duplication, and/or distribution. Not doing so is one form of copyright infringement. The advancements, proliferation, and widespread use of audio technology over the past decade has set the stage for what's commonly referred to as the *digital music revolution.* The rapid development and distribution of all related technologies seems to have far exceeded the ability to manage the protection of copyrighted material and will likely remain a hot topic for some time to come. Unprecedented distribution opportunities online bring with them the challenge of managing digital rights.

Copyright is at the core of any licensing contract since approving any deal that involves music requires permission from the copyright owners. Without copyright protection, there'd be no need to get permission for including music in third-party media, and enforcing the concept of payment for such use would evaporate. That's part of why you should have a copyright symbol © next to all your songs.

What Makes a Song Original?

Originality means the work needs to be unique to the creator. This concept is referred to as the *model of creativity.* Everything you write is not yours; everything that's copied is not copyright infringement. You can't copyright most drumbeats and musical styles. For example, songs falling into the musical genre of "blues" will almost always follow a well-established harmonic progression commonly referred as the "12-Bar Blues." By itself, this chord progression isn't eligible for copyright protection because granting it to a single individual would limit all others from creating music in this genre. What make a blues song eligible for copyright protection are layers of additional elements that include original melodies and lyrics.

Keep in mind that copyright also doesn't protect rhythms, chord progressions, orchestration, arrangement, or musical style. If it did, it would seriously restrict if not completely prevent others from exploring creative endeavors in the same musical genre. Once you record a song you wrote, it's important to register it with the Copyright Office, either by mail or through its website (which is cheaper), www.copyright.gov. While you do own the copyright once your song is put into a tangible format, registering it gives you proof. And, it's imperative to have that in copyright infringement situations. If you're tight for cash, you can register a group of songs under one copyright and call it a collection. Once a song will be licensed, you can register it on its own.

Copyright Infringement

Copyright infringement is, in one word, *stealing*. For musicians, it's the unauthorized use of your music or lyrics that are protected by copyright law. No one has the right to violate any of the copyright owner's exclusive rights, such as the right to copy or perform the copyrighted work. No one is allowed to use your music unless you give him or her permission—in writing.

Proving that copyright infringement has occurred can become a challenging process. If you feel that someone has illegally copied your copyrighted music, you'd have to successfully prove that there are two factors: *similarity* and *prior access*. Similarity means that you can show the resemblance between your song and someone else's. Prior access means that the person who may have infringed had an opportunity to hear your music before writing their song and could have been subconsciously influenced by hearing it or just stole some of it on purpose. Proving that someone had some form of prior access to a song is easier if a song has already been performed in public, recorded, commercially released, or broadcast on radio, TV, or posted on a website. But, it is possible that both of you had the same idea.

Without having any prior access, it could just be a coincidence that someone has a song that has similarities to yours, which isn't copyright infringement. For example, if a songwriter living in Las Vegas, who has never performed or released a song, is convinced that the copyright to his song has been infringed upon, he will probably have a difficult time proving that another songwriter living in Boston, who has never been to Nevada, blatantly stole his song. In this case, the songwriter in Boston never had the means to access a song that's only been in Las Vegas. Because songs in certain genres of music share certain stylistic attributes, even when written by different songwriters, similarity alone is not enough to win a case.

Another problem for proving copyright infringement is that there can be a fine line between two songs sharing one or more similar musical characteristics and two songs being close enough to warrant awarding copyright infringement damages. How close is too close? Making this distinction is difficult, which is why pursuing copyright infringement lawsuits of this nature can be challenging. Pursuing an actual copyright infringement case will require contacting a federal prosecutor and filing a formal complaint that adds compelling credibility to the merits of your claims. Based upon the information you provide, a decision is then made as to whether to pursue the case. A slight variation is to pursue a civil lawsuit in order to seek damages and losses that have happened as a result of stolen property. The outcome of a civil suit of this nature will hinge on your ability to show that the defendant had access to your song.

Unauthorized Use

Another form of copyright infringement, and more relevant to the world of TV and film, involves instances of the unauthorized use of a recorded composition without having documented permission (clearance) from the copyright owner. If you as the copyright owner discover your song has been used without permission, your decision about how aggressively to pursue this type of infringement probably depends on the extent to which the film or video has been exhibited, publicized, distributed, or sold.

It may come as a surprise to learn that this form of copyright infringement has become a fairly common practice in the world of independent film production. The reason stems from the fact that the cost of making a film has dropped significantly in recent years. Therefore, more people are making movies than ever before. One possible explanation is that younger filmmakers, who are accustomed to peer-to-peer (P2P) MP3 file sharing online, are uninformed when it comes to gaining proper clearance for a film and don't know enough about copyright laws. Film distribution deals have been jeopardized or retracted once it's learned that proper clearance wasn't in place.

Regardless of the extent of this type of copyright violation, the film owner or production company is the target of liability. Infringement is much easier to prove in cases where the film has been exhibited in a public place, such as a theater or film festival, or broadcast in some capacity. What can you do if your music was used without your authorization? The copyright owner, whether it's you or your representative, must get an attorney to send a cease and desist notification. That requires the filmmaker to recall and destroy all copies that are in violation. And, you're entitled to ask to be reimbursed for the legal expenses you paid to the attorney who had to confer with you, review the case, and draft the letter.

You also have the option to sue the film owner for the unauthorized use and inclusion of one or more of your songs and/or recordings that are protected by copyright. The film owner will be fined and forced to recall and destroy all circulating copies that are in violation and pay all legal expenses of the plaintiff. This is the reason proper clearance and documented licensing is taken seriously in the world of TV, film, advertising, and elsewhere. Producing a movie, commercial, or video is very expensive in terms of time, money, and human input. Copyright infringement litigation is avoided at all costs. In fact, this is usually why many companies refuse to accept unsolicited material. Their concern about being sued for copyright infringement makes them leery of allowing people to send in music that might not be cleared properly. Some companies only accept CDs from an attorney, agent, manager, or a trusted referral.

Sampled Content

Sampling is taking the sound of a recording made by someone else and using it in your own recording. For some genres, especially hip-hop, it's considered a creative part of the music. Young musicians like to lift beats and sounds and hooks from other people's records to add flavor and interest to their songs. But, however cool people may think these sound in your music, unless you get permission to use a copyrighted sample, it's considered unauthorized use of a sound recording, which is copyright infringement, and you can be sued. Unfortunately, it also makes the production company that licenses your song liable, too.

The technique of sampling involves isolating a precisely selected small section of a larger audio clip. It could be a song, solo instrumental part, sound effect, drum beat, political speech, or anything else that has been recorded. Once this section is marked, the sample can be extracted or archived for future use elsewhere. Digital technology has come a long way in this department. Samples can be stretched or compressed in duration, greatly expediting the once difficult task of aligning the sample's tempo to that of another song. It is also possible to transpose samples into other key signatures. Sampling has made the art of remixing accessible to the masses, while opening a Pandora's box of copyright issues in the process. Regardless of your ability to manipulate or process a sample protected by copyright, usage of it in your own recording is illegal if you lack permission to do so.

Prior to marketing, pitching, or representing your music in some capacity, almost all companies will require that you sign an agreement that among other things, officially and unequivocally states that your songs are free and clear of any unauthorized or illegal sampled content. Furthermore, if you enter the agreement and it's later discovered that there actually are unauthorized samples in your songs, the burden of any resulting lawsuits or other costly mishaps will completely fall upon your shoulders.

The appearance of sampled content goes beyond the stereotypical notion of lifting a few choice sound clips off a classic R&B album while praying that no one will notice. Music supervisors, who understand the legal ramifications of illegal sampling, are very careful to check that the music they select for their projects is free of any rights issues.

Sampled content also comes in the form of "loops" or preformatted audio data that are typically sold on CDs or DVDs, or can be downloaded online (more in Chapter 15). Most of these products use and include phrases like "royalty free" or "license free" as part of their product marketing. The common understanding is that audio content of this nature can be incorporated into user song projects without restriction. If a resulting song becomes commercially successful, no royalties are owed to the company who sold you the content—most of the time. However, you need to make sure this is the truth each time you use a loop, so take special care to read the terms and conditions that are outlined in the "user licensing agreement" that was either included on the disc or as part of the download (more in Chapter 15).

To clear a sample, you must get in touch with the legal department of the record label that owns the sound recording and pay a fee for using their master recording. They can ask anything they want. Some labels are more cooperative than others. You also need to contact the owner of the copyright for the song and negotiate what portion of the royalties they get. It can be a lengthy and expensive process.

Work for Hire

Work for hire is a term used to describe a specialized form of employment. It addresses the issue of creating original work on somebody else's dime and clock. What's tricky is that two things are actually happening: You're being hired to perform a service, and by doing so, it creates something original during the process. Should both occur under the definition of "work-for-hire" employment, you acknowledge and agree that the original work that's created during the employment in fact belongs to your employer and not you. This happens all the time in many types of businesses and industries, but tends to be a more sensitive and delicate issue for those involved with the entertainment world, especially those who may not fully appreciate its meaning, benefits, or consequences.

For an emerging artist, *services* refer to any number of tasks that the artist pays someone else to do for them. Generally speaking, service providers offer specialized skills or a craft. They charge an hourly or per-project rate. Things potentially become fuzzy when whoever is performing a service adds to the creation of your tangible product during the process. This could be the photographer who takes photos for your press kit, produces your recordings, shoots your video, etc. Assuming that you're paying for the service, the question becomes who actually owns the creative byproduct that comes as a result? Unless specified, the service provider can successfully argue that any payments that were received only applied to performing the service itself, and did not apply to a transfer of ownership of the resulting content.

The only way to avoid this potential loophole is to clarify, in writing, that whatever fees are being paid include the cost of a) the services being provided and b) ownership of the resulting content under the definition of it being a work-for-hire situation. Work-for-hire employment situations have a bad rap in some sectors of the entertainment business. The problem isn't with the business model itself. But misunderstandings can occur from a lack of clarity, understanding, and communication between two parties from the beginning of a business transaction, if each party had a different set of expectations about the terms and conditions that guided them.

Many people don't fully understand that signing a work-for-hire agreement means they give up their right to ownership. There can be confusion about being hired, or in the case of a songwriter, hiring someone else to provide a service with the understanding that the terms of this employment will be regarded as "work for hire" or "a work made for hire." This type of arrangement absolutely requires that the employer (the artist, producer, or whoever hires someone to perform services) state the details of the terms of the agreement in writing. All participants must sign the agreement. In these situations, it's to your benefit to have the person you hire sign a contract/release form before you give any money.

This agreement should make it clear that all rights, privileges, and ownership in relation to any content that's created by performing the specified service, and for the duration of the employment, is the property of the person writing the check. Some common examples of work-for-hire scenarios that need this kind of agreement in writing are:

- A studio musician is hired solely for the purpose of performing on one or more recordings of a preexisting composition. He is not contributing to the creation of the composition itself.
- An arranger is hired to create scores and/or alternate orchestration of a preexisting song or composition, such as a classic punk rock song getting arranged for a big band orchestra. This song and its copyright already exist.
- Vocalists are hired to sing jingles, commercial spots, and voice-overs or to demo entire songs. In these cases the song—the lyrics and the melodies—have already been written and are provided to the hired vocalist either before or upon arriving at the recording session.

Many musicians complain that a producer they paid to help with the production of music that was already written made claims of ownership after. They didn't think to have an agreement stating otherwise. Talk to an attorney before you hire anyone to work on your music and have an agreement ready for all collaborators to sign—before you pay them. You don't want problems down the road!

Employee or Collaborator?

It's important to note that any slight variations that are applied to the situations discussed above have the potential to alter the dynamics of a working relationship in such a way that what first began as a work for hire starts to assume elements of being a collaboration. Which is which? Who decides? Any lines that get drawn are, at least in the beginning, completely negotiable as long as everyone can live with the terms that are decided upon. Someone working with you may feel as though she's participating more as a collaborator. However, if the contract that was signed describes a different arrangement, lamenting will be of no legal or financial benefit, regardless of how much or how little collaboration actually transpired.

In most cases, the person being hired and paid in a work-for-hire capacity is not getting screwed. Actually, being paid on a song-by-song basis is usually more financially advantageous for the hired musicians than for the songwriter. The odds are against any one song becoming a hit or going on to generate sizable royalties in the future. The songwriters are investing in their songs. The people hired get paid for doing the work immediately. They don't have to wait to see if the song gets placed or for back-end royalties to generate months or years down the road. There's no high degree of certainty that each song will make more money than was paid to record it.

Songs are often written and recorded on spec for what may seem to be an opportunity worth pursuing. Typically, any and all initial production costs, including studio time, gear, rentals, hiring musicians, engineers, etc., associated with the recording rest upon the songwriter/producer. These costs (in theory) get recouped if the song/recording ends up being selected for the opportunity at hand, and a financial loss ensues if it doesn't get chosen. In contrast, regardless of the outcome, anyone who participated as a work-for-hire employee gets paid. They give up claims on the song but get compensated no matter how well, or how poorly, the song does.

The line that separates that employee status from actual collaboration is fuzzy. The best and only way to avoid a slew of potential problems, misunderstandings, and hard feelings that can result from crossing this line is to spell out the terms and definitions that guide the project from the start. This is the most comfortable time to address such things. Human nature makes people more open to suggestions at the blueprint stage. Once production is underway, it's far less likely to be the case. At that point, asking or needing to change the terms of the business structure will probably be met with resistance or animosity, unless you're offering to give them more money and rights.

Some service providers may take issue with a work-for-hire arrangement, especially if they're paid little or nothing for providing a service or equipment access that's time-consuming or expensive. They may be willing to grant you unrestricted use of any of the music, video, or photographic content for promotional purposes; however, they will retain actual ownership of the material. This has the potential to become complicated if a third party wants to include or embed this content as part of their own, and are willing to pay a licensing fee in order to acquire this right. The third-party contract will stipulate that you must have the right to grant such permission.

Common Contractual Terms and Provisions

Contracts can seem like they're written in an alien language with all the legalese terms and phrasing. It's good to be at least familiar with some of the important terms and how they're used. As I said earlier, you don't want to negotiate a contract on your own but you do want to be able to understand your attorney's explanation and suggested changes and requests. Below is an overview of some of these common terms and provisions that you'll most likely encounter in the world of music licensing.

Term and Expiration

The *term* section of a music licensing agreement specifies when a license goes into effect and if and when it will expire. The duration of a given term may be as little as a few weeks or it can last as long as "in perpetuity," which means forever. The notion of an infinite term is dubious in nature, especially when one realistically considers the question of whom, if anyone, would enforce such matters light-years from now. Abstract and mind-bending concepts such as "forever" and "throughout the entire universe" extend beyond the grasp of what is comprehensible for most of us, with the notable exception of lawyers.

The length of the term that's being suggested or required by an agreement is among those factors considered for the purpose of determining an appropriate and acceptable payment. There is often a direct correlation between term duration and fee rates. In some cases, failure to acknowledge or fully appreciate this relationship has the potential to become a point of contention or to create a need for further negotiation. Some examples of terms are:

- Term: Perpetuity
- All of the rights granted herein may be used in and in connection with the Episode for a period of two (2) years, starting from the date of the first syndicated broadcast of the Episode.
- The term of which this license is issued shall commence upon entering agreement.

Territory

Territory is the term used for defining where the license is in effect. The most common territories referenced are "the world" and "the universe." However, some agreements are less ambiguous, and will place restrictions on the scope of the territory. For example, a film festival license is a special-case synch/master agreement that clears the rights to include music in the film, but is limited to film festival exhibition only. The territory defined in the agreement may be restricted to a specific town or city, or a venue that's hosting the film festival, and specifies that the license expires on the festival's last day.

Grant of Rights

This section of a licensing agreement involves *verbs* presented in the form of permissible actions to be performed. Most of what is being sought in the way of rights acquisition is closely related to mechanical procedures that are necessary for replication, which means the right to make copies for public exhibition, in one or more locations and for entertainment purposes. Whatever rights are included in this section of the contract are understood to be permissible throughout the term of the agreement. The rights granted within this section are those that are often required or mandatory because they will allow the licensing parties to remain in a position to carry out their own business affairs in relation to media they own, along with the inclusion of some amount of licensed content.

Copyright is all about making copies. Though the licensors own copyright protection, in the grant of rights sections they give a licensing party the right to make copies of whatever media will include some portion of the licensors' copyright material. For example, as part of a synchronization licensing agreement, it's customary for the licensor to grant to the licensee the non-exclusive right, privilege, and authority to record, copy, and publicize the song within the context of the media for which it is being licensed. Here are some common grant of rights provisions in connection with synchronization licenses and some common contractual provisions:

- Right to RECORD Composition: "The right to record the Composition in any manner, medium, form, or language in synchronism or timed-relation with the Film, throughout the Territory…"
- Right to COPY Composition: "The right to make copies of such recordings and import said recordings and/or copies thereof into any country throughout the Territory…"
- Right to PUBLICLY PERFORM AND PUBLICIZE Composition: "The right to publicly perform or televise for profit or nonprofit and authorize others so to perform or televise the Composition in the exhibition of the Film throughout the Territory by all means of television now known or hereafter devised. Licensee shall not be obligated to use the Composition or any of the rights granted herein, and/or in connection with Film."

Subject to whatever terms are presented in a master licensing agreement, the licensor will also customarily grant to the licensee the nonexclusive, limited right, license, and authority to record and exhibit the master recording and possibly more. There are common grant of rights in connection with a master license. Here are some samples of these rights and the contractual provisions:

- Right to RECORD Master: "Licensee shall have the right to record, rerecord, and dub the Master and use the Master in synchronism or timed-relation with the Program."
- Right to EXHIBIT Master: "The right to exhibit the Master as embodied in the Episode, and portions thereof, to audiences

for entertainment throughout the Territory and by any and all methods or means of television now or hereafter known…"

- Right to use NAME, LIKENESS, and BIOGRAPHY(S) in connection with Master: "… the right to use the name, photograph, likeness, and biographical materials of all artists who perform on the Master in and in connection with the Episode, in all advertising and publicity therefore and subsidiary and ancillary uses thereof, including merchandising and commercial tie-ins, but not product endorsements."

Name, Likeness, and Biography Provisions

Some licensing agreements, though not all, feature a provision that gives the licensee the right to also use the artist's name, likeness, and biography in connection or "in-context" of the film or TV series and song that's being licensed. These provisions give the licensee an opportunity to make good on any prior mention or assertion that participation in the project has the potential for more than just financial benefits. An artist may be told that licensing the song will also be an opportunity to get good exposure and can be a great mechanism for generating free publicity.

As a caveat, these kind of provisions may need to be modified or excluded from a licensing agreement if the artist's name, likeness, and/or biography are restricted, prohibited, or under the control of preexisting terms of exclusivity that are in effect. An artist may have a preexisting agreement(s) with other parties, such as a manager, record company, sponsor, model agency, merchandiser, etc. If you have an agreement with any of these make sure you have the right to sign a contract where your name, likeness, and/or biography will be used. Be up front with all parties in the deal to avoid problems later.

Moral Rights

Most artists recognize the value of opportunities for exposure. They're happy to get a deal that offers potential benefits to generate some good publicity or advance their career. However, there's also the possibility, albeit slight or unintentional, that somehow a particular project may generate exposure that's not flattering or helpful. Perhaps the film is very controversial, politically polarized, or highly offensive. The messages or political nature of the film might be in direct opposition to your own, and as such, you'd never want your music associated with it. But an authorized representative or exclusive publisher could license it for such use without your having a say before the agreement is signed. Is there anything that can protect you from this situation? Yes, an article of copyright law addresses this.

Moral rights, sometimes referred to by its French translation, *droit moral*, is another protection that's afforded to authors via copyright. For the purpose of this discussion, moral rights are used in reference to one's faith or religious tenets. There can be a personal and, at times, deep connection between an artist and the work you create. Regardless of any monetary value that might become associated with the music, there's also the value of one's reputation in relation to the eventual use of this work in the future. So while on the one hand, you may be eager to start seeing some royalties from your music, on the other, you may still have limits on how and where that money can come from.

The provisions for moral rights offers protection from any unauthorized alterations, revisions, affiliations, or manipulations that serve to distort, devalue, or defame either the work itself, or the reputation of the author. This principle stands, regardless of who owns the work. On occasion, some agreements will include a provision that requires you to waive this right. The decision to agree to this, or to remove the provision from an agreement, is a judgment call that should be considered with care and on a case-by-case basis. Speak with an entertainment attorney when in doubt. Here are some examples of moral rights provisions:

- Licensee has requested Licensor to waive moral rights: "Licensor hereby expressly waives any rights of 'droit moral' that may be afforded Licensor under the laws of any country either as an author, composer, performer, and producer or in any other capacity in connection with the Master…"
- Representative for Artist acknowledging moral rights: "Should company administer an agreement on your behalf, we agree not to license to such visual media as porn, religious, political, and drug-related programming without your permission."

Representations and Warranties
A *representations and warranties* clause is a standard provision found in virtually all contracts, usually near the end. In a nutshell, it serves to confirm

and verify that the persons and/or parties who are entering into the agreement and granting all specified clearance rights have the sole authority required for doing so and are also fully accountable for any claims and/or damages that may occur, if at all to the contrary.

- "Licensor represents and warrants that it owns or controls one hundred percent (100%) of the copyright in and to the Composition and Master Recording for the Territory, and that it owns or controls all rights necessary to enter into and fully perform the terms hereof."

For the purposes of a song licensing agreement, I'm illustrating a loose translation of what is being said—a simplified translation of the legal mumbo-jumbo:

Dear Licensor:

I am writing you this note as a courtesy reminder that should you enter into an agreement with me, you guarantee what you have promised me, and the situation you appear to be representing is the truth. However, if for whatever reason you are being dishonest, I must insist that you proceed with a complete willingness to take full responsibility should your deception cause the shit to hit the fan one day in the future. This means you foot the bill for any damages, monetary loss, lawsuits, or any other consequences that come as a result. The choice to be honest is yours, and the ramifications for not doing so completely rest upon your shoulders, and we are in no way to be held accountable.

Yours truly,
Licensee

So who, if anyone, would be inclined to make a fuss? One possible candidate for filing claims of this nature would be a disenfranchised (and until now, ignored) entitled party, whose existence, for whatever reason, was intentionally excluded from all discussions while the other entitled party green-lit the deal. The problem is that consent from all entitled parties is required to properly grant the clearance afforded by the agreement. Anyone omitted or ignored by the party who entered the agreement can stop the deal from happening, even if leaving out the aggrieved party was unintentional. Contracts have these standard representations and warranties clauses to add a level of protection to the deal and make you liable if there's a problem later. Some examples of things you agree to are:

- You own and control all rights in and to the composition and master and have the sole right to grant both licenses.
- You verify that there are no additional payments, royalties, or consents required from any other parties. "Other parties" could include, but aren't limited to, any music producers or musicians who may have contributed to the music and whose consent would be required to grant clearance and use of the composition and/or master as authorized by the licensing agreement.
- The use of the composition and master being licensed doesn't infringe upon or violate any rights of any third party (additional copyright owners intentionally omitted from participating in the agreement).
- The song does not infringe on any rights of copyright or otherwise of any third parties or entities.
- Licensor shall indemnify licensee, its employees, and its associates, including but not limited to any financiers or distributors, successors, designees, licensees, and assigns, from any and all claims, demands, suits, losses, costs, expenses (including reasonable counsel fees), damages, or recoveries which may be obtained against, imposed upon, or suffered by licensee, its employees, its associates, successors, designees, licensees, and assigns, by reason of licensor's breach, in whole or in part, of any of the representations and warranties herein contained resulting in a final, nonappealable judgment in a court of competent jurisdiction or settle with the prior written consent of licensor, which consent shall not be unreasonably withheld.

Assignments/Transfer of Licensed Rights

Assignment allows the licensee to transfer any of the rights and provisions granted through a licensing agreement to one or more third parties in the future. For example, let's say an episode of a TV series that features one of your songs first airs on network television. Several months later, the producers of this series enter an agreement that offers the entire season through a video on demand (VOD) pay-per-view service. Because VOD was included as one of the options granted as part of the licensing agreement used for clearing your song, the licensing rights are simply transferred to the VOD service, without the obligation or need for paying additional licensing fees or entering a second licensing agreement for your song.

> "Licensee shall have the right to transfer or assign its rights and/or obligations pursuant to this License to any other person, corporation, or entity and shall be relieved of its obligations to Licensor hereunder to the extent such person, corporation, or entity assumes such obligations."

Jurisdiction

Certain laws vary from state to state, and country to country. If two parties enter into an agreement and each happens to reside in a different state, or different countries, it opens the door for some gray areas and/or possible loopholes for enforcing the contractual terms, interpreting applicable business laws, and having an effective ability to pursue legal action if necessary. Should allegations of a breach of contract begin to surface, the notion of "unlawful" is sometimes dependent on the location. When both parties agree to a single jurisdiction, the laws of that state or country are what are applied and upheld for the purpose of fulfilling the terms of an agreement.

> "This Agreement, regardless of its place of execution, shall be construed, interpreted, and enforced in accordance to the laws of the State of California, United States of America, applicable to agreements executed, delivered, and to be performed within such State."

||||||||||||||||||||||||||||||||||||||||||||||||||||||||||||||||||||||||||||||||||||||||||||||||||||||||||||||||||||||||||||||||

CHAPTER 6

Show Me the Money!

While the ego trip of telling friends that your song is in a cool show or film is fun, it doesn't always pay the rent. This chapter is an overview of the different sources of income from licensing. Understanding where the money comes from helps you to keep track of it when your songs are placed in income-earning projects. While others will help to collect it, you are still your own best advocate and therefore, should understand the process.

This chapter explores payment arrangements, negotiating master and synchronization licensing fees, publishing advances, broadcast royalties, soundtrack album mechanical royalties, and how to acquire a knack for knowing when to hold, and when to fold. While you can't control everything in this business, you can control your own business by understanding how the money side of licensing works.

Valuing Your Talent and Skills

I was thinking about what we do in order to create great music that is up to licensing standards, and all the time we put into it. Over the years, it's easy to forget just how complex a job like ours can be at times, and why it's okay—or actually your right—to ask for a respectable rate. I also believe that your value goes up when you have the ability to provide additional assets that not everyone has. Can you offer any of these?

- The technical expertise required to record, mix, master, edit, and deliver a piece of music that meets the deadline and addresses any of the nitpicky technical requirements that, at times, can be a challenge.
- The gear required to make a good recording. It's expensive, and it takes time to learn how to use it all, keep it updated, and make

it work seamlessly. If you have access to the necessary equipment and software to get a recording done properly and on time, you're ahead of many people in what you offer.

- The ability to understand and dissect what it means to sound like a well-known band by being able to identify all the signature elements and, from there, create something original with the same flavor.
- The ability to listen to what kind of music someone wants for a project and be able to interpret their nonmusical descriptions to give them what they seem to want or to convince them what you give them is what they want.
- The disposition to balance your creative nature with the realities of a business transaction.

Then comes the potentially awkward question, "So what are your rates?" This might be in reference to licensing fees. Or, if you're asked to write and produce an original piece of music for a project, you'll quote a price that covers both the cost of production and the licenses for the paying client to use this end product. Rather than just blurting out a number, ask if they have a music budget in mind or a limit to what they can pay. Otherwise, you might outprice your competition.

When I calculate what seems like a fair and reasonable charge, I try to think about how many hours it will take, while factoring in the very real possibility that one or more additional tweaks, adjustments, or last-minute changes end up being necessary later. This happens frequently enough to be considered a normal part of the process. People change their minds or hear something you did that they like, and then want more of it. Sometimes the project itself changes slightly, so be prepared to revisit what in your mind may have already been finished. You need to take into account when you set a fee to create music that there is always, "Oh, and just one more little thing..."

If you're serious about making a living from your musical talents, eventually you'll find yourself at a symbolic crossroad, where the continuation of these efforts requires that you distinguish yourself as a professional or an amateur. The key distinction is that professional licensing situations imply that any goods or services are provided in exchange for payment. Sometimes in film and music production situations, two parties agree to exchange certain products and services with one another. This is fine as long as both parties are satisfied with the outcome of the transaction. Amateurs willingly give their music in exchange for gaining experience, exposure, or affiliation. In some instances, amateur opportunities do include a payment, though considerably lower in scale than professional rates paid under comparable circumstances. When you feel confident enough to call yourself a professional, expect to get paid.

Cash Advances from Publishers

One of the most tempting aspects of exclusive publishing deals is the up-front advance. For these agreements that make you transfer your rights to them, they don't buy now and pay you later as is done in other types of deals. Instead, they buy now and pay you now. A vast majority of exclusive publishing deals will include either an up-front cash advance against future earnings or a lump-sum payment, which serves as a buyout fee that's payable upon signing. The amount of advances varies. There's nothing standard about them nor are there any legal precedents guiding what's offered. What you get depends on the songs, the songwriter/artist, and the publisher. Up-front advances against future earnings that are paid by a publishing company typically span between $1,000 and $10,000 per song for a deal that involves great songs by an unknown artist.

Being paid an up-front advance for publishing deals that involve terms of exclusivity is a customary practice, but even here, there's no standard. On more than one occasion, I've heard panelists speaking at music industry conferences mention that for them, the baseline advance (on a per-song basis) for an exclusive publishing deal should be a minimum of $1,000. Ultimately, you'll have to be guided by your professional instincts when presented with agreements that involve terms of exclusivity. On occasion, there are licensing opportunities mandating that any music submissions must have exclusive representation. A notable example is the television network ABC, which wants music sent in only by you (with the ability to offer 100 percent synch/master clearance) or your exclusive representation that could do the same. Remember that, as with record deals, an advance is money paid out against future earnings. If the deal is exclusive, which means they represent all of your deals, they should pay you for that privilege!

A lump-sum buyout can be much higher, depending on the circumstances and players. A publishing buyout agreement is more often encountered in the world of advertising, jingles, and commercials. Sometimes there's a buyout in television in special cases, like for a theme song, where the music being purchased must remain exclusively linked to a certain product, TV series, or advertisement and used only for related purposes. If you have a nonexclusive agreement, there probably won't be an advance but you will also retain at least some, if not all, of your rights.

Mechanical Licenses and Royalties

The term *mechanical rights* is used in reference to the right to manufacture and sell copies of a recording. Permission for doing so is granted through what's known as a *mechanical license*. This is the type of license that is involved with recording contracts, soundtrack albums, DVDs, compilations, or any music collections where copies are manufactured and sold. The revenue stream generated from selling copies of a recording is called *mechanical royalties*. A mechanical license is not necessary or required for the sole purpose of licensing songs for use in a television series, film, advertising, etc. But it is necessary if your song is on a soundtrack album or other recording that's offered for sale.

If you're in a situation where entering a mechanical license becomes necessary, the details should be addressed in a separate agreement between you and the party who will be selling copies. At the time of the writing of this book, the statutory mechanical royalty rate set by Congress for a physical recording (such as CDs and cassettes) and permanent digital downloads is $.091 for a song lasting five minutes or less. The mechanical royalty rate for songs that are over five minutes is determined by multiplying that number of minutes by $.0175. Each song gets that royalty.

MECHANICAL ROYALTIES

SONG LENGTH	MECHANICAL ROYALTY	CALCULATION
5 minutes (or less)	$.091	Fixed
5:01–6:00 minutes	$.105	6 x $.0175 = $.105
6:01–7:00 minutes	$.1225	7 x $.0175 = $.1225
7:01–8:00 minutes	$.14	8 x $.0175 = $.14

Let's say you wrote a song that's less than five minutes. It gets included on a soundtrack album that sells 500,000 copies. In this case, your mechanical royalty earnings would be 500,000 x $.091 = $45,500. If another song featured ends up running seven minutes and thirty seconds on the same soundtrack album, this track would earn 500,000 x $.14 = $70,000. Copies of music that's purchased for mobile media offers still more impressive royalty returns. The current statutory mechanical royalty rate for ringtones is presently set at $.24 per copy sold.

Front-End Fees

The *front-end fees* for licensing are those paid for the synchronization and master licenses. These are licensing fees paid initially for the use of your music. As previously discussed, the synchronization license clears the composition to be used for a specified amount of time. The master license clears the sound recording of the song itself. The size of these fees paid usually take into account the program type, scope of media rights that are granted in the licenses, how the song will be used, and for how long. There's no standard fee for these licenses. If the offer seems too low, it's your choice to turn it down. If a music supervisor wants your song badly enough, there can be room for negotiations. Each project has a budget they must work with.

The highest licensing fees are most often associated with shows that air in prime-time on the television networks—NBC, ABC, CBS, and Fox—or cable TV shows such as those that air on HBO or Showtime. The fees can also be influenced by whom the artist is. A well-known one may be able to demand higher licensing fees than one who is still under the radar. Most fees will often fall in the range of $1,000 to $15,000. The average rate is probably around $2,500 for a commercial-sounding recording with vocals. But there are always exceptions. You also may encounter situations that pay artists no up-front licensing fees. If you agree, you'll give a *gratis use* license. This is the business model most often used by MTV and some other shows. Many artists agree for the cachet of having their music in these shows. However, this really isn't the same as allowing your music for free, since you'll still collect the back-end royalties (more below). Or you may be offered $50,000 as a flat-rate buyout agreement that involves a transfer of copyright.

There are three mistakes that can eviscerate a writer's earnings: first, failure to register properly with his performing rights society; second, failure to prepare and file a proper cue sheet with his performing rights society; and third, some step deals should permit audits and these should be explicitly provided for in the license agreement. Another mistake often made is that a grant of rights is made to use a song in a film, and it ends up being used in a manner, or behind a scene, different from what was anticipated. This can be avoided by attaching the script page to the license agreement, which I insist on without exception.

PETER M. THALL, Esq.

Back-End Royalties

When music is used on a television show, it's considered a performance of the song. In most cases, the use of music in this capacity isn't a live performance, but rather is considered to be a retransmission of what was performed live during the recording. Television networks and cable stations pay annual licensing fees to the performing rights organizations. This license grants TV networks and stations permission to include music written by their members as part of its programming. The scope of the network or station's broadcast range is directly related to the cost of renewing these annual licensing fees with the PROs. A television network that broadcasts nationwide pays higher licensing fees than one that only broadcasts locally. Performing rights organizations (ASCAP, BMI, and SESAC) periodically pay their members broadcast performance royalties, often referred to as *back-end royalties* since it's money that can keep coming in long after the license is issued.

Several administration issues need to be addressed to ensure that you get all the royalties your songs have earned. Receiving a payment requires that your songs are registered and appear in your performing rights organization's database. This process is straightforward and easily done online. The writer or publisher is responsible for handling this. If you have a publisher or cowriters, be sure to clarify who will take care of this and make sure that it gets done. Unregistered song titles, even when featured as part of a broadcast, will result in major delays or, more likely, omitted royalty payments.

The best way to get the most out of your PRO is to stay in touch with your representative and keep them up-to-date on what you are doing musically. Being in touch allows the staff at SESAC to keep you in mind when opportunities come up. The other important thing a writer must do is to register all of their songs that are being performed in their SESAC catalog. A SESAC writer can manage his catalog online via our website.

LINDA LORENCE CRITELLI, Vice President,
Writer/Publisher Relations, SESAC

There are a few quirks in the system. For example, music that appears in a movie soundtrack being exhibited/performed in movie houses in the U.S. (theaters or cinema exhibitions) will not generate performance royalties, because a U.S. federal court ruling provided movie theaters with an exemption from having to file and uphold blanket license agreements with the performing rights organization. This ruling applies to domestic movie houses (U.S.) but hasn't established an international precedent; many foreign PROs do pay performance royalties for music performed in movie houses. Direct-to-DVD releases don't generate performance royalties because no broadcast takes place. If it's known beforehand that a film's primary method of release will be direct-to-DVD, it's possible to ask for a mechanical royalty based on DVD sales. It's possible for a movie, even one that's not a blockbuster hit, to sell a surprising number of copies.

Mechanical royalty requests are addressed on a case-by-case basis. You'd have an easier time justifying this request if the project is going straight to DVD and the licensing fees offered are ultralow or nonexistent. But there unfortunately won't be performance royalties. The up-front licensing fees may be the only money you'll ever see.

Royalty statements to those whose songs have earned broadcast royalties are distributed on specified dates throughout the year, usually quarterly. The exact dates vary among the PROs. Statements include a check and listing of credited performances. If your music was broadcast as part of a blanket license, this statement may be the first time you become aware of that particular use. Many songwriters who license music consider back-end performance royalties their bread and butter because getting songs broadcast on TV can result in a steady stream of royalties.

ASCAP licenses all major networks, cable channels, and local TV stations. We do comprehensive surveys and samples to ensure fair, accurate, and timely payments. Composers and songwriters can help ASCAP do our job by ensuring that we receive cue sheets (when they can) and by making sure they have registered all of their works with us.

RANDY GRIMMETT, Senior Vice President,
Domestic Membership, ASCAP

Getting paid broadcast royalties requires that someone provide the performing rights organization documentation, most commonly referred to as a *cue sheet*. They provide confirmation to performing rights organizations about which of their member's songs have been used in or as part of a program or movie that was broadcast during a specific quarter. Cue sheets for television include information related to the song titles, duration, usage, entitled parties, and date of broadcast. There's no standard format. In short, songs used on TV, cable, or movies that end up being broadcast in some capacity will generate performance royalties (domestic and foreign), as long as cue sheets are submitted and song titles appearing on the cue sheets are registered. The information logged onto a cue sheet gets cross-referenced against the information on file with the PRO's title registration database to ensure that no one is improperly credited or omitted from receiving a royalty credit. If what appears on the cue sheet matches up to the title registration database, your account is credited.

Technically, the responsibility for preparing and submitting cue sheets rests on the shoulders of a TV/film production company, film distributor, or network. However, it's not uncommon for details that should be on cue sheet submissions to get lost in the shuffle. This is especially the case when working with neophyte filmmakers. To ensure that my songs are not overlooked or filled with errors, I negotiate a provision in my licensing agreements that requires the licensee to provide me a copy of the official cue sheet once available. This way, should they forget to submit a copy to my performing rights organization, I'll have the backup option of forwarding my copy if necessary. When in doubt, avoid leaving these situations to chance.

Getting paid can often take time. Television networks are notoriously slow when it comes to completing and submitting program cue sheets to performing rights organizations of songwriters and publishers whose music was used as part of their programming. The performing rights societies may experience their own internal delays as well. The amount of time that lapses from the original airdate of the broadcast to receiving a royalty statement from your PRO can be anywhere from six months up to a year, and possibly longer. If you have representation, once the licensing fees are received by your pitching service, attorney, or publisher, or whoever negotiated the licensing deal, it's now on to phase two of the wait. Received money must be deposited and cleared. Then they notify payroll and accounting, and at last, mail you a check according to their accounting schedule or practice, less whatever commission fee is deducted.

Step-Up Agreements

For projects on a shoestring budget or whose production costs have them in the red, *step-up agreements* are an option for easing financial strain without sacrificing the desire to include quality music. A step-up agreement is a master/synch license that places a certain number of restrictions on the types of clearance that are covered by the license in its current form, in exchange for agreeing to an otherwise reduced licensing fee. The agreement includes provisions for lifting these restrictions in the future for one or more additional payments as the status of the film changes. Many beginning artists are thrilled to have their song in a film, however small it is, and give away all their rights to additional fees in the initial agreement. They're usually convinced the film won't go further than festivals. While many don't, some do. Don't lose out on the potential for money further down the road if the film gets picked up and becomes popular!

The scope and specific types of clearance restrictions can vary from one agreement to another. They usually make reference to permissible media formats, territories, and methods of distribution, broadcasting, and publicizing and specify if they're allowed at the first step of the deal or excluded from the current terms of the agreement. A step-up deal spells out the licensing fees that will be initially paid for the use of your songs now and lists conditions that will need to be satisfied for making the payment of additional licensing fees/royalties in the future. Factors such as box office ticket sales, DVD copies sold, PPV orders, number of digital downloads, or other uses that generate sales receipts and more will earn royalties for your song.

For example, for every X thousand people who see the film with your music, you'd get a step-up in fees. Let's say your song is licensed for use in a new movie at a reduced licensing fee rate with the understanding that the clearance presently granted only covers usage during the festival and expires when it's over. Afterwards, the movie gets picked up by a distribution company for an international theatrical release. Before this can happen, payment of an additional licensing fee or previously agreed-upon balance will be owed to you in order to step-up the expanding scope of clearance.

If you consent to a step-up agreement, I advise that you protect your interest whenever possible, by stating in the agreement that by agreeing to the initial terms and reduced licensing fees, there will be an ongoing commitment to continue to include the song, should any expansions in clearance become necessary. In other words, you want assurance that a step-up for the film won't allow for a loophole opportunity to replace your song, at least not without your being compensated for any licensing fee balances that remain. Discuss this with your attorney.

‖‖‖

CHAPTER 7

What Music Works Best for Licensing?

Many musicians think that, as long as the music they create is good, they should be able to get it licensed. Creating high-quality music is only half the battle—the music must also work with the images that comprise the licensee's project. This chapter will enlighten you on how to figure out where the best opportunities lie for your music and how to create work habits that make you someone music supervisors turn to for music.

Understanding the Emotion of Music

If you want to license your music, it's important to fully understand how music interacts with visual images. Music supervisors don't look for pleasant songs to include in their productions. They want music that will set the right tone for what's going on in the pictures. Music can evoke a wide range of emotions. A song's ability to capture a specific emotion or message can be a strong asset to its marketability, especially when you respond to music requests that specify a need for that same emotion or message.

> We try to bring emotion to our video pieces. Whether it's through a song's lyrics or the use of certain instruments, music plays a huge role in how we produce our video content.
>
> GRANT MONREAN, Videographer, Editor,
> Producer, and Owner, Monrean Multimedia

Two obvious emotions that are frequently needed in music are *joy* and *sorrow*. Art imitates life, and it should be of no surprise that these two emotions are ubiquitous in film and TV plots. Other emotions music regularly evokes are *anger, betrayal, confusion, fear, euphoria, satisfaction, confidence, adventure*, and *bravery*. All can contribute to bringing major events—and the factors that shape them—to life, including birth, childhood, graduation, coming of age, marriage, divorce, work, change, war, country, friends, politics, success, failure, morality, mortality, money, and death. Music has the ability to create anticipation and clues us in that something is going to happen when you'd otherwise not expect it.

You must do more than simply record a song about an emotion. The performance and the music itself must elicit emotions, too. Lyrics can set a mood or tell a back story that complements the mood on the screen. The music behind the lyrics can have just as much power to make the viewer happy, sad, scared, excited, expectant, or angry. Song quality, performance, and production are also inescapable factors that influence the selection process. A given placement might boil down to having to choose between one of two songs, where both are excellent contenders. One features male vocals, and the other female vocals. Both songs work, though it is finally decided that the scene is better suited for the female vocal track. But with all these factors contributing to a choice, a song must have the right emotional tenor to carry the visuals in the scene.

> *All music sets a mood. You can take any piece of music and put it up against a picture, then put another piece of music against the same picture and you'll hit different emotions. The music might have to bring something to the table that the visual is missing. You can see a very dramatic scene and put a dramatic piece of music under it, and it adds to the drama. But if you have a very dramatic scene and put a piece of whimsical music under it, all of a sudden, instead of people being scared and crying in that scene, they're laughing. Music brings a whole different attitude to what you're looking at.*
>
> ED RAZZANO, Vice President, Business Development
> (North America), Ricall, an online music licensing marketplace

Any given TV show or movie can have a variety of emotions in different scenes. Besides actual shows with a story line, TV uses music for all sorts of other types of shows. Sports television is full of emotions—excitement, ecstasy, and the agony of defeat. Soap operas can be dens of emotions with music highlighting what's going on. Advertising agencies look for music that can get across the appropriate feelings about a product they're trying to sell. Music for video games gets people playing them revved, excited, or even feeling defeated. Music has the power to put people into a variety of moods. It's up to you to identify what moods your music can bring up.

Getting Acquainted with Musical Content

If you want to get the best idea possible of what works for film, TV, video games, etc., watch a lot of them. Begin to pay attention to how music is used. You might be thinking that you've already seen a gazillion films or shows, but watching them to study how the music interacts with the visuals is completely different. Notice how a change in the song can change the mood.

Watch shows you'd like your music on. Turn off the volume and play your song to see if it sets a mood as strongly as does the one used. This is called "playing your music against the picture." That's what music supervisors do to determine if a piece of music works or which section works best. Play videos of movies first without the sound, and then with the volume on, and see how the music evokes the right mood. Then figure out where your music might fit in. The more you become conscious of the role music plays with visuals, the more you'll be able to home in on the right opportunities for your music.

> *Submitting nonvocal versions of your songs is probably the number one way to get placements. Even if I am interested in the lyrics and am planning to "feature" the song in a scene or montage, having the instrumental of that music allows me to lead in with the song under dialogue and then find the right point to come in with the lyric-version of the true song. Nonvocal versions of songs can also be used in many more types of scenes as there is not a conflict with the dialogue in a scene. The tricky part is that lyrics usually have to be applicable to the subject matter of the scene or convey the exact senti-ment that the project requires. Additionally, songs or music cues that have tight, distinctive endings rather than music that just fades out is going to get you many more placements. Strong finishes to songs and completely resolved endings give scenes excellent transitions.*
>
> BRENT KIDWELL, Freelance Music Supervisor

Think about what emotions you hear as you watch. How does music add to excitement in video games? Or make you sad when someone falls in the Olympics? Or make you expect something awful to happen in a film, when everything seems fine? Ask others how your music makes them feel. Begin to catalog your music according to the different moods it evokes. This will help prepare you for when you see a professional request for a specific mood of music.If you don't understand how music interacts with the visuals, you might continue to submit to calls that your music doesn't fit. That can cause music supervisors to ignore your music in the future.

Where Different Genres Fit

Besides adding the emotional elements, music is often used to reinforce a message, idea, or critical plot elements such as culture, lifestyle, an historic period, mood, and the environment that's being depicted in the accompanying visual imagery. The subjective notion of "what music works best for a given licensing opportunity" is most often a function of some combination of these elements.

> *There are two different mistakes that I see artists make when trying to get attention from supervisors and music production companies. The first is that a lot of artists write what they think sounds like a commercial, and in the process lose the soul or unique characteristics of their more personal music. What they might not understand is that the more different you are, the better chance of filling a niche for a specific style you'll have. The other mistake I see is that many artists have unrealistic expectations about the usability of their music, no matter what style it is. Supervisors are always looking to fill a very specific need, whether it's a word in a chorus or a song structure that fits the scene, and rarely, if ever, are they just looking for a "cool track." The chances of your song being the perfect fit for the criteria are slim. That said, making sure that your song is in consideration by actively reminding a supervisor that it exists will greatly increase those odds.*

> ALEX MOULTON, Founder and creative
> force behind Expansion Team

It's hard to say exactly where different genres fit into the picture of music licensing. Below I've listed some of the more common musical genres most frequently sought after in music requests. For each I've given a description of some of the elements they may have that make them marketable for song placement and licensing. Having a general feel for what your music might be best suited for can serve as a valuable marketing tool. Anytime you have an opportunity to get feedback about the best uses for your music, ask and keep the suggestions in mind for future music calls. Mind you, there are many exceptions to all of these generalizations and all music can work when it hits a music supervisor in a way that enhances the feel of a scene.

Instrumental music is most often used as background ambience. All genres can work under the right circumstances. Music without vocals also works well for documentaries and reality TV shows where a lot of music ambience is needed.

Jazz and blues can work well for comedy and romantic scenes. It can also be used to add a nostalgic flavor to the right moments.

Classical music evokes a feeling that can work especially well for historical works, such as biographical shows, period pieces, epic scenery, and transitions from one scene to another.

Electronic music elicits a feeling of action, which makes it especially effective for fast transitions, scenes where motion is emphasized, and chase scenes. That action feel also makes it very popular for use in games.

Hip-hop music creates the feel of urban environments and is often used for nightclub scenes. It can create the feeling of glamour, anger, extravagance, and excessiveness. It's also popular for some reality TV shows.

Country music is commonly used in scenes that take place in Middle America and town and country settings. It can create a hometown feel and work for visuals that take place on farms, ranches, and dirt roads. It can be good to set a reflective mood or innocent simplicity.

Rock music is often played in scenes involving bars, nightlife, and road trips. A classic rock song can be an effective device for establishing a timetable—scenes of someone having a flashback. Rock fits in well with party scenes or those that show good times.

Heavy metal music can be used to emphasize some strong emotions like power and anger. It also works well for scenes that give a feeling of darkness.

Indie rock music is used for scenes that reflect situations that young people relate to, such as rebellion and antiestablishment behavior, and can highlight sarcasm. It also works well for reality TV.

Punk music can be used to emphasize a situation that calls for anarchy or exudes sentiments that are rebellious and antiestablishment in nature. It's also sometimes used in scenes with violence and people getting into trouble.

Brass arrangements add cinematic textures, tone color, and sonority effects. This works well in science fiction films and shows, epic films, and visuals taking place in the deep sea or in outer space.

Percussion music creates tension. It can enhance chase scenes and intensify the fast pace of a scene. It also works well for scenes taking place in the wilderness.

String orchestra music sets a romantic mood. It can also be used to add melodrama or nostalgia.

High string arrangements that feature sustained pitches, tremolo passages, or pizzicato motifs are common musical devices used to add to the suspense, tension, or fear evoked by visuals on screen.

R&B music can add a soulful, sexy, or nostalgic vibe to a scene.

> It's important to really know the style you're writing in so that your music sounds authentic. Do what you're really good at first, whether it's rock, jazz, hip-hop, or whatever. If you want to branch out into other musical genres, do a lot of research and study what goes into the music that really good composers/artists/bands in that genre are producing. The worst music submissions I've ever received were from people who were trying to "put their own twist" on a given musical genre without knowing and respecting what that genre/style was about.
>
> STEVE SECHI, Composer, Producer, and
> Co-owner of two music libraries

Music Clearance and Racing Clocks

The world of network television production is notorious for imposing frequent and tight deadlines on its staff during a stage commonly referred to as *postproduction*. This is the period when the individual components of a film, video, or TV show are assembled, rearranged, and meticulously edited into one single cohesive presentation that's now locked for a scheduled air-date or another deadline. The process of addressing song requests, music submissions, placements, and clearance are all typically dealt with during the late stages of postproduction and are often among the very last items to be taken care of.

There are other technical issues that are handled during postproduction, including video editing, effects, compositing, animation, text rendering, voice dubbing, sound design, score, and song selection and clearance. Schedules and deadlines are generally far less flexible in television production than what one may encounter when working in film. As a result, when music is called for, it's needed fast—sometimes within an hour of announcing the request. The inability to deliver an appropriate piece of music that's close to any specific requirements or that doesn't present difficulties for the purpose of licensing will often amount to a missed opportunity.

> *Slow people with excuses are the worst thing in the world. Under-standably, musicians tend to be a little artsy, which is fine. But procrastinating, working on other things when there is a delivery deadline, and general laziness will not endear you to anyone. If you're hired by a music supervisor to deliver cues or songs for a job, when you've committed to delivering something by a certain time, you need to make that deadline or be ambitious enough to deliver it early. When I am surprised by someone who has music for me a week or a day or an hour before I expected it, that makes me want to work with that musician again.*
>
> BRENT KIDWELL, Freelance Music Supervisor

When you work on a TV or film production that's loaded with tight dead-lines, it can be challenging to be creative while racing against the clock. Severe time constraints seem to affect creativity in one of two ways. It can either sharpen your ability to focus or cause debilitating mental blocks. If you haven't given this much thought, consider your own reaction to stress-provoking situations. How do you handle situations that put you under pressure or that make you feel very rushed to get something done? What techniques helped you deal with stressful situations in the past?

Some people, in a strange way, thrive under these stressful situations. For them, this kind of pressure is actually a necessary requirement. Others get started but experience a meltdown prior to reaching the finish line. There are also those who may be inclined to throw in the towel before even trying. Understanding how you respond to stress can serve as a guide for creating a work environment and schedule that offers the greatest potential for your best work, satisfaction, and peace of mind. For me, creativity has always been the easier part. Coming up with an idea or design for the music I've been asked for can take very little time. The hard part—always—is bringing my ideas to life in a deliverable format and timeframe. Doing so may involve technical or physical constraints that can't be circumvented.

Time can teach you better habits. If you want to create music for film and TV, you need to get very organized. Your work environment should be treated as a shrine that's entered for the sake of getting connected to the elusive spirits of creativity and productivity. Surround yourself with things that will nourish this encounter and forbid those that prevent it. I never take my cell phone into the studio. If you identify what distracts you, you can try to figure out ways to focus on bringing your creative ideas to fruition. Working quickly is a skill you must learn to succeed in this end of the business!

Music Requests

Music requests can come from a variety of sources that include direct requests, referrals, classifieds, and what are often membership fee–based wire services and websites. Regardless of the source, it's common for a request to be accompanied by a set of directions that ends up falling somewhere between being highly specific to having murky details at best. Knowing what to include as part of a presentation that's being forwarded, or at times and just as important, what not to include, is worth some discussion. Once a deal is on the table, you'll need appropriate communication skills for addressing the varying degrees of business correspondence, whether by e-mail, phone, or in person. The artist, a hired service, or a professional representative, may handle this correspondence.

With most situations, the goal of your communication should be to establish a positive first impression that sets the stage for doing business. There are many unwritten rules for responding to a request. Many music requests take an ambiguous direction, leaving you with some room for interpretation. Much of my advice recaps recurring themes that came up during various conversations I've had over the years with people who regularly post for and/or solicit music requests, as well as those who are accustomed to receiving a staggering amount of music submissions as a result of making a request. It's important to understand when you should or shouldn't respond to a request.

Music Requests with Specific Directions

For the purpose of this discussion, I'll define specific directions as being those that are provided as part of a music request and require very little or no guesswork as to what is being asked for. When responding to these kinds of requests, only submit if you have a close musical approximation from within your sonic arsenal. In most cases, it ends up being a waste of your resources and everyone's time if the music you submit is clearly out-of-step with the specific direction being given. Even if you believe your songs are great, and let's assume that they are indeed, using this premise as the justification for making off-base submissions has the potential to backfire. At the very least, it makes a statement about your lack of ability to follow directions.

> In some cases, the songwriter may be asked for permission to reedit a song to make it better fit a scene, or to provide an instrumental version if the lyrics are obtrusive to dialogue.
> SEAN FERNALD, Producer/Music Supervisor, 3Mac Studios

Big egos can motivate sending music that doesn't fit the guidelines of a request. You may truly believe that once someone hears your songs, they'll change the nature of the music to use yours. This never works! Or you may think this is an opportunity to get your music to someone who might use it in the future. This rarely works either. When someone requests something specific, that's all they want to receive at that time. While not everyone will be annoyed by receiving music that doesn't fit the request, tactics of this nature will most likely irritate busy music supervisors, who frequently deal with an onslaught of music submissions, while under pressure to meet their own deadlines. Unintended consequences of not following specific direction could include:

- Ignoring or disregarding submissions you forward in future.
- Getting blacklisted from any future direct music requests.

When a music request includes directions with clarity, detail, and references, it is safe to assume that for the time being, whatever purpose the music is intended to serve has been closely scrutinized. Any opinions expressed within the direction are unlikely to waver, especially when accompanied by a pressing deadline. The music selection process in these instances is guided by the specific requirements that have been outlined in the request, which commonly include the musical genre, tempo, or lyrics with a specific message or catch phrase. Pay attention and respect the guidelines!

Music Requests That Are "Open to Suggestions"

Other requests leave considerable room for interpretation. Why are some music requests vague? There are instances when it is clear that music is going to be needed for the purpose of providing some magic or excitement for a particular TV spot or advertisement clip; however, at the present moment, it isn't clear to the powers-that-be exactly what the "right" musical direction is. Perhaps the nature of the visual imagery involved is such that it easily lends itself to a wide range of musical styles, or any music that has already been suggested and/or tested isn't working. The selection process in these instances is usually guided by some trial and error.

Depending on the amount and types of music available from within your own catalog archives, forwarding a "best of" or "highlights" type of compilation CD is probably the safest bet. Doing so shows that you have access to a variety of musical categories that are available for licensing. Or, forward your best one to three songs. Often, the selection process in these instances can come down to experimentation—they aren't sure what they want and hope that some of the songs submitted will hit them right and provide the missing direction.

Music Requests for Temp Track Replacements

Arguably, the most frequently encountered phenomenon in the business of music requests involves the hunt to find one or more replacements for a temp track. A *temp track* is a piece of music that's used during the editing phase as a guideline for what emotion or atmosphere the director wants. Temp tracks serve as a reference for the music supervisor and the director as they try to find the right style of music for each scene. The genres of music that might be used in one can span the gamut. They're often songs that are either currently popular or well-known classics. In the case of underscore, a common source for temp track music is music from a preexisting soundtrack album or music library CD.

Why aren't the original temp tracks used in the finished product? As discussed earlier, they may be too expensive or time-consuming to license, despite how well they work. Yet directors and producers become very attached to the overall flow of a given scene that has been assembled with a piece of temp music. During the mad quest to find a convincing replacement, the dubious term *soundalike* may enter the conversation, as the powers-that-be listen for songs that share strong similarities with the temp track.

A director or production company may hire an artist who's capable of writing and recording a song that straddles a fine line between being a good impersonation of the artist/song being replaced and a blatant rip-off. Creating soundalikes brings up a potential artistic moral dilemma: Is it right to capitalize on the unique gifts of a fellow artist? Like it or not, soundalikes are a part of the music licensing business. Musicians and artists who've made an impact past or present have developed a sound that becomes their own signature, or becomes identified with an era, generation, or culture. Often a director or production company may want to capture the essence of these talents in the music they use.

Cover Songs

In some cases, when none of the replacements that have been submitted demonstrate the enigmatic qualities that the temp music provides but the project's producers can't afford the original track, they may record a new master of the temp music, known as a *cover song*. For this strategy to provide a viable solution, a number of preconditions must first be taken into account.

Compulsory Mechanical License
Let's assume that a production company has been editing a pivotal scene in a movie using a temp track. It turns out that it's a popular song that has

been commercially released. The production company decides that, rather than try to replace this music, which already works quite nicely, they will first look into licensing it directly. For the purpose of clearing the synchronization license, the production company contacts the song's publisher, who is willing to accept their $10,000 flat fee. Okay, good, they are halfway there. Now it's on to the next step: clearing the master license.

The production company then forwards a request to the song's record company, which *rejects* their offer of $10,000 for clearing the master license. A representative from the label apologetically mentions that, for the recording in question, $50,000 would be the minimum acceptable offer. Furthermore, this fee is subject to *increase* depending on the scope of the film's release and distribution (national, international, theatrical, DVD rights, etc.). The record company's baseline fee is beyond what the film's overextended budget can afford.

What can be done? Is there a solution? In this case, there is.

The film production company could become what is in essence an ad hoc record company. They would hire an artist to record a cover version of the song, while also covering any of the associated recording and production costs. This approach may end up costing less than they had originally offered to the record company. The interesting spin in this case is that the film production company now owns this new master. As long as the publisher remains on board and enters a licensing agreement, this could be a viable solution.

Compulsory Mechanical License Exceptions

Certain situations do not require a compulsory mechanical license. Rather, permission from a composition's copyright owner for the purpose of making a recording will be needed. These exceptions include:

SONGS THAT HAVE BEEN RECORDED, BUT AT LEAST AS OF NOW, HAVE NOT BEEN COMMERCIALLY RELEASED Example: Years ago your band recorded an album's worth of original material that was never released by your then-record company. Somehow, a filmmaker manages to get his hands on a bootleg copy of these recordings. Because the songs on the album have not been commercially released, the filmmaker would have to get your permission to record his own version of these songs.

SONGS THAT HAVE BEEN WRITTEN, BUT AS OF NOW, WERE NEVER RECORDED Example: You attend a performance by a local artist in a café. Although she performs regularly, no recordings have been made of her original material. During the show, one of her songs strikes you as having hit potential, especially if recorded with male vocals. In this case, no recording of the song in question yet exists, and thus the notion of compulsory mechanical licenses is meaningless. Any thought of recording one of her songs will definitely require getting permission.

Making Cover Songs Work

Others take issue with the idea of playing, performing, or recording cover songs. Perhaps this is a result of pride or a sincere belief in the merits of their own original material. I've known bands and musicians who worried that playing covers during a gig would give the impression of being an amplified wedding band or hotel lounge act, one that can't write its own music.

When you play live, the goal should be to entertain. People are most likely to be drawn in to your show when they hear something recognizable. If your band can play a cover song that's a damn good approximation of a well-known and respected song (vocally and instrumentally), it may be to your advantage to record these songs the next time you're in the studio (a demo mix is okay). Licensing opportunities that involve requests for cover songs come along frequently enough for you to prepare for them ahead of time.

Cleared Music

I've said this before but can't emphasize it too much. Every note of your music must be cleared before you accept a licensing deal. If you wrote it all and own it all, chances are there will be no problem. But sometimes songwriters forget about small deals they signed that never went anywhere or a songwriting partner who has a claim on the song. Or, you may have uncleared (or illegal) sampled content in your music, which is a big concern for people who license music. Every sound coming off your recording must be either yours to give permission for or you must have clearance in writing from any parties that control it. A breach of this can ruin further chances to get your music licensed.

Accidents can happen, even when you try to be careful. For example, I once wrote a song that was published with EMI. Prior to getting that deal, I'd given a copy of the song to a guy I worked with who was pitching my songs. Once the deal with EMI happened, I notified him clearly, in writing, that this song title was no longer available for him to pitch. He acknowledged my letter, saying, "Thanks for the heads-up, cool." I don't know how it happened—maybe he had forgotten about the letter—but the song remained in circulation, without my knowledge. A year later, he called to let me know about some recent song placements he'd made because he needed the publisher information for the cue sheets. One of the song placements was for a TV show that had all already aired.

Unfortunately, the song used in that show was the one I'd notified him about that was published with EMI. It was like dumping a bucket of cold water on what had been a warm and pleasant conversation. To avert any misguided accusations, and while we were still on the phone, I went to my laptop and e-mailed him a copy of the letter I had originally sent him about the EMI deal over a year ago. Though it wasn't my fault, I still felt bad about what had happened since we had a good relationship. I really liked him, and other than being a bit disorganized when it came to paperwork, he had done a great job marketing my music. I didn't want this to sour our relationship or cause anyone trouble. So I offered any assistance he thought would be helpful, and, in the end, it was straightened out, though I have little doubt that it was a complete headache for the guy who had pitched the song!

Music clearance issues aren't limited to television, and can happen when clearance for the use of music in film isn't addressed fully and completely. A friend of mine who works for a film production company relayed the details of a music clearance situation that turned unpleasant. A new marketing company was representing a band, and as such had entered into a song licensing agreement on the group's behalf. After the offer was green-lit, the song was included as part of the final edit of the film and 500,000 copies of the DVD were manufactured. It turns out that the song was from a CD financed by a regional independent record label. Once copies of the DVDs were released in stores, the record company found out and contacted the film company to inform them that they, not the band, owned the master recording. They demanded immediate payment of a hefty mastering license fee or they'd pursue a copyright infringement case. The film company filed a breach of contract lawsuit against the marketing company. Regardless of where blame should rightfully get placed, the marketing company, record company, and the band are blacklisted from the film company's future projects.

If someone else paid for the recording, they might own the master. You might not even be aware that they do. Make sure your paperwork is in order and that the master is yours before trying to license it. If you ever signed any agreement for someone to represent your music, however insignificant it may seem, make sure the agreement is void before you move forward. You may have given someone permission to shop your music but they became inactive and you assume they're out of business. But, if your song begins to make money, they may still make a claim on it. Agreements you didn't take seriously can rear their greedy heads when your songs attract moneymaking situations. Get an entertainment attorney to read over any agreement you ever signed. As I said earlier, some licensing services include taking part of your publishing. Make sure no one else controls your copyright if you're giving a music supervisor the right to use your song.

If you use an unauthorized sample in something that's licensed and it's discovered, that might be the last song you license.

One way to get around this is to record something that's similar to what you may have wanted to sample from someone's recording and sample from *that* recording, since you own it. Then your sound recording is cleared for licensing purposes. You would still have to negotiate the publishing share with the copyright owner of the song, if you copied something that's protected by copyright. But this won't interfere with granting the master license.

||||||||||||||||||||||||||||||||||||||||||||||||||||||||||||||||||||||||||||||||||||||||||||||||||||||||||||||||||||||||||||||||||||||

CHAPTER 8

Making a Game Plan

In this industry, at times you may need to comfort yourself with a coat of iron. It can take a long time to get work or even just to have a sense of forward momentum. It's imperative to have an excellent reel on a CD. Make sure that anything you send out is exceptional and can realistically compete with what's currently on TV, film, or in record stores. Music supervisors and directors whom I've worked with haven't had the time or patience for any disclaimers. Making excuses for imperfections will blow future opportunities. If necessary, wait until your recordings are done to your highest standards. I can't stress this point enough. Your CD reel has to be excellent to be in the game.

Getting your work licensed all comes down to good music and reliability. If you have good music, you have a shot at getting a placement. Most directors, unless they're related to you, won't hire you as the show's actual composer without some sort of track record. That means you have considerable professional experience as a composer, musician, producer, and engineer. You can expect to be called upon to be all three. For this reason, these days many film composers are former rock stars, like Danny Elfman and Stewart Copeland. When you first get started, you'll need a demo, a marketing strategy, and a proverbial wall of steel surrounding the tender part of your ego. All of these are important to prepare for if you want the best chance of getting into doors and making those contacts count.

Mental Preparation

||||||||||||||||||||||||||||||||||||||||||||||||||||||||||||||||||||||||||||||||||||||||||||||||||||||||||||||||||||||||||||||||||

Protecting your ego and your feelings is necessary for when you encounter phrases such as "no thanks," "I'll pass," "I'm not interested," and "It's the wrong approach." If you take it all personally, you'll quickly lose your desire to continue. You need to be strong mentally to persevere after getting turned down! Learn to embrace rejection because it's a reality. Comfort yourself knowing that just about anyone you admire, see on TV, or listen to on the radio has confronted these same responses at some point in their careers. Several record companies passed on the Beatles! With a few exceptions, no one licensing deal is going to make or break your musical career. Not getting the gig is just a part of the process on the road to successful licensing.

It has been said that you're never as good or bad as you might think. I've learned that it's important to avoid buying too much into either highly elevated praise or very negative criticism once you allow your work to be exposed to public scrutiny. Subjectivity plays a big factor in why one person feels that a certain piece of music works well within the context of a given scene, while another reaches an opposite conclusion. Keep in mind that polarized responses may have little to do with production quality, and instead could be the result of some predetermined musical objective or atmospheric feeling sought by the project's creators.

If you're offered constructive criticism, embrace it and learn from their suggestions. That's a surprisingly rare commodity. When someone appears to know what he or she is talking about, and takes the time to provide you with honest, competent, and thoughtful feedback and suggestions, embrace it as being a gift. You'll rarely know why your music wasn't selected. In the vast majority of cases, you'll have to assume that whoever posted the request simply didn't have time to provide a courtesy update to those who submitted music that wasn't selected. It might feel a bit rude or imply a lack of appreciation. But it isn't worth investing a lot of time and mental energy into trying to second-guess or figure out the reason why. Like it or not, radar silence is most often the method used to respond in these situations, especially when the music request generated a huge number of submissions. One request can attract hundreds or thousands of songs, so you can't quite blame them for turning you down without actually letting you know.

In most instances, the goal and incentive for responding to music requests is to achieve what's commonly referred to as a *song placement*. Music is submitted for consideration for use during a particular scene, on a per-song basis. You should forward individual songs that closely approximate the details that were specified in the request, not an entire CD. Nor should you submit music that doesn't fit what's asked for in the directions. Members of the production company, the director, and quite possibly, the music supervisor have worked out the specific requirements listed in the request beforehand. They typically make reference to the desired musical genre, a description of the scene, and any other nitpicky considerations that you should use as guidelines for choosing the music you will submit.

There's a bit of a double standard in the world of music licensing. You'll often be expected to respond to a music request very quickly. However, the sense of haste often stops there. Receiving notification and confirmation of a song placement, and all the other related correspondence that eventually follows, tends to happen very slowly. Be prepared to have lots of patience.

How Songs Get Chosen

Music requests kind of fall into three categories. The first is a *direct request*. Maybe your friend played golf with a movie producer who mentioned that he needed music for a new film he was involved with and your friend gave your music glowing accolades. As a result of his referral, they call you. That's probably the best-case scenario, because if it works out, it's a direct conversation with the source, minus any middlemen. These are hard to come by but networking makes it easier.

The second way to find out about music requests is through your representation. A publisher, agent, or lawyer will pursue opportunities on your behalf. Having someone else go to bat for you saves you the time and stress of trying to open doors yourself. The third method is to try it without the luxury of serendipity or representation. You can dive head first into the world of licensing music on your own; pound the pavement, search classified ads, subscribe to music publications or websites like www.Taxi.com, designed to connect you to powerful people in the entertainment world. When you begin, try every opportunity you can until you're more established.

> *The most difficult part of pitching music is really nailing exactly what the supervisor is looking for and then hoping that the director or producer or client that has final say agrees that is the exact fit. Oftentimes you can get right to the last minute and your song falls out in the final edit.*
>
> MICHELLE BAYER, Artist Representation and
> Pitching Songs, Shelly Bay Music

If your song isn't chosen for an opportunity you submit to, don't allow yourself to take it personally or you'll drive yourself crazy fast. There are many common explanations for why otherwise good music isn't selected for a given film or TV placement. Not being chosen doesn't necessarily say anything bad about your music. Here are some of the most common factors that influence a song choice.

Timing/Deadline Constraints

Even though you responded to a music request and your CD arrived before the deadline, it still might be relatively late in the game if a lot of good songs got there before yours. If another song was received sooner and found to be satisfactory, even if it clearly wasn't as cool as yours, it may end up being selected if they're in a hurry. That's why it's good to submit as soon as you see the request instead of assuming that the deadline gives you some leeway.

Good Song but Wrong Fit

If the request specifically asked for a singer/songwriter track with female vocals that conveys a message of optimism and you're in a death metal band, ignore it! Even if you've got a crowd-pleaser that you feel is close to the requirements of the request, that hint of death metal ballad in the song will lead the licensees to scream, "Next!" after listening to it. Don't risk alienating them by sending the wrong music when they were specific about what they wanted. One day your music might fit but they'll remember you wasted their time in the past and may not open your submissions for it.

Submission Saturation and Overload

A music request that's posted in a national entertainment publication will generate several hundred submissions by mail. A small production company that places the ad might not expect the onslaught of aggressive and international submissions that their posting generates. If they have to wrap up postproduction quickly, they may end up selecting music from the first group of CDs that arrived, while the other three hundred remain unopened in a storage closet. This is another reason to submit your music immediately.

Lyrical Content Conflicts with Visual Cues/Plot

The song you submitted may work in terms of genre and pacing, but the message in the lyrics may conflict with the story on the screen. Again, this has nothing to do with the quality of your music or whether they like it. The lyrics must match what's going on in the story.

Correct Lyrical Content, Wrong Genre or Tempo

Earlier I talked about how music contributes to the mood, emotion, or excitement of what's happening on the screen. If a song is either too fast or slow for the pacing of the visual transitions it gets passed on. There's nothing you can do to avoid this except to think very carefully about the details in a request before you send something.

Right Idea, Wrong Mix

At first a director might have been excited about including a certain song but later discovered that the mix of this song accentuates a certain bandwidth of frequency that's creating an undesirable conflict with the ADR (automated dialogue replacement) track. It makes it difficult to understand parts of what the actors are saying during the scene and is a bit distracting. In spite of fiddling with equalizer (EQ) levels, the sound editor has a hard time striking a good balance and moves to the next song that might fit.

Failure to Assure or Grant Clearance

A song that's been imported into the film and by all accounts works perfectly can still get cut. A problem comes if the production company absolutely needs complete clearance in writing from all entitled parties by tomorrow afternoon for this song to remain in the film soundtrack permanently. Hearing this might make you cringe if you know that complete clearance involves getting the go-ahead from a few people on your end fast, since it might not be possible.

For example, your song may have been recorded years ago and, since then, you've lost touch with the guitar player on the recording. If he's on the copyright as a cowriter of the song, you have to track him down fast. You make a considerable effort to find him, but he's MIA. Plus, the drummer for that recording technically owns the master because he willingly covered all recording and engineering expenses related to the creation of it.

Last summer, he moved and you lost touch with him, too. If all parties aren't available to sign off on the agreement, the licensee will say, "Next!"

Make sure everyone is involved and onboard with the music you're submitting before sending it. One way to avoid this type of headache is to assign one or more band members the right to represent the song in a marketing capacity. This applies to band situations where one member is very proactive about pursuing opportunities while others aren't. It's similar to allowing a marketing company to perform the same service. However, there could be a conflict of interest if the band member now-turned marketing guru wants a commission rate that ruffles the feathers of the others. A fair decision must be worked out between the entitled parties, but this process will be worth it. Songs can have a much longer life than the bands that recorded them.

Bad Behavior

While you need to watch out for your rights, don't drag out the process with negotiations that show you're either a novice at licensing or you're too demanding. For example, your song works and a licensing agreement is offered for it. You're new to the business and decide to get some advice from your associates. But you may get a little too much advice and respond to the offer with a revised contract that reflects numerous changes and a list of additional provisions that are over the top. If your reply is filled with demands and intimates that you might be inclined toward legal action, the production company will sense that dealing with you in the future brings with it the potential for difficultly. That will probably make them retract the offer. Have a good lawyer who's experienced in licensing deals look over any agreements you get. Be reasonable, especially if you're an unknown artist, or you'll stay unknown in licensing circles, or be known for making the process difficult!

Honing Your Sales Pitch

As you embark upon submitting your own music, it's important to consider:

- Can your music meet the specific directions that have been outlined in the request?
- Are the benefits of this opportunity, monetary or otherwise, worth your time, resources, and energy?

Licensing music boils down to you, or a representative, taking on the role of a salesperson who is offering products and/or services to potential buyers of licensing rights. This nuts-and-bolts analogy is a good one to keep in mind since it's often overlooked. You must develop an understanding of the needs and concerns of the potential buyers you plan to approach. Overly aggressive sales pitches often feel like a form of harassment, especially when prospective customers are being pressured into buying something they really don't want. Many people keep their phone numbers unlisted or private to avoid these kinds of unsolicited sales tactics. However, when someone politely or casually brings a product or service to the attention of someone who might be able to use it and it fits their need, it may feel more like finding a solution. If the price works within the budget, chances are that the product will sell itself.

> *I search everywhere for music for films—concerts, critics' pages, recommendations, networking, conferences, the radio. I try to listen to everything. I prefer to listen to entire songs rather than samplers of bits of songs. I remember songwriters and musicians and keep them in mind for years, even if they don't fit a current project.*
>
> CARLTON BUSH Jr., Filmmaker

Do your research before approaching people! A blind sales pitch will give the impression (probably correct!) that you didn't do your homework to learn the potential buyer's needs. Jumping in cold may be the least likely way to get a desirable outcome. It tends to elicit responses that are on par with receiving junk mail. I've found that it's better to focus on those opportunities that have the best chance of yielding a favorable outcome instead of pursuing each and every request I might stumble upon. The trick is to develop a realistic sense of those that present odds more in your favor and are worthy of your time.

You may come upon opportunities that mesh with your particular musical expertise, but seem amateurish or involve a tiny budget. These requests could burden you with costs that probably won't be recoverable. Do you want to pay fees for a studio to change a recording to someone's specifications? Do you want to pay a remixer? Perhaps you're passionate about the project, even though it comes with built-in liabilities. Just keep your expectations realistic, and carefully balance the pluses and minuses of your involvement. Think before you sign that agreement.

Budgets

A music request is typically accompanied by the budget that's available for the licensing fee. This dollar amount can be agreed upon on the spot or may require additional negotiation. As the number of parties involved with these negotiations increases, so does the amount of time required for reaching an agreement. As I said earlier, too many delays or back-and-forth price haggling can make the licensing party lose interest. Any factor that leads to the impression that there might be complications, now or in the future, can sink a licensing offer. The fact that there are no standard rates further blurs the art of negotiation as it applies to these situations. Knowing when to hold and when to fold comes from experience.

The licensing party creates its budget keeping in mind potential issues of liability, litigation, and the huge expenses from the inclusion of a song that's not fully cleared and needs to be removed later. Should this actually happen, the production company faces the challenge of locating and clearing yet another suitable replacement. Replacing a song may appear simple on the surface, but may at the very least require rendering a new master edit, readjusting and producing a new sound mix, and disregarding or discontinuing the use of copies of the movie that are in circulation. At its worst, this could become a nightmare scenario, and explains the increased presence of music supervisors in recent years. Independent filmmakers, who are careless with these details, sometimes pay a hefty price.

Is Free Worth the Price?

In the world of entertainment, most new projects resonate with a certain degree of promise. However, it's common for people who want to license your work for free to try to offset financial compensation with a convincing talk about the possibilities that can come from having your music in their project. These offers boil down to an offer of barter, where you give your music for free, and you get the project's exposure potential in return. For a struggling artist, possibility, even when vague, is a tempting proposition. Almost every artist I've known has willingly "paid his or her dues" by doing apprenticeships and internships and working for free. Some have done so for years! Agreeing to participate in these arrangements makes sense, especially in the beginning, since being hired in professional situations can be based on past experience. This raises the murky question: How much experience is enough experience?

There are many licensing opportunities where little if anything is offered in up-front fees. The person calling might try to entice you to let him use your music by mentioning that his film project is potentially "a great exposure opportunity" for many reasons. Because of the realities of the film business, I find myself referring to such contingencies as the "myth of exposure." The payoff may be that it provides you with some experience and a credit. In the beginning these things can be more important than money. I used to equate them to paying tuition for enrollment in the school of learning the ropes, a few doors down from the school of hard knocks. Each opportunity must be weighed carefully before you jump into letting someone use your music. You may hear things like:

- "This doesn't pay much, but will be a great exposure opportunity for those involved." No one can know if a project will do well. Chances are, if there's no budget, it won't have big promotion.
- "We've gotten incredible feedback." From whom? This is as vague as the exposure you may get. People will hype their projects to get you to give them music for free. Watch out for words with no substance. If a top critic loves a film, that's great. But the feedback they refer to can be from family.
- "This is a gem of a film and I'm sure it's festival-bound." Sundance is one of the top film festivals. The odds are roughly seventeen in five thousand that a film will be selected to be shown there. Even lesser known festivals have discouraging odds. Most festivals feature fifteen to fifty films per festival with an average of twenty-five hundred submissions. Applying to Harvard Medical School is a safer bet. So their intentions to get into a festival very well may not materialize.
- "We can't really pay you anything for this project, but expect a much bigger budget for our next film." This one is tempting indeed! Doing a favor for a fiscally strapped production company with the

understanding that there are bigger projects in the pipeline sounds like a good opportunity. In truth, once the company grows and starts to acquire success and real money, they may want to license songs from more established artists.

> *If you're a hip-hop or an electronic music producer and you're churning out music day and night, I wouldn't be that concerned about [licensing a song for free]. If you're placing a little hip-hop beat or something like that, where a hip-hop producer can produce two or three of those a day, it's not so precious. But if you're a band that has blood, sweat, and tears in these songs, you don't want to give away your copyright for nothing.*
>
> KEATLY HALDEMAN, CEO, pigFACTORY

Most of the time, promises of exposure won't play out as expected. There are exceptions, but these are quite rare. It's not my intention to be a pessimist. But since time is one of your most valuable commodities, it's worth examining some of the myths and misunderstandings that shroud the promise of exposure. While the promise is usually made with good intentions, in the end, it's hard to quantify or predict the exposure potential since it's offered based on a best-case scenario. The promise of exposure often hinges on a system of cause and effect, as in, "We're not able to pay licensing fees now, but allowing your music to be in our film will be a great exposure opportunity." What's usually missing are definitive steps or actions that will be taken to help generate exposure in your direction, regardless of a film's long-term success.

If these details are left unaddressed, and most often they are, it's a contingency. Here's a hypothetical example of a better deal. A student filmmaker receives your CD and says, "I really love your CD and want to discuss using a few songs in my new movie. Unfortunately, I can't pay licensing fees at the moment, but if you agree to provide a gratis use license, I'll film your next music video free of charge." This is a bit like a barter deal but instead of just settling for gratis use, both parties get something in return and the benefits don't rely on how circumstances in the future play out.

You may decide that some gratis use projects are worth your time, energy, and resources, despite there being nothing left in the budget to pay for music.

Situations like these can be a good opportunity to get a credit and gain some hands-on experience, as well as exposure. When you can show directors and music supervisors of other films and TV shows, for instance, how well your music worked in that gratis-use project, it can lead to more opportunities. It also adds a little spice to an otherwise generic bio.

I was paid $500 to score my first film in 1997 and did so without having any real expectations. The movie went on to win a number of film festival awards the following year. I was able to ride the coattails of this success. It eventually led to opportunities for doing projects with larger music budgets. I am convinced that in a few cases I was hired solely based on what I had done. It was my credit list, as opposed to the excerpts featured on my demo reel, that got me in the door for licensing deals. I don't think these people even listened to my demo first. Seeing my credits got them to pop my CD in to check out my music.

> *A foot in the door is a foot in the door, but don't sell yourself cheap. If you give your music away for free, don't get upset if you get other calls asking for free music. To give yourself perspective, be in tune with rates from production music houses and what indies as well as majors are charging.*
>
> BARRY COLE, Music Supervisor on over seventy features, SPOT

So do you let people use your music for free? There's no right or wrong answer. Each case is individual. Many musicians find it helpful to work for very little at the very beginning to pick up some credits. But, you must set boundaries if you want to get paid. Otherwise, you'll be the go-to songwriter when there's no budget. Once you've proven yourself in a few projects, build your own confidence enough to start expecting to be paid. Network with other musicians who are licensing music to get more familiar with the going rate. Join songwriter organizations that have meetings so you have more inter-action. Assess each offer individually. Licensing music for MTV to use for free gives you good exposure and you'll get the back-end royalties. Letting an indie film use your music might not be worth it after getting a few credits. When you value yourself enough to expect to be paid for your services, it's much more likely that you will be paid.

Sometimes the best way to break into the licensing side of the TV business is to offer your music for free to cable and network programs and then get paid on the back end through royalties from your performing rights organization. A music supervisor will be much more likely to place a track if he doesn't have to get the company to cut a check. After your music is placed, then you have developed a relationship with the music supervisor and you can begin to work on ways to expand the licensing relationship and even get the opportunity to write music for the specific needs of that music supervisor.

RAMSAY ADAMS, Music Supervisor for film and television

Preparation Exercises

Grab a pen and paper. Your assignment, should you choose to accept it, is to answer all of the following questions as accurately and completely as possible. When you're done, you will have created a profile of your three best songs. These profiles will clarify some essential details that will help you market your music more effectively. This information can aid you when you're pitching someone who knows nothing about you, and isn't sure at first what can be done with your music. The answers can be short, so long as they are on target.

For each of your three best songs:

- Find two well-known songs that fall into the same musical genre as yours. The first track should be able to comfortably play right before yours, and the second right after, as part of a playlist rotation for a radio station. Who are the artists? What are the song titles?
- Is there anything interesting or unique about your music?
- List the names of all the songwriters involved and their performing rights organization affiliations, including your own. Are there any publishers?
- Have you filed a copyright for the song? What year?
- What's the tempo of the song? If available, you can look up this piece of information from the audio program/application that was used to record and produce it. Look for the song project's "bpm" (beats per measure).

- What is the key of the song? If you don't know, try to ask someone who could figure it out.
- Pick ten short phrases or keywords that come to mind when you or someone whose opinion you trust hears this song.
- List any TV shows or movies that feature music that is similar to your own area of musical expertise.

Begin with an understanding of how and where your music—your style—might fit into the cultural landscape. What sorts of films or television programming could you imagine hearing your music in? What sorts of advertising/commercials? Is your music classically oriented? Alt-rock? Acoustic? Softly melodic or relentlessly edgy and rhythmic? A mix? This self-awareness will help you identify the producers and production companies to approach first.

LYLE GREENFIELD, Founder and President, Bang Music

Writing all of this down helps you to be more aware of different aspects of your music and have the information at hand when you make a good connection.

||||||||||||||||||||||||||||||||||||||||||||||||||||||||||||||||||||||||||||||||||||||||||||||||||||||||||||||||||||||||||||||||||||||||

CHAPTER 9

Cultivating Contacts and Relationships

Making contacts is a key ingredient for success in any business. When it comes to the entertainment business, making contacts is a matter of necessity. People in your circle of contacts become a network you can turn to when you have something new to shop or when you've reached a point when all of the required or necessary preparation is in order and you're ready to pursue more opportunities. It has been said that success is all whom you know. If you don't know anyone, that can be discouraging. Instead, think in terms of whom you *can* know. If you use all the resources available, it's possible to connect to people who can help you get your music licensed. The more relationships you build, the more people you'll be introduced to. It begins with connecting to the first contact and working it from there.

Starting Out

||||||||||||||||||||||||||||||||||||||||||||||||||||||||||||||||||||||||||||||||||||||||||||||||||||||||||||||||||||||||||||||||||||||||

You can pursue contacts and leads on your own. In the beginning, making contacts will include developing relationships with some of the players that were discussed in Chapter 2. The networks these key players have built for themselves will determine how effective they can be in representing your interests. You can find ways to reach these people with research and persistence, or use the suggestions in this chapter to develop your own contacts.

Your path to having success in getting your music licensed begins with having the right type of product for the right type of industry contact. Don't spend all your efforts on making contacts for the sake of making contacts. It's much better to focus on pursuing the right types of contacts for your goals. It's also important to know when it is or isn't the right time to approach a potentially good contact. The best time is when you're prepared to deliver on your end and the contact you pursue has the time, ability, and willingness to work with you right now. Timing can be critical to making contacts and actually approaching them.

Even if you don't live near one of the major music licensing hubs, you can get started wherever you are. Any music-related establishment in your town might have someone who might know someone, from the people who work in music stores to local radio DJs and personnel, recording studio staff, and anyone else who deals with music as a profession. Search for songwriter groups in your area that you can network with and get support from. That's how the chain of finding people begins—one contact at a time as you meet people who can introduce you to others.

Making progress is not just *whom* you know; *when* you know them makes a difference, too. Sometimes you can be at the right place but it's the wrong time. Years ago, I was introduced to a manager whose client list included some bands that were enormously popular and successful at the time. This introduction put me on a first-name basis with someone who was, without a doubt, an excellent music industry contact. However, it was quite apparent that he already had more on his plate than he could probably handle. At that particular time, I could see adding yet another client to his already filled-to-capacity roster just wasn't an option. So I didn't pursue it. He was, however, someone I could turn to if I needed him later on. Had I pushed for him to represent me then, he might have seen me as a person to avoid.

You also need to be aware that not everyone you meet, even if they seem to be connected, is up-to-date on everything related to licensing. When pursuing contacts or following up with those you've already made, keep in mind that what they provide may have an expiration date. People change positions and companies in the entertainment industry quite often. As with any business, there's always the possibility that one of your established contacts may have been laid off or left the business so they're no longer there when you call.

When you're introduced to someone who offers to help you then and there, don't assume the offer can be put off until it's more convenient for you. Usually, a window of opportunity will expire if not followed up on in a reasonable timeframe. Not only do people change positions, they also forget you. You may meet someone who says he can hook you up with good people, but you want to go back to the studio first and remix your songs.

Or your plate is full, so you wait for a better time. Guess what? You've just lost that opportunity! Relationships are warm when they're first offered. They can cool off fast if you don't stay connected. The enthusiastic guy you met at a conference may meet three other great songwriters next week and forget all about the promises he made to you.

Exploring every new opportunity for the purpose of pursuing success frequently involves diving into uncharted waters. In the world of music licensing, it can lead you to make difficult decisions at a moment's notice. If you do meet someone and you're not ready to send music, at least drop a note or find a good way to stay in regular touch. That way, if she moves, you'll hear about it. She might be with another company that can use your music. You need to stay on the radar screen of your contacts!

Initiating Relationships

If there is a holy grail of the song licensing business, it would be having the ability to supply high-quality media content and knowing when, where, and whom to pass it along to. Developing ongoing and mutually beneficial relationships with solid industry contacts can open doors that may have been closed until now. It can create pathways out of thin air, where none had been. All avenues can be worth pursuing if you have time. Networking can be the best tool for advancing your career in licensing music, as long as you have quality recordings that are up to the standards required. People resources in the entertainment industry are priceless.

A contact list is a very valuable commodity. The advantage of having solid representation is that you don't need to spend your own time trying to make contacts. The commission fees you're charged by those representing you (publishers, agents, managers, etc.), are in part payment for having access to their list of contacts in the industry. A high-profile agent or manager should be able to pick up a phone and set the wheels of your career into motion, with a level of efficiency or effectiveness that would be difficult to match on your own. Established agents or professional representatives gain attention for their clients because their contacts trust them, have professional respect for them, and/or owe them favors. This can lead to your music being considered for a licensing deal where it may have slipped under the radar otherwise.

The excitement of creating a new song or CD is often followed by the challenging question, "So what do I do with this now?" As I said earlier, there's an important distinction when it comes to pursuing contacts in the entertainment industry. Does the contact have the ability to get your song licensed? You should focus on connecting with those who believe in your music and have a willingness and ability to work with it to either license it or help you find people who will license it. Establishing a solid relationship with a person or company that becomes a good industry contact requires time, follow-ups, staying in touch, and in some cases wining and dining them; some need to be schmoozed.

Successful and capable industry contacts are busy. They're constantly pursued. Find ways to make them want to make things happen. If you get one on the phone, ask if it's a good time to talk. Acknowledge that you understand he may be busy and that you would appreciate just a few minutes. Be as prepared and organized as possible before you reach out to anyone who could open a door for you. It's to your advantage to already have a clear sense of your product, its market, and its value. Make sure you have the ability to clearly articulate the goal you have in mind or what you'd like to accomplish. Be as polished and prepared as possible. Don't contact someone if your goal is beyond the scope of his specialty. You can turn someone off by pitching him for something outside his niche.

If you show great potential but your experience is limited, you might come across as being a diamond in the rough. A skilled representative might recognize that achieving a professional standard will require more time and fine-tuning before your content is ready to be pitched. There was a time when the entertainment industry was open to working with promising artists for development. This trend has faded. The time and resources required to develop the skills and creativity of an artist are a burden that is now the artist's responsibility. The right time to pursue contacts is when you have something that's available and ready to go that can stand on its own merits with no need for disclaimers. A music licensing contact will probably be able to help you only when you give them something to work with. They want product, not potential.

It's essential to put your best music forward the first time. The initial impression you make on someone will stick. Industry players know that there are plenty of other artists out there who have material ready for licensing right now. Few people have time or patience to guide you to make the quality recording needed. Get feedback from people with good ears before approaching a contact so you don't waste the opportunity. And if you're told that your music needs more work, keep your ego in check and listen.

> *I believe in the "six degrees" approach (or is it "three degrees"?): You know somebody who knows somebody who can help introduce you to the person you need to know. The personal approach is always best. But it does not replace the need to make those "cold calls," using the applicable production and music directories. Don't be afraid—be charming, direct, and brief. Do not blanket the world with a CD mailing. Do not send cryptic e-mails with links to your website. Industry professionals are busy as hell! Remember, music may be your passion—but it's their business.*
>
> LYLE GREENFIELD, Founder and President, Bang Music

Chance Encounters

It's said that good opportunities have a way of finding you when you're not looking for them. Based on my own experience, I'd agree, but I might tack on the old cliché that success is when opportunity meets preparation. When I began, I was led to meaningful opportunities that mostly occurred under ordinary, day-to-day circumstances. Anything you can do that keeps you connected with your art, gets you out there, and allows others to become aware of your talents, interests, and passion is worth doing. Over the years, I inadvertently made a contact or became aware of a promising outlet for my music in many unconventional ways—giving music lessons, being asked to play piano at someone's birthday party, taking a class, buying a second-hand video camera, or performing a local gig. You never know who might be listening!

Years ago, I struck up a conversation with a bartender while waiting for friends to arrive. This bar had an excellent jukebox. A song was playing that we both liked and it sparked a conversation. At some point, I mentioned being interested in doing film scoring work. He responded with, "Really? Head down to the end of the bar and I'll introduce you to the guy sitting there. He's a good friend and a director. He's working on a documentary about this bar!" After an abrupt introduction, we hit it off. At the time, he was the senior editor at Getty Images, the industry go-to source for licensing stock video and still images. This informal introduction eventually led to working with him on several of his movie projects, in addition to entering a deal with Getty Images to provide music for their promotional videos.

Let everyone you talk to know what you're looking to do. You never know when a chance encounter may occur.

Creating a Network

A good contact is anyone who shares her own knowledge, experience, guidance, suggestion, or resources and in doing so, helps you to reach your career objectives. Don't take people for granted. Many assume that a good contact must be a stereotypical Hollywood or entertainment industry power broker. This really isn't always the case. I can't stress it enough—good contacts include all the people who have had a positive effect on your life and career path. You never know who might know someone who knows someone else who can help you!

A positive network is the complex web of short-and long-term interactions with anyone who influences your creativity for the better. These include music teachers, musical idols, the guy in the local music store who let you buy equipment at a "VIP" discount for years now, the musicians whom you form bands and friendships with, the people who have recorded and mixed your songs, and anyone who's taken the time to listen to your music and provides you with thoughtful suggestions, constructive feedback, and honesty. Anyone involved with any aspect of music has the potential to give you your next good contact! Don't take for granted those contacts that initially seem humble in nature. As insignificant as they might appear to you at the time, they absolutely matter and can lead to lifelong bonds.

When you go somewhere that could have good networking opportunities, whether it's a party, conference, or a class, it's good to have business cards and pens on hand, especially when you attend an event that's specifically for networking or an industry workshop. A phone number or e-mail address that gets written down on scrap paper as a last resort is very easy to lose or be thrown away. Keep the cards you get from others separate from your own. If possible, make notes on the back of the cards you receive to remind you what you talked about.

As you meet people, ask if it's okay to contact them in the future or forward them your music. If they agree, find out their preferred method for doing so. Some people don't like CDs and prefer to listen to a song that's streamed on a website. Others find e-mails overwhelming and like having a CD to play on their stereo. Perhaps that person who finds you charming and talented has his hands full and isn't in a position to offer help the moment you meet him. If you really hit it off, stay in touch and perhaps he'll have time in the future. The best way to proceed is to do as they indicate.

It's a good idea to have copies of your CD on hand. But, whether you give one to someone in person depends on the circumstances. Some people might be happy to take it if they're not inundated by too many. It's often better to hold off handing over a copy if the person didn't ask for it. For example, if a popular music supervisor is a guest speaker at a workshop and throughout the day attendees give him CDs though he gave no indication that he wanted them, he might take them as a matter of common courtesy, but as with other cattle-call situations, he may never listen to them. Plus, he may not want to carry them back to his office, so they may be left behind.

Imagine that sitting before you is a stack of three hundred CDs and you have to listen to at least thirty seconds of each, possibly more if what you hear grabs your attention. Going through each disc would take a lot more time than you could imagine. While evaluating them, it's also necessary to write down some notes so that the details of CD-34 are not confused with CD-248. Meanwhile, you have requests for music that must be filled and songs that must be cleared. That's why they can't always listen to everything. So, if you meet someone in person, it's best to make a nice impression with your conversation and professional demeanor. Ask if it would be okay to send a CD later, acknowledging that they probably wouldn't want to take it then. They might appreciate your consideration and listen to it when it arrives.

When you approach contacts, you're asking to be provided with their time, advice, resources, and so on. Their willingness or hesitation to do so is usually based on the method and style you approach them with. This is why it really helps to learn about them, their current situation, and their circumstances beforehand. It's helpful to find out what a person or company may or may not realistically be in a position to provide you with. This keeps expectations in check. Disappointments are often the result of misguided expectations. Part of establishing meaningful and long-term contacts is to care about the people you work with and not just see them as a means to an end. Take an interest in what they do, and stay mindful of ways in which *you* might help *them*. That helps build relationships!

Following Up

If you meet someone, you can't just put her card away and expect to be able to contact her easily in the future. Contacts need to be nurtured. Send a brief note shortly after saying it was nice to meet her. E-mails are fine but a personal, handwritten note can go far. The music industry is built on relationships. Take advantage of any opportunity to build one.

Besides helping you, contacts can help you make other contacts if you're not afraid to ask. If someone says she likes your music but can't use it, ask if she can suggest anyone else to contact. Having a referral can get you into a lot more doors. If you call someone, get friendly with the one who answers the phone. Ask for his name. Use it when you call again. If an assistant or receptionist is friendly to you, ask for a little advice on when to catch the person you're trying to reach and if there's something you might be able to do to get his attention. One contact can lead you to another when you're friendly, courteous, and have great music that would work in projects that license music.

Being Someone They Want to Work With

Often overlooked, though profoundly influential over the long run, is the importance of having good communication and people skills when dealing with music licensing players. Since the music industry is built on relationships, it will serve you well to strengthen any social skills you possess. When a music supervisor knows and likes you, she's more likely to call on you again when music requests come in. When someone finds you pleasant to work with, it's more likely he'll want to work with you again. If you're punctual, flexible, likable, and turn around work quickly, chances are he'll continue to call when he has music requests. Having your own studio and the ability to create music easily can score extra points.

The following are lessons I've learned from working with music supervisors and on a few occasions, being one myself. How you present yourself makes the first impression. Personal skills create impressions that last. You can impress music supervisors—beyond just presentation—by following these tips. These will help you build relationships, which will be crucial even if you don't get your music licensed immediately.

> *Flexibility is key for music placements. Musicians are entitled to be the "artists" that they want to be and write, record, and perform the style of music and songs that they prefer. But if a music supervisor is hiring you for a job, your goal should be to listen to the request and deliver the music as it is being asked for. It's fine to be creative, but paying attention to the style and the details of the request is very important. There is nothing worse than having to go back to a band or a musician or a composer and needing them to redo the music. It holds up editors and the production and makes the music supervisor, as well as yourself, look bad.*
>
> BRENT KIDWELL, Freelance Music Supervisor

Learn to Be Patient

If you submit to an urgent music request but don't get an instantaneous response or final decision announcement, don't bombard the person with calls or e-mails. Wait. If they want you, they'll get in touch. If they don't, contacting them probably won't help. But it can make you seem like a pest and someone to be avoided. Patience is a quality that's appreciated in this business.

Respect Other People's Time

Music requests often come during a time crunch. Be sensitive of people's time constraints and it will be appreciated. Also, avoid excessive or unnecessary correspondence and other tangential activity that is ultimately a waste of everyone's time. If you talk to a music supervisor, ask if it's okay to call again. If the answer is "no," respect it.

Provide What's Being Asked For

When time is of the essence, forwarding music that you know is off the mark of what was spelled out in the details of a request, regardless of how good you think the music is, tends to do more harm than good. It gives the impression that you're not able or willing to follow directions. Music supervisors want to know that if music comes from you, it will comply with the specifications they asked for. Otherwise, your music may never get listened to again!

Take Ten Deep Breaths

Even if you have a legitimate right to be angry, try to avoid flying off the handle or overreacting if a particular opportunity isn't going the way you'd like. This happens to everyone. Don't take it personally (really!). In the face of disappointment, responding to a music supervisor with a piece of your mind won't help and will probably be held against you in the future. Keep in mind that music supervisors rarely have the final say about what music gets licensed. They're employees. For all you know, the supervisor may have preferred your song. My grandmother used to say, "The unspoken word doesn't come back to haunt you." When in doubt, say something like, "I really appreciate your time and consideration; please keep me posted with your music requests in the future."

> Try not to push too hard. There's nothing that will turn off a music supervisor faster than someone pounding down the door. Try to look at it more as a numbers game; when you find the right match, it will click!
>
> SEAN FERNALD, Producer/Music Supervisor, 3Mac Studios

Have Grace Under Pressure

Although it's not always easy, try to be polite. People want to call on those who've been easy to work with. Difficult personalities can quickly cast shadows upon quality work or legitimate talent. Everyone is replaceable once a threshold barrier gets surpassed. Minding your manners is appreciated, even if the person doesn't acknowledge your good behavior outright. Getting called again for a second project is acknowledgment enough!

Move On

Not every music supervisor will be pleasant. Some may be so unpleasant you can't tolerate it. If you feel that you've been treated disrespectfully or judged unfairly in a situation, cut it loose and move to greener pastures. Chances are excellent that doing so will have zero negative impact on your career path and will make you feel better.

Understand the Competition

Although the entry-level barriers for many licensing opportunities have been significantly reduced, it's still a very competitive environment. Your competition is not only other indie artists, but also songs and artists being pitched for the same opportunities by major labels. Set the bar high when you record your music. It can't just be good. The quality must stand up to highly produced recordings. And if a music supervisor says that your recording isn't up to his standards, don't argue. You won't change his mind. If possible, ask for advice about how to improve it.

Stay Open-Minded to Advice

Be willing to take advice or constructive criticism when it's offered. Learn to embrace feedback instead of bristling or taking it personally. Address the issues and let them hear results or improvements in the future.

Don't Say "Yes" to What Can't Be Delivered

Avoid agreeing to provide or deliver anything that's unrealistic—the specific things they want or the tight deadline. Take the time to think a request through before you agree to it. Some people say "yes" or "no problem" because they're afraid that disappointing a music supervisor will kill future opportunities. The opposite is true. Being honest about your inability to fulfill a request earns respect and you're more likely to get requests in the future.

Humor Is the Best Medicine

It's important to take things seriously by being responsible and professional but don't forget to laugh. Certain aspects of this business are a bit absurd. People love to work with those who have a good sense of humor. Lighten up when you interact with people. That makes you more pleasant to work with.

Resources

You can tap into many resources for making contacts. Some cost money, some don't. You can take advantage of all of them to pursue people who can help you get licensing deals or to reach the people who need music on your own. For example, Global Media Online (www.gmocorp.com)

publishes guides and directories focusing on the film and television music industry, and also provides job leads, educational seminars, and courses for the industry.

Connecting Digitally

> Ricall is a searchable database with independent music writers, producers, record labels, as well as the big commercial people. We're going to be branching out for production music. Pretty much people with all categories of music can come to us to put their content up on our website. When people go to the site to search, their music will be in the mix. They can search by content, genre, year, instrumental, tempo, keyword, lyrical content, and almost anything else or combination.
>
> ED RAZZANO, Vice President, Business
> Development (North America), Ricall

Online sites, such as Pump Audio (www.pumpaudio.com) and Ricall (www. ricall.com), allow you to place music on them and connect with people who need music content. People with licensing opportunities come to these sites and can search their databases to fill their music needs by genre, lyrical content, vocal or instrumental, tempo, and many other factors. They're both nonexclusive and don't take any rights to your music. You just give them the right to license it on your behalf. Follow their instructions to register your music, and it will come up in searches made by people looking to license music. They take a cut of the licensing fee but you get all performance royalties that the music earns.

> The key to Pump Audio is the theory that independent music is as good as much of the "label" music out there and that licensees of all kinds want good music, no matter the name or source. Pump Audio is a place that if you are selected, you have just as good of a chance as anyone else to get placed and get played. We have many artists who have quit their jobs to become musicians full-time because of the income we bring them—all for just submitting music to us.
>
> LARRY MILLS, Vice President, Marketing
> and Partnerships, Pump Audio

Being on these sites may open doors to opportunities that can continue in the future. They're easy to use—a win/win for both you and the person looking for music. All the music is cleared before going up and they have access to music that they wouldn't otherwise. And, they can search for exactly what they need. Music supervisors with tight deadlines especially like using these sites because all the music is available immediately. If someone finds your music on one of these sites and likes it, they may seek you out for more in the future.

The Film Music Network (www.filmmusic.net), which is part of Global Media Online, has job listings for composers and songwriters. You can check their board or get on their mailing list. There is a small fee to submit to each listing so make sure your music is a good match before you send. You don't want to waste your time and money!

Publications and Websites
You can use one of several directories to find names of music supervisors. This involves a lot of cold contacting but it gives you a chance. The Music Business Registry (www.musicregistry.com) publishes *The Film and Television Music Guide,* a directory of music supervisors, production companies, and many other professionals working in the music licensing world. It's updated every year and is quite thorough in its listings. *Film Music Magazine* (www.filmmusicmag.com) features many insightful articles related to music for film, TV, and composition. The *Songwriter's Market* (Writer's Digest Books) is a useful directory for exploring additional marketing leads. Updated each year, it lists the contact information for hundreds of music publishers, record companies, producers, booking agents, conferences, managers, and contests.

Two subscription-based publications worth mentioning, the *Hollywood Reporter* and *Variety,* cover news, events, and features related to current or upcoming film industry projects. Among other stories, it provides information about projects that are underway and who is producing them. Projects that are currently in the pipeline or that are just getting started will have to address the issue of music, song placements, and clearance at some point. Use the *Hollywood Reporter* or *Variety* to identify one, and then initiate some early correspondence with the production company. This will allow you to establish a connection during a time that, at least with respect to music, may be a little more low-key. It's more of a challenge when you attempt to get noticed later, during the onslaught of music submissions.

Try to contact the production companies. Their websites are usually referenced in the dailies or in directories. As always, keep correspondence short and to the point. Include links to your media (songs, video, etc.) that are both readily and universally accessible. Simply say who you are, how you found out about them or the project, and what you're offering. This can be accomplished in as few as three sentences. Be aware that during preproduction or production, the focus will be on filming, casting, locations, permits, and the rest—not the music.

> *Familiarize yourself with the trades and find out what is in various stages of production so that you have a better chance of tailoring your submissions for specific needs. The "we do everything and are the best" pitch doesn't always get you in the door these days.*
> BARRY COLE, Music Supervisor on over seventy features, SPOT

Proactive correspondence can sometimes work, but don't be aggressive or use hard-sell tactics; don't turn yourself into a pest. The goal is simply to create an awareness of your music and its availability. Leave the impression that you look forward to having it considered for the project at hand, now or in the future.

No one strategy for establishing your own contacts will work for every situation and every time. The same strategy applied in two different situations or with two different personalities may end up resulting in very different outcomes. One may work out while the other doesn't materialize. However, in the end you have a new contact. I encourage you to initiate correspondences for projects that are most aligned with your own personal taste and musical style. This alone can increase the odds of hitting it off with a potential contact. If it does, the project will be a more satisfying opportunity to become a part of.

> *The easiest thing in the world to do, but which takes initiative and persistence, is to pick up the quarterly issue of the* Hollywood Reporter *and* Variety, *which list all of the television shows and feature films that are currently in production. Their office contact information*

is right there. If you contact each production office and ask for the music supervisor, you will probably find a person very eager to hear what you have.

BRENT KIDWELL, Freelance Music Supervisor

Events and Support

Several annual events offer plenty of opportunities to rub up against fellow songwriters, from whom you can learn much about the ins and outs of music licensing.

ASCAP "I Create Music" Expo

In addition to overseeing performance royalty distribution for their members, performing rights organizations host many annual seminars, workshops, and industry events that take place throughout the country and beyond. Keep an eye out for any that are scheduled in your area and try to attend them. Events of this nature can represent a great opportunity for making contacts, as well as getting advice and professional feedback. There's often a small attendance fee associated with these workshops, and they may also require that you register or purchase tickets prior to the date of the event.

Events attended by music supervisors and others who license music are especially good for making contacts. One of the best is the ASCAP "I Create Music" Expo, an annual music conference in Los Angeles that has grown in popularity by leaps and bounds over the past few years. The conference is all about musicians networking, making contacts, getting one-on-one feedback, listening to music industry guest speakers, and gaining expert advice. They have a smaller version in New York City.

Indie-Music.com

Other songwriter groups have conferences, too. Indie-Music.com (www. indie-music.com) has an excellent listing of events around the country. You can subscribe to their newsletter, which lists them for free. The Songwriters Guild of America also has events you can check out. This is a volunteer organization (run by songwriters) that offers other songwriters various services and resources to assist in the pursuit of success in the music business. SGA has offices located in New York, Nashville, and Los Angeles.

TAXI

TAXI (www.taxi.com) is a service that's based on connecting independent songwriters and composers to record, publishing, and film and TV deals. It provides its members access to an impressive list of opportunities. As a member, you decide which ones you would like to pursue.

Because TAXI provides artists with a service, there are fees involved, both to join and for each submission. But they take nothing for any paid opportunities that come as the result of their services, which is fair. So if you license a song for a TV show through TAXI, you keep 100 percent of the licensing fees and subsequent performance royalties. Before submissions are forwarded to those looking for music, TAXI prescreens them. Only music that satisfies the quality standards and meets the requirements outlined in the request is submitted. They claim that by screening and enforcing high quality control standards, TAXI entices companies to turn to them when posting music requests. Members are just one step removed from what sometimes appear to be high-profile opportunities.

While anyone can sign up and join TAXI, you will be charged for responding to requests on a per-song basis, whether or not your song is deemed worthy of being forwarded to the potential licensee. One benefit that you'll be provided with if your song isn't forwarded is a written explanation as to why. This courtesy is rarely provided elsewhere. It's highly recommended that you don't join TAXI until professionals with good ears have critiqued your songs and you know they're up to the site's high standards. Otherwise, you waste your money joining since your songs won't reach the people who license music if they're not up to par.

‖‖

CHAPTER 10

Presentation Tools

There's a good deal of truth in the old axiom "Presentation is everything." The look, feel, style, originality, and most important, the audio content in your presentation make a lasting impression. Don't leave someone with a poor one! The quality of the song itself, along with its ability to satisfy the specific needs or musical requirements of the licensing opportunity, are *the* most significant factors in determining your success. Having great music that works for a project is the primary concern during the selection process. Savvy marketing materials and a professional presentation can be persuasive tools, *if* the music fits the specific needs of the person receiving it. Many music supervisors only care about the music.

Packaging Your Music Effectively

Some music supervisors and production companies say they refuse to accept unsolicited materials. This may have less to do with pretentiousness and more to do with liability or bad licensing experiences related to direct contact with an artist. The right presentation can increase your odds of having your music heard. Some calls for music generate hundreds of submissions. Managing all the packages can overwhelm those looking for music. So the visual is important! How it's packaged can get yours in the door, or the trash.

Even if your music is requested, you should still make a good impression. Just as a resume is sent to apply for a job, people looking for music will usually request a copy of your CD and whatever song(s) on the CD best fit the specifics outlined in the request. Do your best to send a professional-looking package.

CD Packaging
Choosing the best CD package option can be a significant factor in the selection process that determines whether yours is tossed aside or put on a shelf to

be considered. When submitting music on CDs, it can be beneficial to use those bulky, old-school jewel cases that accommodate a J-card insert. Those are more helpful for music supervisors than the newer, popular, slim-line cases or cardboard CD sleeves. Jewel cases are advantageous because:

- They're easier to store.
- They allow for quicker accessibility.
- They provide better visual recognition.

Since you compete with tons of submissions, consider all options to sway the odds in your favor. CDs in a jewel case with a distinct J-card are easier to locate on a shelf with many others. The narrow band on a J-card, called the *spine*, is what's seen and read when CDs are stored on racks. Text and color distinguish the spine, making the music editor's life simpler and assuring that your CD is easy to locate when music is needed quickly. Stick to the standard format in terms of size and type of printed information on the spine and/or J-card insert.

> *Artists often don't give me song or cue titles, which is frustrating. It's the very best when the artist had taken the care to make sure the cues or music they sent include meta-data so that when I load a disc in my computer, the song titles, artist name, and a CD title all come up in my iTunes. It's also important for me to have songwriter information and publishing details, which I will ultimately need to report on cue sheets for my TV series. There is enough finishing work that needs to be done on projects but to have to chase down artists one by one to get their publishing entity, which recording society they are with, and exactly how the songwriter's name is spelled, is a bother. You should always include that information with everything you submit.*
>
> Brent Kidwell, Freelance Music Supervisor

Space for printed text along the spine of a CD jewel case is limited, so only include what is comfortably accommodated, while still easily read. Include the artist's name, CD title, and company name if you have one. In a different color, include a few words that describe the style and emotion of music, such as "ACTION, TENSION, DRAMA," "URBAN JAZZ," "ELECTRONIC

PULSE," "COMEDY & REALITY TV." That gives potential licensees a reference since they're usually looking for music with a specific feel. Make sure your contact information is on the front and/or rear panel of the jewel case and on the J-card insert. Play it safe by also including it on the CD itself. Discs frequently become separated from their cases once screened. If you move or your phone number changes, put stickers with updated information on everything you send for licensing.

Occasionally I see CD artwork that features a very clever design; so unique in fact, that it instantly becomes recognizable. For example I got a CD where both the disc and jewel case are lime green with black polka dots. But it has no text! Although this eye-candy presentation could be viewed as a form of marketing brilliance, its lack of readily available contact and other information is a critical flaw if used to pursue licensing opportunities.

> For me, it's more about the song than the songwriter. When you're going through a stack of demos on your desk, it's the music that's going to speak for you. Another tip is to have an eye-catching sleeve. You would be amazed how many demos I get with no artwork/image attached.
>
> SEAN FERNALD, Producer/Music Supervisor, 3Mac Studios

Have very visible details on the CD. Songs that closely match specifications make the first cut. The CDs are placed in a "worthy of consideration" stack or on shelves that are accessible to editor(s), the director, or anyone who might conduct test runs and green-light music selections. CD cases lacking a spine are more likely to get ignored at this stage. If your music isn't quite right stylistically for the specific project but a music supervisor or director likes it, it will be archived for consideration in future projects. A good package with a clear spine provides the best chance for it being used later.

A CD that's also sold to fans should probably not have all the information needed for licensing, like your cell phone number. However, when sending it to a publisher, lawyer, music supervisor, etc., include more detailed contact and other information. You can add it with stickers and inserts or consider having a version of the CD specifically for licensing, with more details. Potential licensees will want to know: the songwriter(s), their PRO affiliation, whether the song has a publisher, who owns the song's copyright, whether there is a record company involved, who owns the copyright of the sound recording, and whether you can clear both the synchronization and master license.

When you take the initiative to provide this information from the beginning on whatever material gets presented, you eliminate a great deal of potential for guesswork and future misunderstandings. By clearly and accurately including all pertinent information on the CD, you reduce the chance of mistakes, confusion, cue sheet omissions, and complicated corrections later. It also indicates you understand the business and may be professional to work with.

Presentation Styles

Printed materials that accompany your audio content don't need to be fancy. They should, however, look professional. Whenever in doubt, a simple and clean presentation is your best bet. People who license music aren't concerned with helping an artist to get a great exposure opportunity. For them, licensing music is a business transaction, and as such, has a clinical feel.

Music is used to enhance the production value of a project. That's their purpose for licensing it. Period. They just want to find the right music for their projects and have no time to address recurring questions from a neophyte seeking her first licensing deal. For that reason, licensees prefer getting music referrals from publishers, lawyers, or other services, to ensure all clearances are in order and transactions that come as a result will be smooth. Music from referrals is often packaged a certain way, a stark contrast to the type of presentation that comes directly from an artist. I call it the "library corporate look."

This clean and simple style seems more professional. It creates the impression that the artist is more likely to have all clearances available and licensing arrangements will be handled efficiently. But many people looking for musical content like showcasing the hip and emerging artist. Some music supervisors or advertising agencies take pride in "discovering" new talent on the rise. In some ways, they are like the next generation of A&R. This more sterile presentation style will be less appealing to these types, who are also big music fans.

I'm impressed with good music, not with artwork, lyrics, bios, and other stuff I really don't need.

BRENT KIDWELL, Freelance Music Supervisor

For these folks, the pleasure comes from being one of the springboards in an emerging artist's career. Their involvement and enthusiasm can sometimes amount to a golden opportunity. In such cases, it helps to have some local or regional success under your belt, to validate their gut instinct. However, they don't want you to have so much success that what they offer won't excite you. That's why indie artists with a good fan base can be appealing. These music lovers like CDs with artwork, photos, and press, which I call the "artist look." They're music fans at heart and enjoy helping an artist if they can.

Consolidate all of your promotional materials. Too many papers may get lost. Make sure your current contact info is on every sheet! Include a synopsis of your band's relevant biographical highlights, credits, and/or testimonials if applicable as part of the printed text that appears on the J-card insert. Or you can refer them to your band's website for additional promotional content. When in doubt, simply send what is being asked for. If you have a direct conversation with whoever is making a request, ask what they want. Or, create a one-sheet with all pertinent info and a summary of press and other accomplishments.

Submitting Music

Nowadays, more music is submitted electronically. If you respond to a call for music, use the format they ask for. Unless you're a mind reader, you won't know how someone who licenses music wants submissions. Before cold calling, inquire by e-mail. If there's no response, use your judgment. Never send big files to someone who didn't request them. Despite the ease of using electronic submissions and its growing acceptance for song pitching, many requests still require mail submissions. Some might require you to *upload* MP3 files to a server.

MP3 Attachments and Electronic Submissions

Until recently, electronic submissions and hyperlinks embedded within an e-mail were often frowned upon or disregarded. Hard copies sent by mail have been the preferred choice. But electronic submission policies are changing as technology expands and makes it easier for those who need music. A great thing about MP3 attachments, Web link referrals, and electronic submissions is the dramatic cost reduction they will bring you. Depending on how many requests you pursue, shipping expenses can add up!

> *I don't have time to surf music sites in the middle of the day. Remember that most music supervisors are incredibly busy, so try to keep your communications and impressions as brief as possible. I will generally listen to a piece of music if it is embedded in the e-mail (but rarely the whole song), so try just attaching a thirty- to sixty-second snippet of the song (verse chorus is usually best) with a link to the entire song on your website. That way, if there's interest, the music supervisor can follow up. Remember—always leave them wanting more!*
>
> SEAN FERNALD, Producer/Music Supervisor,
> 3Mac Studios

These days you might be asked to upload MP3 files to a server. There are specific directions, requirements, and restrictions about the acceptable MP3 file size and/or resolution. The greater the compression resolution, the bigger the MP3 file's size. If server space is an issue, you'll likely be asked to further squash your file. When in doubt, *256 Kbps, 44,100 Hz, 16 Bit, stereo* is usually the compression resolution of choice for an MP3 file in an e-mail attachment. Sometimes there are e-mail attachment file size limits and restrictions on the receiver end, or their mailbox may be filled to capacity.

There are many ways to modify and customize resolution attributes of a preexisting audio file. Most audio programs offer several options to do this. Launch your preferred audio production software, and open/import the file you'd like to adjust. Once the file is open, select it. You'll now create a new copy (under FILE, choose either SAVE AS, SAVE A COPY, or RENDER). Prior to creating the new file, you'll be given a variety of file types to choose from, and whatever options are available may appear in a drop-down menu in the SAVE AS dialog box. From this list, select the file type that is appropriate (.mp3). Within the SAVE AS dialog box, you should see a button (CUSTOM, SETTINGS, or OPTIONS) that allows you to choose from several common .mp3 file resolutions. Select the suitable one and click OKAY.

When submitting music via MP3 files or uploading or posting on third-party websites, it's common to get specific directions and/or requirements for MP3 file size resolution. MP3 files are compressed audio files; approximately 90 percent of the audio information contained within the uncompressed counterpart is removed during the MP3 conversion process. You have some say prior to making a conversion. Unlike uncompressed .wav and .aiff audio files, MP3s can come in a variety of resolutions. Music submissions being sent or received over the Internet will often have specific directions in relation to acceptable file sizes. For such purposes, 128, 192, and 256 kbps are the most commonly encountered.

As you create, save, and accumulate MP3 files of a given song at differing MP3 resolutions, it's good to indicate variations in resolution as part of the new file name. For example, for a song called "Disillusioned," you can have a music folder that includes *"Disillusioned_128.mp3," "Disillusioned_192.mp3"* and *"Disillusioned_256.mp3."* Then it will always be clear which MP3 is which.

Submitting Music by Mail

Preparing your submission in response to a music request can take a surprising amount of your time. It often involves burning a copy of your CD, printing labels, or, when necessary, creating a customized compilation CD formatted to the specific needs of a request. Before sending a CD that's burned from your computer, play it to make sure it works. Print a bio, CD label, J-card, and anything else that might help make a good impression.

> *Make your package stand out. Don't stick a CD in a manila envelope with a note that says, "check out my music." That will surely end up at the bottom of a pile of thousands of other CDs that a music supervisor gets in the mail. Try sending it Federal Express or in a cool package. Combine it with a gift. Be as creative with your packaging as you are with your music.*
>
> RAMSAY ADAMS, Music Supervisor for film and television

CD packages should be accompanied by a cover letter that tells the receiver who you are, how to contact you, and what request you're responding to. Since music requests attract many music submissions, cover letters, especially those sent to strangers, should be brief. A paragraph or less is usually all you need. A company or band letterhead lends a nice touch. Create it in your computer if necessary. Don't waste time crafting brilliant and lengthy cover letters. To submit music to strangers, a generic prototype might read something like this:

> *Dear _____,*
>
> *My name is _____. The enclosed material(s) is a response to a request for "_____" posted in/on _____. Please feel free to contact me if you have any questions or feedback. One-hundred percent synchronization and master clearance is available.*
>
> *Best regards,*
>
> _____

If you are slightly acquainted with the person you contact, remind him of when and where you met, or other details that might trigger his memory. If you've been referred, include the name of the person who sent you. Most companies that request music submissions eventually acknowledge receiving packages, either by e-mail or phone. If they don't after several weeks, it's typically best to move on to other opportunities. If a music request involves a pressing deadline that requires submitting your CD by priority mail or overnight shipping, use the tracking number to keep tabs on the delivery status online.

Following Up

Should you call the person or company to confirm delivery and try to work some charm to sway odds in your favor? Appropriate action varies from case to case. People skills are probably the most important—and most overlooked—factor in getting ahead in any facet of life. Sometimes proactive calls are necessary, or could be counterproductive. *Never* call when a request states something to the effect of "No phone calls or e-mails please; we will contact you if interested."

Be patient. The music selection and clearance process can take longer than expected, even when "URGENT!" was in the header of a request.

While many companies that request music won't have an issue with your confirming your materials arrived, most busy video production companies and music supervisors would rather not be contacted just for that, unless they contacted you first. Few will tell you that outright, but it's better not to if you replied to a general request.

If your songs are great, they'll be imported into an edit. If they work within the parameters of a given request, chances are you'll be notified. If your songs are great, but not quite right for their project, you may still be notified, if only to be informed that your CD has been archived and will be considered for future projects. I usually don't bother calling, unless I'm on a first-name basis with the requester or if they contacted me directly with a request and specified an urgent deadline. If you simply can't resist the temptation, or perhaps were instructed to follow up later, wait a few weeks.

> *I initially prefer a few MP3s so I can get a feel for the artist. If I need a full-length, I'll request it. A well-done packaging and track listing does make a difference.*
>
> ADAM SWART, Music Supervisor, 35Sound

Keep conversations light and brief. People are busy. Acknowledge that their time must be tight and you won't keep them long. Sharing that your time is limited, too, works to your advantage. Be polite, especially when you don't know the person. There's a delicate balance between following up, staying in touch, and being too pushy, which gets you branded as inexperienced, desperate, or a pest. Aggressive calling rarely works with someone who doesn't know you. Asking many questions and pushing for answers, especially with no licensing agreement on the table, turns many off. When people want to license your music, they *will* contact you. If you do call, here's a sample script to use:

> **YOU:** *Good afternoon. My name is _____ from the (band/ company) _____. A CD was mailed to your attention a few weeks ago in response to a music request that was posted in/on (name of publication). I am calling just to confirm that the package I mailed has arrived safely.*

COMPANY: *Hold and let me check ... yes, I see that it has.*

YOU: *Great. Thanks for your time and I'll look forward to updates.*

WHEN IN DOUBT, STOP HERE.

If you don't hear from someone you submit music to, your music or song(s) weren't the best match for their requirements or they got so many CDs that a suitable match was located before they even got to yours. Your package may not have even been opened. As I said earlier, don't take rejection, or success for that matter, personally. Continue to submit music. And if you don't have a readily available match, it's best not to waste your time and energy pursuing it.

Marketing Songs Online

The Internet opens up a whole new world of opportunities for songwriters who become savvy at using it. It gives you a stage to place your songs where those who need music can hear them and learn about you. If you use it wisely, it's a great inexpensive tool for attracting licensing opportunities. Music supervisors go to websites to hear music and learn more about it. While pictures, bios, and video clips play a role, that material is usually a secondary consideration. The first is finding the best musical match for their needs, that's available and affordable. The most important content on your website is music. Keep in mind:

- Music files posted on your website should be easy to access. Links to them should be highly conspicuous. If viewers need to search for music samples, they might get impatient and leave.
- Many websites stream music clips by default once accessed.
- Make it clear that music on your website is available for licensing.
- On the page with music files, list information such as song title, genre, tempo, keywords, comments, writers, copyright date, publisher, contact info, and copyright protection.

Your chance of getting licensed improves by including pertinent information for potential licensees. Knowing immediately whether your music might work for a particular project makes their jobs easier, which could lead them to come back to you for other musical needs.

At times you may be asked to provide highly detailed information about your song(s) that gets embedded within the audio file itself. This is common when working with companies and/or marketing-type services that provide Web-based infrastructure for hosting online music catalogs featuring a searchable database. Embedding keywords gives users the ability to search for a piece of music having one or more specific attributes. The technical process of adding/embedding keywords into an audio file is straightforward:

- Create a list of keywords in any word processing program. Separate each keyword and/or short phrase with a comma + space.
- Click/right-click on the audio file's properties tab.
- Copy and paste the list of descriptors you have created into the keywords and/or meta-tag data entry box.

Embedding keywords into your audio files is a good viral marketing strategy to help you get picked up by search engines. While doing a search, someone may not be looking for your digital content per se. But, if your content is tagged with keywords that are very close to whatever terms are used during the search, your media appears as a search result. Under the right circumstances, this can generate an increase in traffic to your website and/or media files posted within it.

The more challenging part is compiling a useful list of descriptive words that are both comprehensive and accurate enough to ensure your song shows up as a high-ranking result in a search. Include general terms, like the musical genre. If your song is rock, is it classic rock, modern rock, punk rock, alternative rock, or indie rock? Many other variations could also be included in this list of musical genre sub-categories. I've found it useful to get suggestions from anyone with some musical savvy, and not necessarily a musician. The people you turn to should be willing to lend their ears and subjective opinions. Music lovers have often provided suggestions to me that I would have overlooked or never considered.

Generating Online Visibility

The best way to get your music placed is to develop relationships with music supervisors and other creative professionals who are placing music in productions. There are many good websites that provide networking opportunities. LinkedIn, Facebook, MySpace, and many other social networking sites are extremely useful because not only do they provide opportunities to meet production professionals, they also offer a way for artists to actually showcase work. Posting videos and music to these social networking sites will probably get you more views than posting music to your own personal website. The trick is always marketing. Social networking sites rely on friends linked to friends so you need to spend a lot of time and energy inviting people to become your friend so they see your profile and updates.

RAMSAY ADAMS, Music Supervisor for film
and television

Online social networking websites like MySpace (www.myspace.com) and Facebook (www.facebook.com) have become a standard marketing tool. People who license music increasingly turn to these websites and networks to find new or undiscovered talent. Most of these websites offer a decent amount of free Web space and excellent potential for networking, exposure, and publicity. You can upload music and video files. Be aware that some online user agreements have provisions that grant ownership of any digital content uploaded to the server to the hosting company. Many artists have gotten their music licensed after someone looking for music found them on MySpace or Facebook.

People can hear the music right away on MySpace and find out more about you. No matter where you live, you can connect with people needing musical content from around the world and build relationships with them right on the site. Sometimes if someone hears a song she likes and would consider licensing it, she might do a search for you on MySpace. But just like in the real world, don't agree to anything without first talking to a lawyer.

Sites like MySpace are becoming a valuable resource for new and fresh music. More and more, filmmakers are turning to these sites as a resource for fresher (and less expensive) alternatives to more established recording artists. If you don't have one of these set up...do it right now.

SEAN FERNALD, 3Mac Studios, Producer/
Music Supervisor, 3Mac Studios

Although many social networks are free, it is worth reading the fine print prior to clicking "I agree" while setting up an account. Deeply embedded within some (but not all) of these online user agreements (aka a "contract") might be one or more provisions that would likely raise red flags if a similar deal were being offered in an equivalent offline capacity. In some cases, agreeing to the terms of membership will in effect grant ownership of any digital content subsequently uploaded to the server to the hosting company. In a sense, free membership is exchanged for content ownership. In such cases, it can safely be assumed that the hosting company retains/acquires the right to sell, lease, or license their own website and/or services along with any digital media that happens to stream from within it to third party companies and/or advertisers.

For many artists, the fine print and nitpicky legalese related to content ownership may not matter; the trade-off can be justified in favor of the increased potential for exposure, expanding fan-base, and MP3 downloads/ sales. Just be aware that some free social network memberships are predicated upon business models of this nature, and you are not agreeing to anything that another entitled party would take issue with.

Like all marketing, getting the most out of a social network requires time and ongoing attention. The Internet offers artists the possibility of chance exposure opportunities. Many people who need musical content scour social networking sites. Make it easy for them to learn about you! Have lots of information and music samples on your pages. Link to your main website if you have one. Include a clear description of your music so visitors can gauge if you might have the style of music needed. Many unknown musicians say they got their start by being discovered on MySpace or Facebook. Once you make connections electronically, you can build relationships that can continue for many years!

II

Getting Music Licensed in Television Shows

Television has many opportunities for licensing music. It offers the possibility to earn long-term royalties, even for a single song placement. TV placements often provide an artist with meaningful exposure, too. The number of people who hear your song featured in a network television series can be the equivalent of having it played on several thousand radio stations all at once. At that moment, millions of people hear your song. Some series will go an extra step and provide the artist with a very valuable courtesy: they'll display a brief end-title card that informs viewers who the artist is, what they look like, and where their music is available for purchase. Shows like *Grey's Anatomy* (ABC) and many on CW (formerly the WB) are known for doing this.

Having your music identified in a popular TV show provides real exposure for you if you're an artist. In terms of licensing songs on television, it's a home-run scenario. Many TV series have become more attentive about using their official websites to post and update details related to songs and artists heard during each episode. These music credit listings often provide a link to the artist's own website or a place to buy their music. This is very helpful for generating exposure as well. If the show's official website fails to list credits, it's become common to find one or more unofficial fan websites that are more than happy to do so. On the downside, placing songs on TV has become very competitive. Although TV is indie-artist friendly, securing a licensing deal often requires working with representation, especially in the beginning.

The Licensing Trend

Licensing songs wasn't a normal part of doing business in television production in the not-so-distant past. While music has been a part of television since the beginning, methods and business models that have become far less common accomplished its use and inclusion. Music in a television series was mostly limited to the show's theme song and some occasional underscore. It served to accentuate moments of drama, transitions, humor, and other moods or emotions.

The theme song and underscore for a show were typically written by a single composer who was hired or commissioned to create this work by a production company, studio, or network. Once music was written for a show, an arranger was hired to orchestrate what often began as a melody or piano sketch. He would transform this basic musical framework into a more expansive and robust sounding piece of music, frequently taking full advantage of the colorful timbres that could be provided by an orchestra. Greater priority was given to the string arrangements that often rendered a quasi-romantic or bittersweet style of music compositions, sometimes referred to as "the Hollywood sound."

Each instrumental part had to be written out by hand. Highly skilled studio musicians, all union members, were hired to perform and record the TV theme songs and incidental cues as needed. During a recording session, the scores were sight-read on the spot. Whenever possible, each excerpt was recorded in a single take in order to stay within the production's budget. Creating music for television was a complex and expensive undertaking, and relied upon the skill and cooperation of many. The bulk of the music produced was instrumental and created specifically around the direction and character of a given TV series.

In contrast, today's television theme songs, underscore, and songs featured as part of a television series come from a variety of sources. Music that's selected for use as the show's theme song may not have been written with this intention in mind. Another trend has been to have less emphasis on hiring or commissioning just one composer to create customized music for a show. This tradition has been replaced by a selection process, overseen by producers and music supervisors and officiated through licensing agreements. While some recordings of the underscore still feature some live musicians, when music budgets are strapped, orchestral sounding recordings are often the result of digital audio technology, such as high-end VST (virtual sound technology) sound modules that are triggered via MIDI (Musical Instrument Digital Interface) sequencing. All of this opens the door wide for licensing opportunities in television.

The 1996 Telecommunications Act

From the 1940s until 1984, broadcast limits were guided by the *rule of seven* that specified no one owner was permitted to own more than *seven* FM, *seven* AM, and *seven* TV stations. This limit was increased to twelve in 1984 and several other times until reaching twenty in 1994. On February 8, 1996, President Bill Clinton signed into law the 1996 Telecommunications Act. This law provides definitive steps to both regulate and deregulate the telecommunications industry. The "Broadcast Services" section of this law included a provision that removed broadcast ownership limits as long as owners didn't reach more than 35 percent of all audiences. The government made additional broadcast spectrum available that could be licensed by a network, thus creating a way to digitally broadcast many more stations at once than had previously been allowed. This provided a network the option to split itself into multiple stations and explains why, in the years that followed, the number of stations that have become available to digital cable service subscribers has grown exponentially.

This deregulatory measure not only opened the door for the creation of more stations, it also allowed stations to deliver more specialized content suited to the desires of various target audiences and demographic profiles, such as MTV, MTV2, VH1, VH1 Classic, etc. The creation of more stations created a demand for new programming and, of course, a greater demand for music to keep these shows as entertaining as possible. The 1996 Telecommunications Act opened the door for a series of changes that began to reshape the music industry. In its wake were opportunities in what had been a more obscure and restrictive practice of licensing for use in television programming.

Multiple Revenue Streams

Songs, with vocals or instrumentals, that have been licensed for inclusion in TV programming offer the potential to generate more than one type of revenue stream. Under the right set of circumstances, one single song placement could go on to earn royalties for many years. It can earn the synchronization and master licensing fees (the up-front licensing fees), broadcast royalties (the back-end performance royalties), royalties from inclusion on a possible TV series soundtrack album, and in some cases, renewal and expansion fees should the terms of the original license expire or not include specific media rights that are now necessary to include.

There are many different types of television programming formats, as well as different methods for delivering televised content to viewers, such as digital broadcast, satellite, pay-per-view, and cable subscription services. All of these factors can influence up-front licensing fees. They also influence the calculations and formulas used to determine the back-end performance royalties. The potential for generating long-term back-end royalties is greatest in the realm of television. This potential bonus is what gives certain types of TV song placements extra appeal. Pursuing them has spawned growth in the areas of music publishing and marketing services over the past decade.

A network television show called *Third Watch* was one of the first to license a song I wrote. My song "Jaded Heart" was featured in the second season of the series, which aired on NBC. A music publisher negotiated the deal. To my pleasant surprise, its appearance in the show has generated royalties for both of us ever since. That particular situation represents a somewhat unique case, where certain factors came into alignment that made it possible for the song to continue to earn royalties over the course of a decade. It's important to understand that not all song placements on television will guarantee that you'll receive royalties for years to come. There's always potential, but it only happens under the right set of circumstances.

Royalties that are credited for music used in a television show will continue to come in as long as the show continues to broadcast. A trail of revenue streams can be generated from summer repeats and getting syndicated to air in other countries. Sometimes other stations and networks pick up a show to air in reruns after its last episode airs on the original network or cable station.

But not every television show experiences a prolonged shelf life. It depends on its popularity, the number of episodes that were produced, and its appeal and ability to pull in viewers in other parts of the world. Some television shows only last for a single season. That ends the potential for multiple box sets of a season for the show. But, if production of the series can at least complete its first season, which averages thirteen episodes, before getting cut, it may go on to air in other countries as a one-season TV series for quite some time.

Deadlines and Clearance Requirements

In network television, the production schedule is usually about two weeks ahead of the time it's scheduled to air. A network episode you view this week was hand-delivered to the network as a broadcast-ready edit from someone at the production company roughly two weeks ago. So, if you have a song slated to appear in this episode, signing off on the license request may have happened as recently as two weeks ago. Network television operates on a tight and rather rigid time schedule.

In order for a TV show, or even a commercial, to be allowed to air on a prescheduled day and time, a number of items called *deliverables* must be given to the network beforehand. They have a specific date prior to the airdate to get these in or the show won't be allowed to air. These items include the broadcast-ready edit and a stack of paperwork that includes music clearance forms. As mentioned earlier, the biggest rush in relation to song licensing is getting all entitled parties signed off on a request and clearance form. The actual broadcast of the episode often seals the deal for a legal obligation to pay the agreed-upon licensing fees to the entitled parties. In the case of TV shows that air on network television, fees are usually sent within a month.

Networks are understandably mindful of their susceptibility to potential lawsuits. Adopting some strict policies about mandatory clearance and refusal to accept unsolicited materials is a precaution triggered by past lawsuits. Clearance and approvals for the music must be verified prior to it being allowed to air. One form of copyright infringement involves the public exhibition of another person's work without legal permission. There's no better example of public exhibition than a network television broadcast available nationwide. From a pragmatic point of view, the most significant role of a music supervisor isn't to sift through stacks of CDs to hunt down the next hit artist. Instead, it's making sure that whatever music is included in an episode has been properly cleared. If one of these songs happens to become a hit, all the better, but if not, the supervisor will still have performed his primary duty.

Getting in the Door

Getting songs placed in a television series has become a prized commodity since the marketplace has become increasingly saturated and competitive. If you're new to the business, you'll have a better chance of landing your first song placement if a marketing company, publisher, or attorney represents you. Some are more selective than others about the type or number of artists they represent. Whoever represents your music will ideally have a decent track record in securing song placements on television, or have a direct contact with one or more production companies.

> *I see the demand for licensed songs growing for episodic television and network promos. Supervisors have tight turnarounds and it's imperative that they find a track that captures a specific emotion but can also speak to a wide demographic. The true beauty of a great pop song is that it can be personal and speak to many people simultaneously.*
>
> ALEX MOULTON, Founder and creative
> force behind Expansion Team

You can pursue network television opportunities on your own, but the odds of it getting a placement are better when a person or company that's familiar with the process, has experience pitching music, and knows the right people to send it to is doing it for you. You can pursue placements on your own while keeping your eyes peeled for those who might be able to represent you. In the beginning, there are things you can do to help open doors.

Prioritize Songwriting

While learning to play a musical instrument, you know that practice makes perfect. It can take a long time to feel like you own your craft. The same can be said for songwriting. As an art form, it should be given the same time and attention that's dedicated to learning an instrument or rehearsing with a band.

It's a myth to assume that a skilled musician is also a skilled writer, just as it's a false assumption that a great vocalist is a strong lyricist. Whenever possible, attend songwriting workshops, join songwriter groups, get feedback from professionals, or ask friends or musicians you know and admire for advice. Study other people's songs, especially those that inspire you. When you hone your craft well, you're more likely to get noticed.

Attend Music Industry Conferences

Try to attend at least one conference that's related to the music business. Going to them is an excellent way to make contacts, meet someone who can provide you with a referral, or become aware of a company or services that can help steer you in the right direction. Conferences that involve publishing, entertainment law, digital media, technology, gaming, and marketing could all be useful. There's no best one. Many times the people who end up helping you most are discovered in places or situations where you don't always expect to find them.

Approach Marketing and Pitching Services First

If your material is very strong and it's clear that there's a market for its use, you'll generally experience less resistance by first approaching a person or company in the business of pitching songs, unless they simply can't handle representing any more clients at the moment. Many will probably agree to screen your CD. If it's good, they might take you as a client since they, too, stand to earn a profit by placing your music on a TV show. Music supervisors are typically up to their necks with music submissions. In addition, it's common for people who work at publishing and marketing companies to actually do the music supervision for a project.

Theme Songs

A *theme song* is usually the first piece of music you hear when a TV show begins. It's part of an introduction presentation that often accompanies a visual montage of the cast, locations, plot overview, and credits. Unlike a song that is licensed for use in just a single episode, the theme song is usually a fixed part of the opening credits and introduction shown at the beginning of every episode. Musically speaking, it becomes the thematic signature for the series. When you hear this piece of music on television or elsewhere it's readily identified as linked with the show. A television theme song is found either through a selection process, where a music supervisor or producer screens a pool of submissions, or the music supervisor is asked to find and hire someone to compose an original piece of music specifically for the show.

Occasionally a TV show's theme song has enough mainstream pop appeal to appear on the Billboard charts and radio station playlists. TV theme songs from *M*A*S*H*, *Cheers*, and *Friends* are some of the theme songs that have crossed over to the Top 40. For a TV series with a more robust music budget, the theme song might be an edit of a well-known songs or artist, like the use of The Who's classic "Won't Get Fooled Again" during the opening credits of the very popular series *CSI: Miami*.

Sometimes the production company commissions the theme song for a series. They hire a composer or music producer to write and record a piece of music based on a list of directions and a set of musical requirements. This may happen before a show airs on a network, or even before they get the deal to air. A TV show can begin with a single episode, produced as a pilot episode. Once complete, it's pitched to a TV network or cable station. If and when the pilot is signed, the network/cable station provides funding to produce more episodes to air over the course of a season. Pilots are often produced in February, March, and April.

If the theme song used for the pilot receives a stamp of approval from the network, it will likely remain in that spot. Theme songs have traditionally been commissioned as a work-for-hire gig. However, mandatory terms of exclusivity are not as much of a given as they used to be. Overall television production budgets have been on the decline in recent years. For TV music licensing, the trend has headed in the direction of a songwriter agreeing to lower fees in exchange for licensing terms that are nonexclusive. This is a fair trade-off, because the privilege of ownership should be accompanied by a price that is respectable and on par with a product's value.

A theme song is very valuable. It's usually the only piece of music that's all but guaranteed to appear in each episode. This can't be said of a song cleared by a single-song licensing agreement, or other source music used in the show. As long as the series airs, now and in the future, domestically or internationally, the theme song will continue to generate performance royalties. Theme songs have their own classification for cue sheet logging and royalty crediting ("main title"). On a per-episode basis, they don't pay as much as a song that's featured in the same episode. But over the long run, a theme song racks up credits from its recurring performances. Theme songs can generate additional revenue streams through mechanical royalties if DVD copies of the TV show are sold. Additionally, license renewals, term extensions, an expansion of rights, or any licensing fees associated with the theme song's use that occurs beyond the scope of the series itself, such as a video game based on the show, a soundtrack album for the TV series, printed sheet music, or other merchandise sold in the future, can all result in additional income.

Agents and Composing for TV

The practice of music licensing as the go-to source for music in TV has overshadowed the role of TV composers. There are only so many places in a given episode that will need music. The question for a music supervisor becomes: "What type of music should we use, licensed songs or original score?" To further blur the distinction, it's now possible to license an instrumental piece of music that serves the same purpose as the score. I refer to this practice as *licensed score*. It has become a common practice. Yes, it's less personal, but from a production standpoint it's often less expensive, especially when it's from a library CD and the right to use this piece of music is covered by a preexisting blanket license.

Landing a TV composer gig is most often the result of being referred by or working with an agency. Finding one can be a little frustrating since they prefer working with clients who are already established. Agents work on commission and breaking in a newbie can require some additional effort or risk. However, big rewards always involve risks. I have found, and this applies across the board, the more prepared, self-sufficient, and capable you seem, and the less time or energy that appears to be required in order to do business with you, the better your chances will be of winning over someone who is either sitting on the fence, or doesn't seem interested at first.

Music Uses

The term *usage* refers to how a piece of music is used within the context of a TV show or film. As each piece of music or cue gets logged onto a cue sheet, it's tagged with an abbreviation that identifies the context in which it was used.

CUE SHEET—COMMON USAGE TERMS

ABBREVIATIONS	USAGE TERM / DESCRIPTION	EXPLANATION / NOTES
VV	Visual Vocal	Vocal track; song is the primary audio content being heard and used to support accompanying visual imagery.
VI	Visual Instrumental	Instrumental track; composition or "cue" is the primary audio content being heard and used to support accompanying visual imagery.
BV	Background Vocal	Vocal track; song is used in a background capacity; provides atmospheric or incidental texture underneath the main dialogue occurring during one or more scenes.
BI	Background Instrumental	Instrumental track; song is used in a background capacity; provides atmospheric or incidental texture underneath the main dialogue occurring during one or more scenes.
SRC	Source	Primarily instrumental music cues; the source of which is most often a production music CD or library collection covered by a preexisting blanket license agreement.
MT	Main Title	Music featured during opening credits.
ET	End Title	Music featured during closing credits.

The different usage categories influence the dollar amount of the broadcast royalties. Each usage type is given a certain royalty point value or weight. The term "cue" refers to any piece of music that appears in an episode, regardless of its duration or volume. So music excerpts are technically cues of some sort, but not all cues have the same value for the purpose of royalty calculations.

The royalty value is determined by both how a cue's usage is defined and how long it was used. Usage definitions vary in value. The longer a cue plays during the episode, the more it earns. So a cue that's assigned a less valuable usage definition but is played for two minutes during an episode will more than likely generate a higher royalty credit score than one that's assigned a more valuable usage definition but only plays for twenty seconds.

Sometimes a specific cue appears in more than one spot per episode. This is referred to as an *occurrence*. Usually a given cue happens once per episode but when it's used more frequently, it increases the occurrence value, which also augments the royalty crediting per episode. So on a per-episode basis, a cue's usage point value is multiplied by the length of time it was used and the number of occurrences. Other factors also influence the royalty calculation that determines the final dollar amount. These include the day of the week the show aired (weekday or weekend), time of day, series type, and scope of broadcast (station or network). Each usage description carries a certain point value that influences the bottom line. The formula, usage values, and calculation methods for determining royalty amounts differ slightly among the performing rights organizations.

For TV, the highest performance royalties are earned by songs that have vocal tracks and are listed for the usage description section on the cue sheet as *features use*. A song that's featured as part of a television episode is typically heard either at the beginning or end of the program. There's little or no dialogue occurring when this song plays. Feature use means that the song stands out and isn't part of the background environment. For the song to be paid the highest dollar value, the show that features this song must be broadcast on a national television network, such as ABC, NBC, CBS, or Fox. Access to this channel must be part of basic TV service and available anywhere around the country. The scope of broadcast affects how much royalties are earned. A national broadcast pays much more than a local one.

The most money is paid for music airing on a show on a weekday during prime time (usually shown between 8:00 P.M. and 11:00 P.M.). It also helps if most of the song is heard, since the duration of use also matters. If all of these conditions are met, it will be a performance in the top royalty bracket. Feature vocal tracks generate the highest paying broadcast royalties, and can be considerably more than even the show's theme song. But not all song placements involve feature track usage. Songs also appear as part of the background texture or environment. Background use doesn't pack the same royalty punch that feature use does. But regardless of how noticeable or inaudible the cue appears to be as part of the background texture, you'll still receive the same royalty credit regardless of volume since it falls into the general usage description of *backing track*. If a conversation happens over your music during a scene, its usage will be logged as a backing track.

What follows is an overview of broadcast royalty potential from my own experience and what I've seen commonly occur. This is only intended to provide you with a ballpark approximation of relative royalty earning power for pieces of music that are used for a fixed amount of time, and per single performance basis. These values are relative to program type, and can be easily influenced by other factors.

MUSIC IN TELEVISION OVERVIEW

PROGRAM TYPE	COMMON FORMS OF MUSIC USAGE	MOST PREVALENT LICENSE(S)	REQUESTOR (LICENSEE)	MUSIC PROVIDERS (LICENSOR)
NETWORK TELEVISION SERIES	Songs (vocal tracks), instrumental tracks, source/library music, original score	Master, Synchronization, Blanket	Network Studios	Music Publishers, Record Companies, Marketing Services, Attorneys, Library and Music Catalogs, Composers (usually represented by agency), and Songwriters
NATIONAL CABLE SERIES	Songs (vocal tracks), instrumental tracks, source/library music, original score	Master, Synchronization, Blanket	Video Production Companies	Music Publishers, Record Companies, Marketing Services, Attorneys, Music Libraries, Producers, Composers, and Songwriters
NETWORK TV MOVIES	Instrumental/ background; score; may also include vocal tracks	Master, Synchronization, Blanket	Video Production Companies, Film Studios	Music Publishers, Record Companies, Marketing Services, Attorneys, Library and Music Catalogs, Composers (independent or with agency), and Songwriters
CABLE MOVIES	Songs (vocal tracks), instrumental tracks, source music, original score	Master, Synchronization, and possibly AFM Deal may be a Work-for-Hire Composer Agreement (buyout rights)	Video Production Companies	Music Publishers, Record Companies, Marketing Services, Attorneys, Library and Music Catalogs, Composers (independent or with agency), and Songwriters
SPORTING EVENTS	Instrumental/background	Blanket	Network Studios, Cable Stations, or an affiliate production company	Music Libraries and Catalogs, Music Publishers, or "in-house" library that has been purchased and is owned by Network (buyout)

MUSIC IN TELEVISION OVERVIEW, cont'd

PROGRAM TYPE	COMMON FORMS OF MUSIC USAGE	MOST PREVALENT LICENSE(S)	REQUESTOR (LICENSEE)	MUSIC PROVIDERS (LICENSOR)
TV SPECIALS	Music specifically written or commissioned for special, or licensed prior to airing, vocal tracks, instrumental tracks, source music	Master, Synchronization, or possibly Work-for-Hire Composer Agreements (buyout rights)	Video Production Companies, Network Studios, or affiliates	Hired/commissioned composer
INFOMERCIALS	Source/library/catalog music	Blanket	Video Production Companies	Library and Music Catalogs
SOAP OPERAS/ DAYTIME DRAMAS	Instrumental tracks/ source music	Blanket	Network Studios	Library and Music Catalogs
TALK SHOWS	Instrumental tracks/ source music	Blanket	Network Studios	Library and Music Catalogs
NEWS	Instrumental tracks/ source music	Blanket	Network Studios	Library and Music Catalogs
CARTOONS	Instrumental; score and background use	Master, Synchronization, or possibly Work-for-Hire Composer Agreements (buyout rights)	Video Production Companies, Animation and Game Production Companies, Networks	Composers (represented by agency or independent), Music Production Companies
REALITY TV SHOWS	Songs (vocal tracks), instrumental tracks, and source/production music	Master, Synchronization, and possibly AFM Deal may be a Work-for-Hire Composer Agreement (buyout rights)	Video Production Companies	Music Publishers, Record Companies, Marketing Services, Attorneys, Library and Music Catalogs, Composers (independent or with agency), and Songwriters

‖‖

CHAPTER 12

Getting Music Licensed in Films

There are many opportunities to get music licensed for use in films. The net sum of all music used in a movie is referred to as the *soundtrack*. Traditionally, each musical excerpt (as in TV, called a *cue*) from a movie falls into one of two main categories: *song* or *score*. Songs as part of the soundtrack are often written and recorded by different artists. The score is most often written by one composer but plenty of variations are possible. As with all things involving digital media, there's room for more flexibility. For example, it's possible for a movie soundtrack to be entirely comprised of only songs.

> *Music must inspire from the opening notes. Mood, color, palette, tone — it pains me as a writer to say it, but often the least important aspect is lyrical content because, given time, we will try to change it or use it for contrast. The most important thing is whether the music can tell a story all by itself, whether it has a motif that bears recalling again and again and can tolerate varietal changes. Pacing and rhythm must complement a story by advancing the emotional heat.*
>
> CARLTON BUSH Jr., Filmmaker

Music has a remarkable effect on our perception, feelings, mood, and reaction to visual imagery. In the case of scary movies, viewers who cover their ears will get through the experience with calmer nerves than those who cope by covering their eyes. Music can drive the mood and anticipation in each scene. In film, the underscore elevates the audience's reaction to visual imagery. It's important to do it in a way that doesn't steal the show or become distracting. Creating an appropriate level of imagery and knowing the limits is tricky in the beginning. This chapter discusses the process of licensing songs for movies and provides an overview of composing music for movies, which can also involve licensing content that's written specifically for a project.

The Lure of the Big Screen

There's a certain prestige or hip factor that comes from being associated with a project that's destined for the big screen. A project doesn't need to be a blockbuster or include a star-studded cast for it to have value from a publicity standpoint. A renegade film project that's all indie, a bit underground, or touches on a hot topic will often appeal to journalists who write for local music publications or college newspapers. When you have music in projects like this, forward a brief (250 words or less) press release to publications in your area. If you get a response, be accessible and down-to-earth about it. They may offer to run a story that provides press for you and the film, whose creators will probably really appreciate your proactive approach to marketing.

Indie filmmakers and bands have to assume some responsibility for marketing. Bands are fairly accustomed to promoting an upcoming gig or CD. Most filmmakers have less experience with this mindset. Not long ago, if a film landed a distribution deal, the distributor would handle publicity and advertising for it. However, just as artist development is history with the record labels, indie filmmakers now face the challenge and burden of also having to create a buzz for their film projects to solidify interest from a distributor. This creates a connection between film- and music-makers. Working together can be an incentive to cross-promote and help each other with marketing and publicity in ways that may not be possible or practical if your music is used for a hit TV series. Licensing music for television has its own set of advantages, but at the upper echelons, often feels like a straight-ahead business transaction. It's less personal and welcoming.

The use of music in a film is carefully considered, and at times, painfully scrutinized or debated since, in the end, selections for each scene have to work in concert with the visual images. The directors I've known often want a certain style of music in a scene because it adds to the story, sometimes in very subtle ways. For example, consider a scene where a man approaches a woman who is standing in the lobby of a building, waiting for the elevator to arrive. At last the bell rings, the doors open, and they both step inside. Elevator music is background music, both in real life and in a movie. But since this story is in a movie, the type of elevator music used is chosen carefully, even in a scene like this. While it may seem ordinary on the surface, there was probably careful consideration given to the type of elevator music that should be used.

Decisions for music are made to reinforce a subliminal message. Maybe it's to indicate a light-hearted flirtation, or it could be to prepare the audience for something more sinister. The music serves as a tool of persuasion and manipulation. It can serve to clue the audience in to something that's funny or a bit out of sorts. Thoughtful music selection or direction can sway this balance either way.

Most indie filmmakers I've met are very open to symbiotic cross-promotional opportunities. For example, you may be able to make arrangements for a fun, hip, red carpet–type promotional event with a double billing that includes your band performing at the movie's premiere. Or you might be allowed to include clips from the movie as part of an upcoming cross-promotional music video or other project that promotes your music. These kinds of ideas would be more complicated to get approval for and might be forbidden altogether, if you suggested one related to a TV series.

Although being asked to appear in the film itself is a rare occurrence, it does happen. Years ago, I played in a rock band called Fuzz Box. I saw an ad in *The Village Voice* for a film that was looking for music. We not only recorded music for the movie but were also asked to be performers in it since the plot was music-oriented. It was a cool experience. Our scene was filmed at CBGB, which was rented and temporarily closed to the public for normal business. Our performances were lip-synched. We performed the same songs over and over in front of a fake audience of extras. I remember it being very hot and we had to use hair dryers just to cool off. There was lots of stage lighting and after four hours, our pleather outfits didn't look or feel good. But it was still fun to play in a film.

There are also downsides to doing music for films. As with television, licensing songs for film can pay a respectable licensing fee that may span a few hundred to several thousand dollars per song. The final dollar amount that's settled upon depends on the film's music budget. In general, however, most independent films don't have big music licensing budgets. Many films won't generate the performance royalties from being played in theaters since they're released directly on DVD or for downloading on online retail sites. As I discussed earlier, none of these uses constitutes a broadcast. So getting your music into films provides more opportunities for a satisfying experience while imposing more limits on how much money you can make. But even if you don't get paid much, the relationships you build can lead to more profitable ventures down the road.

> *Understand what your niche is and what your music works well with and pursue music supervisors and production companies that specialize in the type of films that work well with your music. Connect with emerging directors and do pro-bono work to get entrance into the marketplace and develop those relationships.*
>
> DRAZEN BOSNJAK, Q Department

Music Uses in Film

Music serves a variety of roles in a film. The soundtrack consists of the score, which is the original music that's specifically written for the film, and songs in any genre or style that have already been recorded and are licensed. These songs may be featured in the opening or closing credits, or during a pivotal scene. Or they may simply appear as part of the background texture, such as when a song is heard playing on a car radio underneath the dialogue. Creating the soundtrack is a process that usually includes a lot of input from the director, and possibly the producers as well.

There's a long proven history of using soundtrack albums as a means of marketing and promoting a film. In many cases, the music featured on the soundtrack may in the long run become what defines the film or the era in which the film takes place, such as, *Saturday Night Fever, Purple Rain, Pulp Fiction, Rocky,* and *The Bodyguard.* The use of songs in movies is sometimes linked to an established and proven marketing strategy, where one or more singles from a soundtrack album are released just prior to the film's debut in theaters. With enough radio airplay and aggressive marketing, these songs climb the charts while providing additional perks or advertising for the movie.

The most common uses of music in a film include the following:

Opening Credits

Music used here establishes the major musical theme of the movie. Combined with the visuals, the music explains the starting point of the story, where it's happening, the time period, and sets the mood.

Underscore

This is a general term for what's most often presented as the supportive or background musical texture. It serves to reinforce the mood, the setting, or the atmosphere depicted in a scene. Underscore can also be used for comedic purposes to indicate tones such as exaggeration, mockery, or chaos.

Musical Transitions

This is music that accompanies scene transitions. They're often used to accentuate motion or plot transitions, such as an epic journey, challenge, mission, quest, search, flashback, etc.

Background Textures

This is underscore that's used to reinforce a mood, atmosphere, or ambience.

Leitmotif

This is a recurring musical theme that's always associated with a particular character, place, or object in a movie, play, or other dramatic work.

Understanding Filmmaking

It's good to be a little familiar with the process of filmmaking, at least the portions related to music. It will help you get the most out of the experience and also to be someone filmmakers find easy to work with.

Film music begins with a *spotting session*, which is a scheduled meeting to address all the film's requirements, share suggestions, and give direction about the role of music in it. Spotting sessions have traditionally involved score-related discussions between the director and composer. But it's not uncommon to also discuss scenes where songs, or both songs and score, may work better. Spotting sessions that I've attended are often daylong events.

Everyone watches the movie in piecemeal and every spot that requires music is discussed. Notes are written down according to time code display. Some directors give lots of input about the music. Others leave most decisions to the composer and/or music supervisor. A spotting session might be just one meeting, or can be split into several sessions. The movie's director and composer will most likely attend, and other postproduction sound crew, such as the music supervisor, sound editor, film editor, or producer(s), may also join in. This meeting usually happens in the middle of postproduction.

> *What I like in a songwriter is flexibility—whether it's to tweak songs quickly if needed or "knock off" a well-known song, and the flexibility to work within the parameters of the music budget.*
>
> ADAM SWART, Music Supervisor,
> 35Sound

Postproduction refers to various stages of film editing. A film has entered postproduction when all the shooting is complete, or very close, and all of the video content is being organized, assembled, and edited to deliver its story. During postproduction, technical issues related to the video processing, effects, computer graphics, and animation are addressed. Scenes are shortened, rearranged, and sometime cut all together for the purpose of establishing the right pacing and to tighten up transitions between scenes. Because music is synchronized to the video, it makes more sense to focus on the music once a working edit of the film is available. During postproduction, temp tracks start being replaced by the score cues delivered by the composer, or with songs suggested by the music supervisor that have been cleared through licensing agreements and fees that work within the movie's budget.

If you get asked to do music for a film, don't hesitate to ask questions. I try to get as much direction, input, and suggestion, as possible. The best time to probe for this information is in the beginning. I often take notes or bring a tape recorder to meetings. Since time is limited and scoring can be so much work, clear communication and understanding of the director's intentions will help prevent you from making a false start by inadvertently taking the wrong stylistic path. A client's feedback can guide you in the right direction. Not all directors will want a Hollywood, big budget, cinematic-sounding score.

Some situations may involve receiving a lot of feedback and direction. It's important to remain open to what may turn into an ongoing stream of input throughout the duration of the project. Don't take this personally. Many directors and producers simply regard it as being part of the collaboration process. However, I have worked with a few directors who have given surprisingly little guidance beyond their requests that it should "sound good" or "work within the genre." Be prepared for anything!

I scored my first film in 1997. Since then, it's been amazing to witness the quantum leaps that have transpired in audio and video production technology. Back then, computer-based music and video production gear was in its infancy stage and equipment was very expensive. There was a lot of stigma associated with the idea of creating a MIDI-based synthetic score. Most filmmakers didn't see it as a preferred option. A synthetically derived score sounded … synthetic. Since then, vastly improved audio and video editing software has changed how scores are produced. It's become much easier to experiment. Anyone with a computer can basically dive right in.

Indie Film Advantage

As with music, the equipment and production costs associated with filmmaking have dropped considerably in recent years. More people have gotten involved in independent filmmaking as a result.

Pursuing licensing opportunities in film can turn out to be a little more accessible, because the person in charge of its direction will probably be accessible. Most low budget independent films don't have music supervisors. It's possible that in some cases you might end up becoming friends with the director or producer of an indie film. Things tend to be a bit more low-key and production may be conducted under a less severe time crunch. When pitching music for network television, you might not have any direct contact with the show's producers since they're a step removed from the clearance process and a music supervisor addresses music issues. If someone represents your songs for TV, you'll be two steps removed from the producers and may have no direct contact with the music supervisor either.

From a practical standpoint, waivers on mechanical royalties, synch rights, and publishing for festival and theatrical screenings are important for budget-minded filmmakers. Musicians who wish to underwrite some of their fees in exchange for mastering costs may wind up at the head of the pack.

CARLTON BUSH Jr., Filmmaker

An independent filmmaker who needs music may post a classified ad on a free website or in a local newspaper. If you submit a CD and it seems right for the project, they'll probably call or e-mail you directly. When I became interested in film music, I followed every lead I could find and made some good friends this way. Every once in a while, one of these people will work on something that's really interesting, or reach a new plateau in her own career. Many bonds in the world of filmmaking are established over the course of a considerable period of time.

Many independent films don't have a budget to begin with. The production company in this case might be a one- or two-person operation, possibly a film student or someone having a story to tell, a camera, and a laptop computer. If they know what they're doing, you might not realize that what you're watching was assembled and produced on a shoestring budget. Sometimes a production company might have raised investment funding but went way over budget during filming and/or editing and spent the money set aside for music clearance and licensing.

If a small indie film company is crying low or no budget, remember that a commercial exploitation is better than none; but also remember that the film might succeed. Therefore you should bet on success and make every effort to obtain a step deal. In addition, (1) try for a most favored nations protection, (2) make sure there is adequate credit, and finally, (3) make sure that a proper cue sheet is prepared and filed with your performing rights society.

PETER M. THALL, Esq.

Most independent filmmakers try to get their films screened at film festivals. Some are harder to get into than others. If they get in, the hope is often to be able to attract distribution, PR attention, and/or financing. That's why so many independent filmmakers will ask for the festival license for free. At this point the film usually isn't making money. If you agree, they can use your music when they screen their films. It's important to understand that there's a big difference between giving them your music gratis and agreeing to a free festival license. Once the festival is over, they can't use your music without a broader agreement. I discussed step deals in Chapter 6 but must emphasize the value of having one in place from the get-go. If the film gets picked up at a festival, you want to have good terms for going forward.

Film festivals are a good place to meet up-and-coming young filmmakers. If you can get to a festival, even a small one, bring lots of business cards, some CDs or DVDs, and a big smile. Independent filmmakers are the most accessible and willing to work with indie artists. If you can develop relationships at the ground level, you may get to take a ride with them as they grow successful, if they like your music, and you. Sundance is one of the most popular film festivals where you can meet young filmmakers. SXSW is another that can yield productive contacts. You must meet as many people as possible if you want to attract licensing opportunities in film.

Film festivals also offer the opportunity to meet music supervisors, producers, and others involved in filmmaking who may be too big to connect to outside of these events. Every year, more film festivals pop up throughout the world. Check out sites like www.filmland.com, www.filmthreat.com, and www.UltimateFilmFest.com for up-to-date festival listings.

You can also find young filmmakers at film schools, like New York University. Students need music for their films. It's a good way to get a feel for how music works in films and have something to illustrate how your music works against the picture. Try to watch a film before agreeing to let them use your music. If you feel yourself cringing, stay away from the project. But if it seems to have talent behind it, it may be a good way to get your feet wet. Remember, even if there's no money in the budget for your music, be sure to enter into a licensing agreement with the filmmaker to protect both his work and yours. Every successful filmmaker began at the bottom. That's the best time to develop a relationship that can generate better licensing deals.

Musicians' Union

Unions are very important organizations that represent the interests of their members. The extent of a union's power or ability to enforce its policies is directly related to the number of members it represents. As a collective body, a union can demand and contractually enforce a set of baseline employment standards that apply to any of its members. These include standards related to hourly pay scale, maximum number of hours permissible in a workday, safety at the workplace, getting breaks, and other policies, all of which are intended to ensure that employed union members are treated fairly and not unnecessarily or unreasonably placed in harm's way.

The end result is a set of regulations that are periodically reviewed. Revisions are suggested when necessary as part of contract-renewal meetings that happen between these unions and studio executives. If both parties fail to reach an agreement, the last resort is implementing a strike, which can make the entire industry come to a standstill, like the writers' strike in 2007. It resulted in economic consequences for both the industry and local communities. Almost every profession associated with TV and film production has its own union or guild. For composers, orchestrators, arrangers, copyists, and musicians involved with film and television scores in the United States, it's the musicians' union, the American Federation of Musicians (AFM).

Being eligible for certain high-profile gigs often requires being a member of this union. The tradeoff is that, as a member, you're technically not allowed to accept employment that fails to satisfy union approved standards, most notably the pay scale. The reality is that most low- to medium-budget independent film projects can't afford these rates. On these projects, the fee for hiring the composer will usually need to include her out-of-pocket production costs, such as the cost of hiring musicians (union or freelance) in addition to renting a sound stage or a decent recording studio for a couple of days, which will often not only wipe out what has been budgeted for the composer fee, but will also accrue debt in the process. I've personally experienced this more than once.

Union musicians are generally more expensive to hire on an hourly basis than freelance studio musicians. For a major film studio production, these additional costs can be justified. By and large, union musicians are seasoned pros who can nail down parts in a single take. For a production company to hire a union member for studio session work or other music-related services on a film or television recording project, someone with the production company must become a designated signatory with the AFM. This individual must sign and submit what's called an *assumption agreement* with the musicians' union. This is a contract that outlines pay scale requirements for any studio work provided by union players, and creates a legal obligation to pay for it.

These agreements also include other provisions that may require making additional payments in the future, depending on the scope of commercial success related to the recordings. For a while, film companies used to circumvent these expenses by outsourcing specialized or technical work to people in other countries, whose employment standards are less expensive to address than those mandated domestically. Recent technology has made it possible to cut production costs related to recording film, TV, and game scores. Huge advancements in both audio software and hardware products allow composers to create quasi-synthetic orchestral recordings that can sound like a big-budget sounding score.

The appeal for opting to license prerecorded music that's suitable for a project's underscore is that it circumvents a long list of requirements, expenses, and other complexities that are an inherent part of producing new and original score recordings for film. Of course, a film that licenses certain tracks could see that music show up in another project down the road. However, at present, this consequence doesn't appear to be a strong deterrent when it's weighed in against the convenience and relative affordability that licensing musical content offers.

Independence offers artists freedom, but often with a price. The constraints imposed by unions for TV and film production often create an indie project's primary incentive for keeping all aspects of filmmaking independent for as long as possible. Because of this, the pay scale in an indie film is often much lower than that which would be earned for an equivalent union gig. In many cases, your involvement should be motivated by reasons other than monetary gain alone. The silver lining is that as you compose music for indie film projects in a nonexclusive capacity, which means you agree to work for next to nothing but retain ownership of the music you provide, you'll begin to amass a back catalog of instrumental music that already has a track record for working in films.

Eventually you may have enough music filed away to categorize it into genre-specific collections that can be marketed and licensed to others. It's a different form of payment, but can eventually provide exponential returns. Be patient and work on projects that inspire your best work and creativity. This is the key to making it work and retaining a sense of purpose and satisfaction.

Breaking In

Most of the movie projects I've worked on have come to me as the result of a referral or my having already worked with the person/company in the past. This can often be traced back to a time when these collaborators and I were less established, less experienced, and just getting started. Unless you have the luxury of being born into the business, everyone faces the same lack of experience and hurdles at the starting line, in all areas of licensing, be it film, TV, or advertising. Since that's a given, all you can do is control the way you respond to the decisions that are made by others—which usually have more to do with a potential licensor's talent and potential. Beethoven is arguably one of the greatest composers to have ever lived, and even his undeniable masterpieces may not work for a number of film scoring situations.

> *Do the homework and approach me about a project that I am working on. Have a few cues ready based on the subject matter and send your best couple of tracks as opposed to an entire library. Someone can find out through the trades what I am working on and contact me, by post or e-mail, specifying for what project the contents are intended.*
>
> BARRY COLE, Music Supervisor on over
> seventy features, SPOT

Bonds and connections gel and solidify over time. Most people prefer working with those they like. Movie projects can involve lots of back and forth correspondence between the various people involved, as well as concentrated periods of time working at a single location, often under mildly stressful conditions. If you don't like the person with whom you're in such intimate and protracted contact, it can be a nightmare!

Referrals play a considerable role in determining the cast, crew, and music that is considered and/or used in a film project. It's a practice that tends to save time. Suggestions for whom to bring in for various roles often come directly from a person who is a trusted source and who has prior experience working with whoever is being referred. Establishing personal connections and mutual respect while working with directors, producers, music supervisors, and editors increases the likelihood of working with them again sometime in the future. The converse is also true. The impression you make can hurt any future chance. Good working relationships can become as valuable as your skills.

Stay on top of today's popular songs, artists, and soundtracks on the mainstream charts as well as those associated with underground culture. Directors, music supervisors, and publishers have a habit of making references and comparisons to popular songs, artists, or albums. These descriptions are usually included as part of music requests, especially for temp music replacements such as, "We're looking for a suggestion to replace the following three songs…" Similar kinds of references are also used when describing the direction that's being sought for film scoring.

As you're breaking in, you will quickly discover that the scope of responsibilities associated with licensing music for film has evolved. Composing original music now often includes a fairly wide spectrum of tangential services that, until fairly recently, were each addressed by other specialists, such as orchestrator, conductor, arranger, copyist, sound editor, recording engineer, producer, and sound designer. Depending on the gig, you may need to wear some or all of these hats in addition to composing the music. I often remark that creativity is the least time-consuming part of this job.

> *You can gain direct access to filmmakers at Q&A panels and advance screenings. Always have a copy of your demo with you. You never know when or where you'll bump into someone who might be able to lead you to a song placement!*
>
> SEAN FERNALD, Producer/Music Supervisor,
> 3Mac Studios

To increase your value to a film, improve your skills and learn new ones. If you aspire to get hired to work with audiovisual media, you'll probably divide your time between being an artist and addressing technical issues. If you don't know anything about the technical end, the production company may pass on using you if they can get someone who wears more hats.

I spend a lot more time mixing and editing music than I do composing. If your ultimate goal is to do film scoring, the process of getting there will seem more manageable if you learn the skills needed:

- Learn to master one or more musical instruments. If it's an option, take lessons, since it will save you time by ensuring that you address technical issues related to playing the instrument properly. Poor or inefficient musical habits can be extremely difficult to break.
- Learn to read music. Study music theory, orchestration, and music history to have a better understanding of it.
- Become familiar with as many different styles of music as possible, including music that features unique or unfamiliar instrumentation associated with cultures other than your own.
- Get comfortable working with video. Take video classes, especially ones that address the basics of video editing.
- Practice by rescoring scenes from your favorite movies, short video clips, or images that inspire you. Scoring a film is very similar, although you will probably have to score between ten and twenty video clips per project. Learn to edit audio clips.
- Become the best musician that you can. Spend time with musicians who are more advanced than you. Their good playing may help improve yours if you play together.

Many movies on DVD will include an "extras" or "bonus section," especially when it's a *special edition* or *director's cut* version of a film. Watch them for some insightful information. You'll hear a director, producer, cinematographer, editor, or other member of the production crew explain their thoughts, methodology, and subtle factors that influenced their decision-making during the production. The information they share and the perspective they offer can be quite insightful. It's given me a fuller appreciation for the intricacies that go into producing a film. This commentary often provides insight into the type of things that interest, or possibly are a point of concern for, a director. If they hire you, it's important to be on the same page and understand the more subtle elements that can influence or assist making well-thought-out musical decisions.

||||||||||||||||||||||||||||||||||||||||||||||||||||||||||||||||||||||||||||||||||||||||||||||||||||||||||||||||||||||||||||

CHAPTER 13

Getting Music Licensed in Advertising

Using music to make advertisements more entertaining or memorable is a well-established practice. A concentrated area of jingle houses were located in Tin Pan Alley, a section of Manhattan that was famous for housing music publishers of popular song. For many years, musical jingles were used effectively to reinforce a memorable expression or slogan that became indelibly linked to a product. The use of jingles in TV commercials has been considerably phased out and replaced by the practice of licensing songs or commissioning original music that's less blatant in delivering a sales pitch. Gone are the golden days of the jingle houses, replaced by an era of licensing old hit songs or new ones by unknown artists. Covers by new artists can also work well for advertising.

> *We are responsible for a lot of the regional marketing activities for our clients. We look to see how we can make the brand more relevant on a local level. Sometimes regional artists who are known in a market may not have national appeal but have a strong appeal in that area. That helps a product connect more to that region.*
>
> REGINALD OSBORNE, Senior Vice President, Director
> Multicultural Marketing, Arnold Worldwide

Benefits of Licensing Music for Advertising

One of the main perks of licensing music for advertising is the up-front licensing fees. Generally speaking, they're sizable in contrast to those frequently offered in film or television. An indie band might be able to secure a few thousand dollars for a song licensed for use on a TV network series or a film with a budget. Yet a national advertising campaign might pay ten times this amount to license one song. Over the years I've seen request quote fees that were close to $100,000. Licensing fees can even go far beyond this if the singer has star power. Since these opportunities often have bigger up-front paydays, they're competitive. Establishing solid contacts with the bigger ad agencies requires a lot of ongoing effort.

Part of the challenge is that ad agencies pull music from a variety of sources, depending on the details specified by their clients. The opportunities that exist in advertising are pretty evenly split into two categories. For the first, an advertising agency opts to search for, locate, and license preexisting music. For the second, a person or company is hired to create something original that will be custom tailored around a theme to help drive a marketing campaign forward. Advertising campaigns are designed around capturing the essence of a simple message, theme, idea, catchphrase, or slogan. Music is a highly effective, proven device that can be used to reinforce the concept.

Forming a Network

We rely on music production houses. We have in-house producers at the agencies and they work with production houses and also recording studios. If someone thinks they have a perfect piece of music for a product, the best way to try to connect is through the producers at ad agencies or the music houses. What happens is we'll create a concept. If it's a commercial focused on music, we will seek out producers who have the expertise to do it. For example, what McDonald's decided to do to strengthen their focus on music is they're working with a well-known producer out of Chicago. This is an avenue because he has many relationships with other producers and probably writers and recording artists. Going through these well-known producers or experiential marketing companies are good avenues to try.

REGINALD OSBORNE, Senior Vice President, Director
Multicultural Marketing, Arnold Worldwide

If you want to break into doing music for advertising, it may be worthwhile to contact music production companies to offer your services on a freelance basis. They'll want to hear some tracks. It helps if you can show them commercials you've worked on. If you haven't done any, ask if they'd e-mail you a few short video clips they have on file from past projects or clients. Offer to score them to demonstrate your potential. When they see your work, it gives them a good taste of your ability. If they're impressed, you may be added to their roster. Most music production companies are open to this, especially if you can fill a void in their roster. This is a good strategy to consider since, once you're in, you can piggyback on their established list of clientele.

Production companies tend to be musicians with a good instinct for business and the ability to work well with other business professionals beyond the arts. Give them the impression that you're easy to work with. Show that you have the type of personality that responds to constructive criticism without throwing a temper tantrum. They're looking for people with talent, who are dependable, and have a willingness to listen and learn. These personal attributes can get you further than talent. I've known many musicians over the years who were blessed with extraordinary talent—way, way above average. But they weren't able to work well with others, which put serious limits on what should have been endless potential. Merging music with advertising requires having a strong ability to interact well with others.

> *Partnering up with the right brand can be a great marketing exercise.*
> *Try to do nonexclusive with a limit on territory and length of usage.*
> *Be open to tailoring and remaking the track to tell the story.*
>
> DRAZEN BOSNJAK, Q Department

Music production houses tend to focus a lot of their attention on developing, maintaining, and nurturing ongoing relationships with their advertising industry contacts. When a new project gets in the pipeline, the creative contacts will likely be the first to get called if it requires music. In these situations, a music production company or team of skilled music producers join forces to pursue opportunities to bring something to the table that's often difficult for equally talented individuals to compete with—the power in numbers.

Many advertising agencies feel reassured to know there's a team of experts working to address an issue and trying to find a solution, rather than just one person. Even if a competing individual tries to get hired for the project and has considerably more talent than any single member on the production team, a potential client will often focus on the total package offered by the qualified team.

Try to form a team once you network and meet some good professionals. A network of audio specialists that can share responsibility and use the greatest strengths of each team member can work together to create music for advertising. When an opportunity comes up, your team can pool its resources. Demonstrate you're a professional by making deadlines, delivering the goods, and following instructions.

> Work the relationships you can make with people at production houses and agencies. Figure out which ones do music well. For example, BBDO has a long history of doing music. They have accounts like Pepsi, a very music-driven account. From a strategic standpoint, look at which advertising is music driven and find out which agencies are responsible for the production.
>
> REGINALD OSBORNE, Senior Vice President, Director
> Multicultural Marketing, Arnold Worldwide

Radio Commercials

Most of us think of music on the radio as songs played in rotation as part of a station's playlist. But for every hour of radio that's aired, approximately twenty minutes or more is dedicated to advertisements — corporate-sponsored commercials and event promotions. That means the demand and outlet for a wide variety of music extends considerably beyond the playlist of the month. As with many video production companies, the frequent go-to sources for musical content are tracks featured on music library CDs and compilation discs that are on file at the station and are precleared through blanket license agreements. But there are other options. The nice thing about radio, from a songwriter's vantage point, is that commercials and programs often play repeatedly. Because radio is a broadcast transmission, this generates performance royalties. In the same way it works for television networks and cable stations, the bigger the station, the greater the royalties. Music is also used on radio during talk radio shows, ads for the radio station itself, and in news clips and product advertisements.

The music used for radio can be an original piece that's specifically written for a commercial's overall conceptual theme or it can be a song or composition that's already been recorded. It's used as what's often referred to in both the radio and TV world as a *commercial edit*. This is a full-length version of the song that's been digitally spliced, diced, rearranged, and possibly time-stretched in order to synch up with key entry and exit points, or to add emphasis or exclamation to the commercial's overall theme. If this involves a well-known or famous song, issues related to licensing and clearance are often addressed beforehand. Sound editors who are employed by the advertising agency do any required audio and video synchronization editing that's subsequently performed, in house.

> *The song that best connects the product or game to the consumer and creates an impression on the consumer has the best chance of getting licensed. Sure there are trends that might come and go, but the standards and songs that have a very broad appeal are always getting licensed. Usually music that is accessible to a very large audience finds its way into an ad but again, there are exceptions to that rule as well.*
>
> DAVE PETTIGREW, Senior Vice President, Strategic Marketing, and Head of Advertising and Games, Warner/Chappell Music

You're likely to find that the music for a radio commercial needs to end with a sting or hit. A *sting* is a musical device used to emphasize a moment, like a crash of cymbals followed by a pause. This accent device usually happens near or at the end of the commercial. However, stings can be used at any point along the commercial's time line.

The ad agency or someone who assists them in finding the right piece of music may provide you with some ballpark references (previous radio spots that have been used by the company, or one linked with another company they happen to like). Whatever the case, you'll need to be comfortable working with video and music files to do it effectively. It helps if your editing skills are on par with the agency's sound editing staff. It's always best to deliver suggestions, presentations, mock-ups, or prototypes that look and sound like broadcast quality. Your edits should be good enough to air when you deliver them.

When working with an ad agency, it's possible that all of the correspondence and file exchanging required for a given project may entirely take place over the phone or by Internet communication. The need for in-person meetings has become much less of a priority than it used to be. I've worked with a few companies without personal contact and feel like we know each other rather well after collaborating on a number of projects together over the years. We've had many phone conversations, yet it's funny to think that none of us would recognize each other if we passed on the street.

Television Commercials

Music can be used in television commercials in the foreground or in a background capacity. Your song will have the best potential exposure opportunity if it is the primary audio source and is used throughout the commercial. Apple's iPod commercials are an excellent example. Since the product being advertised is music related, it provides equal exposure for the song and the product at the same time. Most commercials are thirty seconds long. The exact duration of a commercial puts obvious constraints on the length of music needed. Scoring, editing, and synchronizing music set to preexisting video is frequently accompanied by a set of directions and markers expressed in standard time code.

	HOUR	MINUTE	SECOND	FRAME
Time Code	00:	00:	00;	00

Some types of television commercials highlight music more than others. For example, car commercials tend to allow music to dominate the audio channels because there's little or no voice-over to vie for the sonic attention. However, when there's a voice-over track, the music is mixed and relegated to the background. Many commercials don't highlight music. The priority is always focused on the product being advertised. Music is just one of the media elements that can be used to reinforce the message and enhance the overall presentation. It's important to keep in mind that music licensed for use in commercials is chosen because of its ability to work within the framework of the bigger presentation. It's one part of an equilibrium that's balanced by other factors such as the story, pacing, visual effects, animations, voice-overs, and sound effects.

> *The advertising world is a different animal because the musical goal is to communicate a brand message to a specific demographic. This is usually better accomplished with original music scored for the specific needs of the campaign. When licensing an existing song is decided as the best solution, I find that it falls on two sides of the fence—either the brand wants to capitalize on nostalgia by licensing a well-known or classic song for a large budget, or they want to reinforce their cultural relevance by licensing a song from an emerging artist, typically for very little money in exchange for increased exposure for the artist.*
>
> ALEX MOULTON, Founder and creative
> force behind Expansion Team

Music licensing opportunities in TV commercials are fiercely competitive, so it can be advantageous for an independent songwriter to submit music that's already in commercial edit form. You'll make an even better impression if you can get access to a video clip of the commercial and use it as a reference guide and benchmark for editing the song accordingly. It's not just a matter of having a commercial edit that's thirty seconds long. It's better to have a thirty-second edit that works within the constraints and context of the visual imagery, overall pacing of scene transitions, and possibly a voice-over track. Striking this balance is a critical aspect of showing that a piece of music works or that something is out-of-step. This can be true even when the music you deliver closely approximates the stylistic attributes that were outlined as part of the directions in the request.

When a video clip of a commercial is available for referencing, it will probably be accompanied by project notes and someone telling you, "We look forward to seeing what you can come up with." If you decide that it's worth the time, try scoring something original or edit a preexisting piece of music that you have on file. Once you've worked up your pitch, sending broadcast-quality material adds a certain appeal to your work, since your presentation translates into less work for others when it's received. It allows you to deliver a presentation that accurately reflects your take and direction on the music and your editing, and the volume level settings (automation) if a voice-over is involved.

Working with your own preexisting music can provide a convenient option when a TV commercial deadline makes it impractical or impossible to write and produce an original piece that sounds stellar. But, working with preexisting music files comes with a few caveats. Before opting for this choice, it's important that you know the deal for the payment and if the situation involves any transfer of rights or terms of exclusivity. When you license music to an advertising agency for use in a national TV commercial for a brand-name product, you're more likely to encounter work for hire, buyouts, or some type of exclusivity terms. This partly accounts for why the fees associated with TV commercial song placements are often the highest. They generally pay the largest licensing fees, in exchange for acquiring certain privileges, terms of exclusivity, or a transfer of rights.

Income Stream from Commercials

The most obvious income stream for the use of music in commercials is the up-front licensing fees, which can range anywhere from a few thousand to well beyond. It depends on the size of the company, the project's budget, and any terms of exclusivity or transfer of copyright that might be involved. Generating performance royalties is also dependent on the scope of the commercial's accessibility. A commercial may air locally, regionally, or nationally. As with other broadcast media, the broader the scope of viewers and accessibility, the greater the royalties per play. Performing rights organizations address music that's featured in commercials in a slightly different way. Since a commercial is not a TV show or film, a specialized form (not a cue sheet) is submitted to the PROs. It reports the use of one or more songs, written or published by the PRO's member, in a commercial. If your song ends up on a national TV ad, be sure to address this issue. Don't just assume that it has been taken care of. Contact your PRO and request a form used to report music appearing in commercials and advertising.

ADVERTISING AND PROMO MUSIC REPORT

Song Title	
Catalogue/CD/Cut #	
Product-Promo-PSA:	PSA—"Product Service Alert"
Composer(s)	
Publisher(s)	
Commercial Title:	
ISCI #:	ISCI—acronym for *"Industry Standard Commercial Identifier"*—this is code used to identify commercials and/or "spots" that air on commercial television worldwide. Usually eight characters; four letters followed by four numbers. (Ex. "BGKA7829")
Sponsor/Station:	
First Air Date:	
Term of Agreement:	

Media: (Check all that apply)	**Lyrics or Voice Dialogue:**
	Network TV	
	Cable TV	
	Local TV	
	Radio	

Local TV/Radio Broadcast areas:

Enclosed are the following Performance Affidavits:

	Network TV
	Cable TV

Enclosed are the following of additional materials:

	Title Registration Form
	Transmittal Form
	Licensing and/or Composer Agreement
	Lead Sheet
	Voice-Over Script (Advertising Agency Copy)
	CD, DVD, Audio or Video Cassette

Breaking into Commercials

Licensing music for advertising can be easier to break into if you pursue local opportunities first. Pay attention to which local businesses advertise on TV and radio in your town. Which use music? What products could your music be a fit for? When you have a list, call each company and ask who handles their advertising. You may be given the name of a production house or producer that handles the music. Be prepared if you reach the person responsible for it. Say you'd like to send some samples of your music for consideration in a future commercial. Be friendly and polite. If you can begin to develop relationships with local people and companies, there may be work for you down the road when they make a commercial that's a good fit for your music. It also gives you credits you can leverage for work with bigger companies.

Directories list the ad agencies for many products. Some libraries carry them. *The Advertising Red Book* is in digital format so you can do searches on the parent company of the product you feel your music would work well with in a commercial. Big companies often have different agencies for different activities. And since the directories are only updated once a year, they may not be completely accurate. Begin with the contact you see. Call the ad agency and try to find the right person to approach about considering your music. It's a gamble but some people do win the big prize—a good music placement.

Interpreting Music Requests

Music requests can be a little difficult to decipher. Some people give very clear directions. The examples that follow are requests that I have encountered over the years. Learning how to read into these kinds can be challenging, though necessary at times, since they come with decent opportunities. Having a sense of humor helps.

> **EXAMPLE 1:** *We are searching for a track with darker atmosphere and elements of danger; one that doesn't sound electronic; however the ad agency doesn't want a rock song either. The music needs to move, but it can't be too fast, just slightly.*

NOTE: Since the two categories of music that would probably yield the closest approximations have been eliminated right off the bat, finding a solution that fills this void will be more of a challenge. Perhaps something mid-tempo and orchestral could fit the bill.

EXAMPLE 2: *Ad Agency is searching for an upbeat, hip sounding song for a national TV spot for a major department store. High production quality is a must; must be professionally recorded, mixed, and mastered.*

NOTE: Music requests involving national TV commercials (known as spots) will often make reference to quality control. In translation, anyone can apply for this job, but you'd better show up for this interview in a sharp-looking suit to stand a chance.

EXAMPLE 3: *Song should have limited vocals.*

NOTE: In translation, this means mostly instrumental, because there's probably going to be a voice-over used during the commercial. Satisfying this request could require creating an edit of a song that eliminates its prevalent vocals. The other option is to create a commercial mix that mutes the vocals in various places so they're sparse. This is more of a remix strategy than a song file edit. Remixing requires having access to the software, files, and the project file used to mix the song. Editing may only require having a copy of the song as a .wav, .aiff, or MP3. My personal favorite audio editing programs are Sound Forge (SONY) and Wave Lab (Steinberg). Basic audio editing skills are not the same as mixing and are very useful in these situations.

EXAMPLE 4: *There are no specific requirements for the lyrical content, although the phrase "so hot" could work, as long as there are no sexual connotations involved.*

NOTE: This is classic wishy-washy guidance. The phrase "so hot" strikes me as being reasonably specific. It can take a lot of creativity to figure these requests out!

EXAMPLE 5: *The reference track for this spot is "Song Title" by Artist Name—the ad agency really likes the organic nature of this song, and its overall fun and lighthearted spirit, despite Artist in this case being better known for its darker electronic.*

NOTE: Pretentious descriptions like "organic" are most often used by lay people rather than musicians. They're trying to sound a little hip. The problem is that most of the time they don't provide much clarity, despite good intentions. "Organic" in this case probably implies the use of acoustic instruments such as acoustic guitar, acoustic piano, stand up bass, or any other "real" instrument accompanied by a beat that sounds electronic but might be played on acoustic drums. Also, the song they want is apparently a little out of character for the style of music most typically associated with that artist. I'd listen to the track that's referenced. This is probably a request for a no-harsh-chemicals soundalike.

As you can see, the people whom you deal with often don't know what they want. Or they don't know how to express what they want in musical terms since they're not musicians. They may hear the music in their heads but all you'll hear is words and comparisons that may contradict each other or that leave everything up to interpretation. As you do more music for advertising, your instincts can get sharper. Otherwise, this may not be the right area of licensing for you.

Lines of Command

Creative directors and music supervisors often assume similar roles for the process of music selection. As music submissions are forwarded in response to a request, the first hurdle is to win over the support or endorsement of the creative director/music supervisor. However, this accomplishment isn't always enough to lock down, finalize, and secure a song placement licensing deal. Sealing the deal in most instances requires clearing one final hurdle. For music in film, the director needs to agree with a music supervisor's suggestions. For advertising, the client has to agree with the suggestion provided by the ad agency's creative director. Sometimes the client will sign off on the musical choices if they trust and respect those whose job responsibility includes suggesting appropriate music for a project. However, there are times when a client is dissatisfied with the commercial's initial musical direction. The client may ask the creative director for a different suggestion, feeling that the choices he has made are stylistically wrong for the product's intended target audience.

> *The way it won't work, for the most part, is going to the client. Often the music is out of their domain. They probably don't consider themselves the right ones to determine if there's talent or not. So they rely on the experts—at the advertising agency or music production houses.*
>
> REGINALD OSBORNE, Senior Vice President, Director
> Multicultural Marketing, Arnold Worldwide

I was recently hired to assemble the music for a TV commercial that was scheduled to air on Fox. It was an unusual situation. All discussions, details, and selection for the music were addressed before the commercial was shot and edited. The project happened at warp speed. My responsibility was to both provide the music and address any sound editing as it became necessary once the video production company had a working edit of the commercial. This happened late in the evening and the final, ready-to-broadcast version of the commercial had to be delivered to the network the following day at 1:00 P.M. I also had to create and fax a music release form verifying that all music clearance was approved and in order. This documentation is called a *deliverable*—one of the items that must be included in the package handed over to the network or distribution company prior to broadcast or release. At the beginning, all I was given was a storyboard that was e-mailed from the advertising agency in PDF format.

A *storyboard* is a preproduction tool used by some filmmakers and advertising agencies to help guide and organize a shoot. It helps to identify appropriate locations, plan cinematography, and determine what equipment, props, and crew will be necessary to bring these illustrations to life. A storyboard created for the production of a TV commercial usually consists of five to ten illustrations. Each is accompanied by some brief, fairly specific detail, including the duration of each scene, its corresponding voice-over narration if there is any, any musical requirements necessary, and the purpose the commercial is intended to serve.

As you learn to work with audio and video content in an editing capacity, the notion of balance is really important. Diving into a project without keeping this in mind tends to yield work that creates the impression that something is wrong with the overall picture. Even when the music is stylistically correct, if it's presented as part of an edit that sounds out of step with the pacing of scene transitions and imagery, or it overpowers the accompanying narration, the client, agency, or any other powers-that-be will brand the music selection as wrong. Balance, form, and timing are a critical part of making the end product look and sound coherent and unified. It's easy to slice and dice digital content but there's an art to making all of the individual elements fuse so that what emerges is whole and seems bigger than the sum of its parts, at least for the purpose of the commercial.

A good director is sensitive to this equilibrium. Some whom I've known tend to think less in terms of the integrity of a piece of music's composition and more about its function, purpose, and ability to provide support that appears seamless. If your goal in music includes working with video content, it helps to learn how to think along these lines. As musicians, we tend to prioritize our thoughts and actions around the music. Yet others hear this music within the context of something bigger. Maybe it's the story, a message, a mood, or an idea. Whatever the case, all of the elements have to come into alignment. When this happens, the experience that's perceived by the audience isn't segmented into either seeing images or hearing sounds, but rather the fusion of both. Like music, video imagery has a tempo. The problem for this rushed job, at least at the moment, was that there was no voice-over track, nor was there a commercial. I was supposed to provide the music track beforehand.

In the case of my warp-speed commercial slated to air on Fox, I knew that for the music to work it would have to dance around the voice-over script. The problem was there was no voice-over recording or video to work with. My solution was to capture and extract the seven illustrations contained within the storyboard PDF document I'd been sent and use them to create an automated slide show. The storyboard gave clear direction as to how long each scene would last within the thirty-second commercial. Using markers, I mapped out the scene changes along the timeline with a video editing program. From there, all seven images were imported into the project and placed accordingly. Adding a little automation, key framing, and cross fading created a mock-up commercial. The next step was to record a scratch voice-over. Once recorded, the voice-over was aligned to the scene illustrations according to the storyboard directions. Now I had something to work with. Without this reference, it is hard to say how any piece of music will work.

Because of time constraints, recording an original piece of music wasn't a practical option. The ad agency had already given the green light on a preexisting song that I'd suggested but it was full length. For the commercial, the song had to be edited down to thirty seconds and done in a way that would work within the parameters of the voice-over and transitions. For example, in places where voice-over is occurring, it's usually better to use parts of the song with little or no vocals. This gets tricky since chopping up a full-length song is one thing, but reassembling it in a way that sounds natural, within the timing constraints of the voice-over entrances and exits, can be a challenge. There was no way to do this without first creating a mock-up reference.

My music edit was based on the mock-up, not the actual commercial. Of course, any deviations from the storyboard once filming began would require additional editing on my part. Creating the mock-up was extra work than was required or expected of me, but it had to be done so that I would have a reasonable approximation of the music from the start. In this case it was worth it. The edit that was submitted was used in the actual commercial that aired the following week.

While it's not always required, doing music for advertising is easier when you have the extra skills to work on the whole music project. If this is what you want to do, consider taking the classes I recommended. You can also try to get an internship at a production house and learn hands on. Working for free can teach you skills and help you make contacts that are worth more than money.

‖‖‖

CHAPTER 14

Getting Music Licensed in Brand Entertainment and Sponsorships

Brand entertainment is an emerging marketing/media tactic, whereby brands engage with entertainment media platforms at an early stage, to fully integrate their branding and merchandising around the media platform and its talent. A media platform could be a television series, movie, sports or entertainment property, a tour, an event, or a celebrity/artist. Branded entertainment is much more than product placement, and could include brand ownership of properties, for example, Mutual of Omaha Wild Kingdom.

CORD PEREIRA, Chairman and Executive Producer,

BrandEntertain

The idea of *brand entertainment* is a bit like rolling sponsorship, licensing, and advertising all up into one single ball. However, one key distinction, metaphorically speaking, would be akin to a head coach asking the advertising agency to hit the bench, then turning toward the artist with a loud whistle and an extended finger pointing in the direction of the field, making it clear that he's going into the game as the replacement. In other words, the artist assumes roles that might ordinarily be provided by an advertising agency. The conference room is replaced by a rehearsal space. The artist is asked to create content or provide entertainment that somehow, in either subtle or blatant ways, ties directly to a specific brand or product. Getting involved with a brand can help you gain exposure for you and your music and it can also be financially rewarding.

Basic branding comes down to "signage" and trying to connect your brand with a particular style of music and a particular music community. If you do sports, you get courtside signage. If you do film, you get the film release party. Music is kind of a blank canvas, as long as both parties are open to the exploration and finding ways to make it mutually beneficial. So you really can do anything.

MICHAEL AIKEN, Managing Director, Spring,
LLC, a music marketing company

Traditional Sponsorship versus Brand Entertainment

Traditional sponsorship is typically when a celebrity is hired by a company to use their product for the purposes of advertising. Brand entertainment is a specialized form of sponsorship. It's a product endorsement that uses entertainment, talent, and creativity for the purpose of product marketing. A subtle example of brand entertainment is when a product is used as a prop or in the scenery of a music video. It could involve people in the video drinking a particular (and visible) brand of beer or wearing some clothing known for its logo. Product placement is often subtle, and unless you knew otherwise, it wouldn't necessarily be clear if the band had a prior arrangement with the company, or if the lead singer just decided to drink it or wear it because he likes it. A more conspicuous kind of branding is if an artist has a product banner draped across the stage during a live performance.

A celebrity's name and likeness warrants a certain amount of trust from the general public. Their visible association provides credibility to any claims being made in relation to the use of the product they now endorse, and this connection or list of testimonials can add considerable marketing value to a product. Endorsement deals can, at times, be highly lucrative. But those offering the highest paying deals are also often the most selective about whom they work with. The good news is that these days, sponsorships and endorsements don't necessarily require being a household name as long as you have an interesting story or a list of past experiences that would be useful marketing tools for the product. Many companies that specialize in the manufacturing of musical instruments, audio gear, and recording software work with talent that covers the spectrum. This talent ranges from the widely recognizable to the obscure and underground artists who have a cool factor.

Sponsorships have traditionally involved the public announcement of a partnership between a celebrity/recognizable name talent and a company that manufactures a product. The talent is offered a contract and some form of payment in exchange for agreeing to use and endorse the product. It's often an exclusive deal. The arrangements can vary. For musicians, the benefits of getting a sponsorship deal could include:

- a monetary payment
- receiving some free equipment, clothing, and other products
- the creation of a customized or signature line that has your name on it
- becoming eligible for dramatic discounts
- press that results from activities related to the sponsorship and/or product affiliation
- assistance in promoting concert events
- public appearances to perform your music on behalf of your sponsor company
- the prestige of having the direct support of a company that makes a superior product in your field of expertise

> *The beauty of music is there isn't any specific type that works for branding. Each genre technically has its own characteristics that fit any number of brands. We wouldn't use classical to reach a youth market, for example, but classical music is very effective for reaching an affluent, older demographic.*
>
> MICHAEL AIKEN, Managing Director, Spring,
> LLC, a music marketing company

Two-Way Streets

Agreements based on the concept of brand entertainment can involve a company paying an artist licensing fees, but actual contractual provisions in this area may turn out to be more flexible or expansive when compared to other types of music licensing agreements. In lieu of or to supplement fee payments, a *barter arrangement* might be agreed upon, which may stipulate that both parties perform certain cross-promotional services or agree to a list of obligations or duties that extend beyond the use of music (notice I said *both* parties).

The company might agree to pay X dollars in addition to supplying the artist with certain goods or services intended to assist them with career development and exposure (short- or long-term). As part of the agreement, the company might be granted the right to use one or more songs and images that have been selected, and the use of this content will happen in a promotional context. In exchange, the artist agrees to perform certain services that will assist the company with promotion, marketing, and advertising related to this product. Hypothetical examples might include:

- entertaining the public at one or more prescheduled events
- referencing or embedding the company's name and/or products in specific media presentations that the band will release and publicize ("product placement")

Keep in mind that, as long as the key points describing the use of your music are included in a written agreement, and all parties agree to enter into and sign the agreement, and are bound to the terms and conditions, you are working under a license. Remember, a license can be short and sweet or densely bloated with layers of legalese, and the right approach depends on the situation and advice from your attorney.

There isn't a standardized brand entertainment licensing deal, because the terms and conditions will depend on the artist and company, and how they intend to work with one another. However, an agreement of this nature would likely contain the boiler-plate provisions that would allow the company permission to use your music, but will also address additional rights related to the use of your likeness and biography. These agreements and understandings transcend simply using an artist's song(s). And unlike a standard licensing agreement, which may only require that the artist agree to the terms and fees, truly implementing the concept of brand entertainment will require that the artist participate in the delivery of services for the company in return. The tables are a bit turned in the sense that some of the burden of providing exposure now rests on the shoulders of the artist. Under this type of agreement, the artist is in essence agreeing to provide some means of exposure for the product or company licensing their content. This might involve agreeing to a certain number of public performances, product placement that might happen in a music video, recording a song that makes reference to the product, or placing a banner on a band website. Think of it as combining the core elements of a music licensing agreement with one or more other types of deals, including bartering services and resources, cross-promotion, marketing, publicity, sponsorship, and advertising.

Brand Entertainment Licensing and Nonmonetary Compensation

A question I commonly hear with respect to brand entertainment is, "If I allow my music to be used for free, or as part of a barter, is it no longer a licensing deal?"

The licensor has the legal right to demand compensation in exchange for granting another person rights and permission for the use of their music. However, compensation isn't strictly limited to monetary form, as long as whatever goods or services are being offered as a substitute are deemed acceptable, respectable in value, and get delivered. In the vast majority of cases, monetary compensation is most often the preferred choice. However, rather than cash, the licensing agreement can involve barters, gratis use, and cross-promotional endeavors.

It's important to note that, no matter what form of compensation is being granted, the terms of the license are just as binding as they'd be if money was exchanged. A business arrangement of this nature may turn out to be what guides an artist/brand joint venture.

Qualities That Attract Product Sponsorship

It's hard to endorse a product you don't love, much less like. Potential sponsors respond best to enthusiasm and familiarity with the product on a personal level. They will want to see what your relationship to their product is.

Artists should be profiling themselves as "brand" friendly. Getting ahead in the new emerging artist world is about finding and shaping relationships with brands that can help promote the band across its needs. Hook on to entertainment properties that are seeking relationships with brand involvement. The sponsorship world is changing. Whereas brands have traditionally thrown sponsorship dollars at media, talent, and properties, now brands are increasingly aware of measuring return on investment of those dollars. Many brands, thanks to Web 3.0 and the development of their direct distribution channels, will engage with artists on a revenue-share basis, based on tractable sales directly influenced by the artist. When sales happen, the artist is paid. This is a new form of sponsorship that takes the idea of endorsement to the next level.

CORD PEREIRA, Chairman and Executive Producer,

BrandEntertain

You need to make yourself aware of the key qualities potential sponsors look for when lining up deals with musicians. These include the following:

Passion

You should already be using the product/brand and truly love it. It should be something you'd use with or without the endorsement. For example, if you're trying to get a guitar endorsement and the company that makes the one you use and love turns you down, it's not a good idea to go to a different brand for support. If your heart is with the guitar you use, you probably won't fool the other company by faking passion for their brand. It's best to approach companies that make the product you regard as being one of the best, if not *the best*, of all options available on the market. Then your passion can help sell you as someone to represent it.

Connection

Be able to provide a few examples of how using this product has played a role in an experience where you've had some recent success, such as high-profile gigs or a charity event, publishing, record or licensing deals, or an impressive number of downloads. Put on your PR hat.

Ability

If none of the above applies to you or you can't readily find a connection between you and the product, try to show potential sponsors that you're an extraordinary, exceptional, mind-blowing talent in a field that's directly related to the use of their product. This may allow you to circumvent any need to provide examples or demonstrate a link between your use of the product and some recent success. If you're known for your keyboard playing, go to a keyboard manufacturer. But before you do, create a recording or video clip that makes a compelling case. It would need to elicit responses like "Oh my God," or "Unbelievable." When you make people scream, there's a decent chance you'll excite someone enough to want to work with you!

Visibility

Performing at higher profile venues or concert events may result in getting the attention of a manufacturer or product representative, who happens to be in attendance because they endorse another artist who is also performing on the bill. The more you play live, the more chances of catching the interest of someone who works for a company that gives sponsorships to musicians. It can be a long shot but it happens.

Keep in mind that the cost of publicity and advertisement is often the biggest out-of-pocket expense for most companies. An endorsee provides a company with marketing services that are indirectly related to the product and assist in the process of spreading the word. Over the long haul, an artist may end up being a more effective delivery mechanism for this goal than the traditional and often more costly standard methods of using print ads, posters, or TV commercials. Having some visible presence in the public, even at the local level, may be enough to warrant some type of endorsement.

Going for Sponsorship Deals

If you know of a specific product that you'd like to endorse, go to the company's website, and look up their contact information. Some sites may include a page listing specific information for getting sponsorship, including the details and required steps for supplying or submitting materials for endorsement consideration. Follow the directions, and if none are given, mail a copy of your CD, a photo, and a press release that includes details about yourself and your music. You can also find a library that carries an electronic copy of *The Advertising Red Book*. You can look to see who does the branding for the product and try making cold calls.

This business is all about relationship building—face-to-face as often as possible and when not possible, the phone. Call and ask them. You have to understand how much they're getting called. A brand like Coca-Cola probably gets calls for every single opportunity on the planet. So you have to be prepared with a message that shows them that you have something unique to offer. Then you have to be patient.

MICHAEL AIKEN, Managing Director,
Spring, LLC, a music marketing company

If you're friends with someone who works at a local music store, ask him if he knows a sales representative for the company or product you're considering contacting. Product sales reps and music store salespeople tend to be in frequent contact. Your friend may be able to put you directly in touch with someone who works for the company. That person may be able to point you in the right direction or provide helpful suggestions. If you have no friend in the store, make one! Chat with salespeople when the store is quiet and pick their brains at the same time.

What income streams can come from brand entertainment and sponsorships? If you perform on behalf of the product, sponsorship income can happen on multiple levels. Some deals might be limited to a company providing you with some free musical equipment. For example, a company that manufactures instruments may provide you with three complimentary signature model electric guitars for your upcoming tour. In return, you agree to perform with these guitars live on stage so your fans see what you're playing, and continue to do so for the entire duration of the tour. In addition, you also agree to license your name, likeness, and biography in association with these guitars as it will be used and appear in certain promotional and marketing materials released and paid for by the company throughout the term of the sponsorship (posters, flyers, promotional video, print ads).

The deal may also require you to make special appearances at a number of conventions, conferences, or charities to publicize and market the products sponsoring you. In addition, a sponsorship can also include a one-time cash payment upon entering into the deal. The terms of the sponsorship agreement may last for six months, a year, or longer. Once the agreement expires, a new agreement can then be entered if both parties agree.

The perks and provisions of a sponsorship agreement will vary in size and scope from company to company and product to product, and may also depend to some degree on your own star power.

> *We're working with a telecom company now. One component is sponsoring the tour—all the engagement opportunities with the fans available through that tour. But then we're doing stuff that really leverages the new album release of the artist with free downloads, commercial marketing program usage, building unique experiences for contest winners, like a meet-and-greet VIP treatment backstage, all access packages. For all the consumer touches that happen through the program, we build what's called a post-tour remarketing kit. After a tour sponsored by a car company, we took all the ticket information— all the consumers that came—and introduced them to other aspects of the brand experience: "Come take a test drive," invitations to a sponsored event, mailing brochures to their houses, e-mail campaigns.*
>
> MICHAEL AIKEN, Managing Director,
> Spring, LLC, a music marketing company

Branding is more than just using a piece of music in a project. Keep in mind that these types of arrangements will likely involve a licensing deal that could include the use of your music, as well as the licensing of your and your band's name, likeness, and biography. This will grant the company permission to use, include, and publicize your image in direct association with the product, brand, or company name. Image often doesn't matter much to someone licensing a song to be used in a film or TV show. But it does usually play a big role in brand entertainment. Make sure that your image fits with the product you want to endorse.

Sponsorship Backlash

Many well-known actors and musicians have licensed their likeness and image for association with products that often have little to do with their actual craft, such as clothes, perfume, and skateboards, and are sold or manufactured in other parts of the world. These deals may involve strict limits for the territories of the endorsement deal. Unless fans happen to visit those particular countries, they may never know that their favorite drummer endorses a certain brand of sneakers. Setting territorial limits is often done intentionally for a good reason. Not all music fans are receptive to the idea that a band or artist they admire jumped into bed with corporate sponsors, especially if it involves products that have little or nothing to do with their art form. These kinds of endorsement deals have been known to create a backlash effect with some fans. A delicate balance exists between exploiting the spoils of having some commercial success and being perceived as a sellout. The solution seems to be accepting foreign offers.

It seems unfair that die-hard music fans so often turn their backs on artists once they manage to cross over the commercial success barrier. This recurring phenomenon is independent of musical genre. One possible explanation is that most people feel more of a connection with the romantic notion of a struggling artist. Maybe it's because they seem more approachable, yet-to-be-discovered, one of us, or they seem to approach their craft in a way that appears more pure, rough around the edges, and less influenced or tainted by the temptations of commercialism. The part of an artist's story that tends to be most captivating to fans centers around their early struggles and the events that transpired during the process of "making it." However, once they've become successful, they seem less accessible. So you need to be careful about what products you endorse and how you handle it.

For indie artists who are still working hard to develop their fan base, the exposure that can result from having their music licensed and featured for a branding situation that's part of a national ad campaign can outweigh any lofty concerns of being perceived as sellouts. Once in a while, a song that's featured as part of a television commercial goes on to assume a life of its own. Conversely, product placement within a music video accomplishes the marketing objective while assuring that the artist remains center stage. In the future, implementing this new spin on indie band videos as a marketing strategy will help mitigate a recent concern in the world of advertising—how to infiltrate user-generated media. Most people don't go online for the purpose of watching commercials and reading ads; usually we all take great care to avoid them when possible. Many people use spam filters and pop-up blockers to avoid them. In the future, marketing strategists will continue to find ways to break down the barriers consumers currently depend upon to shield themselves from advertising.

Being Proactive

Brand entertainment links a product or a brand name to the process of being creative or providing entertainment. This is an emerging facet of the music business, and is one worth exploring. It's an open forum, and is a flexible model that could be made to work with an international corporation or a mom-and-pop store in your own neighborhood. Making it happen does require adapting a proactive approach. These opportunities are rarely, if ever, posted as part of some classified listing. In most cases, they only happen when one party approaches another with a compelling proposal that the receiving party never would have thought of on its own.

Linking an artist with a brand and presenting all of it in a music video represents a complete role reversal compared to the format typically depicted in most TV commercials. Traditionally the product is featured front and center, whereas any music that might be included in the commercial, regardless of quality, ultimately assumes a secondary role. Some well-established artists have taken issue with this dynamic and rarely if ever allow their music to be used in this capacity, though history has shown that almost everyone has their price.

> *You have to be careful how you try to tie into a product for branding opportunities. It has to be a collaboration between the brand and the artist. You don't want to make it seem heavy-handed. When a company goes to these artists and asks them to make a song and insert the product, it becomes heavy-handed. The fans will know. It starts to tamper with the artistry and the authenticity of that artist to deliver work that their fan base will appreciate. It has to be seamless. It would be great if you could go to a product ahead of time to let them hear a song that would be a good fit. For example, India.Arie has a song called "Chocolate High." Hershey's is one of our clients. If we had known ahead of time that she had this song, we could have figured out a way to get some publicity out of it.*
>
> REGINALD OSBORNE, Senior Vice President, Director
> Multicultural Marketing, Arnold Worldwide

You need to create a proposal to get a sponsor interested in working with you. Your presentation should show that the arrangement you're suggesting won't put the other party into an awkward, compromised, or stress-provoking position. They often need to know that it doesn't require them to provide or supply a disproportionate amount of their own resources compared to what you offer them in return or that you don't want what isn't readily available, such as their time or money. Your proposal should provide them something they actually need—marketing, advertisement, promotion, and some fun. This may require doing some homework. It's important to have a basic understanding of how their business works. Learn whatever you can about the company and the product so you're prepared. Remember that you're trying to help them solve or handle a problem, and not create another in the process.

Your goal should be to outline a situation that's workable, where your creativity, ability to entertain, and media savvy opens new marketing and promotional avenues for the company you plan to approach. Perhaps there's a local boutique clothing store nearby that sells very hip, fashionable items. You've noticed that some of your local fans like to shop there, so there's a mutual target audience. You could approach the store's owner and offer to model some of their clothing in your new music video, with an understanding that both your band and the store will be free to use this video for mutually beneficial cross-promotion. You offer to mention the store's location and website in the closing credits. If they agree to your proposal, at the very least, you'll appear well dressed in the video! In exchange you'll be providing the store with creative marketing which may be a lot cheaper than running newspaper ads and they can boast about having their clothing featured in a hip music video.

This is a simple and straightforward example, but there's plenty of room for growth, expansion, and additional complexity. However, it's advisable to keep things as clear as possible. Only include what both parties can realistically deliver. The key is that *you* may need to be the one who comes up with the proposal and organizes your ideas into a simple written presentation. In some cases, you may also be required to create a prototype or sample content that clarifies what might otherwise sound a bit abstract. High-tech media jargon can be a bit intimidating! Show rather than tell. Make it painfully obvious that what you're proposing is beneficial and worth becoming involved with.

Brand entertainment has the potential to become a dominating factor in the entertainment business in the years ahead. Funding and sponsorship that facilitate the practice of brand entertainment will in essence become tantamount to the record deals of the future and similarly will provide bands with funding that can be used to make new recordings, generate press, or provide assistance with tour support.

Savvy musicians and bands who can land brand entertainment opportunities are likely to find themselves in a position to expand their fan base, exposure outlets, and money-making potential while operating as self-contained advertising agencies. Tours, merchandise, and music videos (having a slightly revised format) can all be used to serve a dual purpose: to promote an artist as well as products that are cleverly incorporated into the overall media presentation. The types of products that might be used to springboard musical careers span the gamut. In general, there should be a connection between the artist's *core fan base* and the product's primary *consumer target audience*. If these two groups share a number of similarities or a common profile, implementing a brand entertainment marketing plan will be an easier sell and is more likely to yield results. Pursue companies to work with that will result in matches made in heaven rather than recipes for disaster. If your music and image conflict with the products of the company that sponsors you, you could wind up alienating fans, which hurts you and the potential for the campaign to be effective for the product.

Your ability to elicit interest from potential sponsors will likely hinge on a delicate balance that considers your look and sound and the demographic makeup of your fan base in relation to the product and its presumed target audience. In order to prove yourself as the right artist for any such sponsorship opportunity, you'll have to demonstrate that your fan base closely fits the lifestyle, values, culture, opinions, politics, beliefs, attitudes, and demographics of a product's well-researched target audience. Although relationships that link artists with a product, sponsor, and with endorsements isn't new, being in the position to accept, or more to the point, elicit any such lucrative corporate backing is a privilege that has been typically bestowed on well-established, sure-bet, household-named celebrities. What's conceptually new is that, in the future, such restrictive factors may no longer be a mandatory prerequisite.

Brands are looking for sophisticated marketing opportunities. So you really have to come up to speed. What are you bringing to the table that's unique, that the brand can't get from other opportunities, and how can you use all your touring and music assets to drive real business for the brand? Just reaching large numbers of fans isn't enough anymore. They're going to ask questions like, "How can we translate that intimate relationship you have with your fan base into new business for [product]?"

Michael Aiken, Managing Director,
Spring, LLC, a music marketing company

Indie artists are being used more frequently as brands recognize their value, and that they can save a lot of money by using an artist who is hungry for sponsorship and has great talent and an appropriate image. A halfway decent garage band with the ability to tout impressive numbers for website hits and a fan base on community websites such as MySpace or Facebook can leverage statistics of this nature to their advantage. The potential glitch in this otherwise exciting and new artist-friendly business structure is that shrewd marketing expertise is stereotypically not a strong point for most artists. Most musical careers that have demonstrated any degree of staying power usually rely on one or more business associates who add their marketing savvy to the equation. But many indie artists are now learning to do it themselves, and do it well! You just can't jump in without a plan.

Artists need to understand their audience in the context of the brands they are approaching. They need to go one step further than their music and actually create the hooks, creative integrations, and exposure value, merchandising tie-ins, and more, in order to be successful with brands. This approach works from the smallest level to the largest level. Artists now need to view themselves as "properties" or "platforms" in terms of supporting their brand partners. It's not just about the music. Artists need to be as sensitive to selling their brand's products as they would be with their own music or tickets.

Cord Pereira, Chairman and Executive Producer,
BrandEntertain

Additional Licensing Options

The focus of this book hinges on the concept of licensing the copyright for recordings and compositions. However, beyond music, deals that license an image or trademark in association with consumer products, services, and lines of merchandise can represent a considerable source of additional revenue for an artist. In the case of musicians or bands, common scenarios include licensing a band name and/or image for the purpose of encouraging the sale of musical instruments, gear, jeans, skateboards, sneakers, perfume, underwear, watches, sports gear, and much more. It many cases, and over the long run, licensing deals that also involve the use of an artist's or band's image or trademark end up being far more lucrative than the mechanical royalties generated by album sales for a record deal.

The traditional role of record companies and what they provided to signed artists will likely become a thing of the past. Consumer options for purchasing media of all types will continue to expand. In the case of music, it will primarily take place via online digital music retailers. For the artist, access to these distribution and retail options has become very accessible. The record deals of the future—the actual financing agreements for the purpose of springboarding an artist's career—will be replaced by financing from companies who are not involved with recordings and album distribution. Companies with products to market will sponsor artists and their recordings, tours, and marketing in exchange for product endorsement and advertising. The artist will still own her music and the profits from it. A shampoo company will be the record company and the sponsored artist on tour will in effect serve as a peripheral advertising firm.

> *Brand entertainment is disruptive to the current music business models, and it's progressive in the sense that smart, strategic, and creative artists can find their way, where three years ago, forget it. Artists need to figure out how to reach brands with sustainable involvement opportunity.*
>
> CORD PEREIRA, Chairman and Executive Producer,
> BrandEntertain

II

Getting Music Licensed in Digital Media

Digital media is the new frontier of licensing and the entertainment business. The rate at which digital media evolves speeds up daily, as technology constantly improves. A digital gadget that is "all the rage" today can quickly fade from the spotlight when something new, smaller, or apparently better appears on the market. Staying on top of what's "in" or "out" in terms of new electronic devices, software updates, website–based services, emerging outlets, or alternative business models can feel overwhelming at times. However the resources discussed in this chapter can help you navigate music licensing in the digital world more productively.

The many recent advancements in digital communication and entertainment technology provide media users with a much greater degree of control, user options, and flexibility as to when, where, and how we idle our time while accessing media or communicating with others. For example, the distinction between viewing shows from a television set versus doing the same from a computer or handheld media device continues to blur, and at some point will all be variations on the same theme.

The proliferation of digital media has vastly expanded the scope and types of content that is becoming available. Gone are the days of "one-size-fits-all" programming. At first, an emerging category is usually referred to as being a "new" or "alternative" media format. However, once a certain threshold is surpassed in terms of use or popularity, "new" becomes "mainstream." Both the development of new digital media forms and the expansion of mainstream outlets provide musicians with a wide array of opportunities to license musical content.

It's obvious to say that the greatest need for music content nowadays is the Web. But I think that is a bit simplistic. I think as video continues to grow as far as being the key component for many parts of the Web, low-cost, high-quality, easy-to-license music becomes even more important. Web designers, new Web broadcasters, advertisers, corporations, and new media teams are just a few of the examples of the growing music customers. Also, with the growth of international outlets and globalization, making a video that has only music, allowing the text to be translated by country, is another reason for online and offline growth.

LARRY MILLS, Vice President, Marketing
and Partnerships, Pump Audio

The Digital World

Compared to media in an analog format, digitized media is far more flexible in its signal output and content delivery. Various modes of communication (text, e-mail, phone, directions, address book), media (music, videos, games), and an entire world's worth of stored digital information (Internet access), are all there for the taking, within the palm of your hand.

Analog-Speak in the Digital Age

As of June 12, 2009, full-power television stations are no longer allowed to broadcast in analog-only broadcast signals. This decision was authorized by the U.S. Congress as part of Digital TV (DTV) transition as a means to free up parts of the broadcast spectrum. The vast majority of movies and video projects are now recorded to digital tape or shot using "prosumer-grade" HD camcorders. It's now rare to find a movie project shot using film. In a similar way, the same can be said for music. In the end, what's distributed, downloaded, sold, or licensed is a stream of numbers—digital media.

The way digital content is seen or heard has created some fuzziness in terms of clarifying restrictions, the scope of its use, and royalty and licensing fees. Is a TV show still a TV show when it's viewed on an iPhone? Is a video posted on YouTube (www.youtube.com) still regarded as a Web video when it's viewed from a television instead of a computer screen? These probably seem like trivial questions, but keep in mind that these distinctions and details influence license pricing, quotes, and royalty distribution. The slippery nature of digitized media can create loopholes from a contractual point of view, which could amount to specific financial benefits and consequences. The transformation from storing information in analog to digital media formats has engendered many opportunities that used to seem like science fiction and has paved the way for creating and licensing digital media of all types.

Serving the People

When digital media is viewed on the Internet from a computer, mobile phone, handheld device, etc., where is it coming from? It could be a live digital broadcast (stream) or you might be accessing content that's already been uploaded to a hosting website server. A server is basically a hard drive (data storage device) or a group of hard drives that are interconnected to form what's known as a network server. Servers store all the digital media that's accessible online, including music, videos, pictures, and text files, as well as encoded HTML files that keep this content organized and user friendly (websites). The Internet is basically an enormous matrix of network servers that interact with each other. When you access a website there's a physical location hosting some or all of this content, temporarily or long-term. What mobile phones, handheld computers, and the rest of these gadgets share in common is the ability to access the broadband spectrum via wireless transmission and get onto the Internet highway.

Digital Licensing Basics

It doesn't so much matter how digital media gets accessed (via phone, computer, handheld device, etc.). What does matter is that the party licensing the content is the party who's hosting it on a network server or that it's being done by a third party who is authorized to do so. When this isn't the case, the familiar phrase *illegal file sharing* enters the discussion. Authorization may take place in the form of a physical contract that's entered between two parties, or by clicking the "I agree" button prior to uploading your content onto another party's network. If you've ever posted a video on YouTube, MySpace, or other social networks, you've (knowingly or unknowingly) licensed your digital media.

Digital Media Convergence

Digital technology—including the growing list of gadgets that allow us to access and deliver digital media—provides more flexibility and interconnection than we've ever had before. In light of these advances, musicians need to adopt a more generalized view of the process of music licensing.

Consider what happens if one of your songs is licensed for use on a popular network television show. As of 2010, the deal that's offered will most likely be an "all-in" agreement. This gives the production company the right to release the episode by various means across a broad spectrum of digital media formats. This begins when the episode airs on national television (broadcast rights). At some point later, the episode/series will be made available for purchase on DVD and sold in retail stores internationally (DVD rights). The procedure for purchasing and viewing the episodes in DVD format requires the identical steps that would be required if purchasing/viewing a movie on DVD. The disc types are the same format and both can be played on the same type of player (convergence). Remember that in the analog world, there was a period of time when movies could show in theaters and TV shows could be seen from television sets—period.

The series that licensed a song will probably also become available for purchase through an online digital retailer. For simplicity's sake, let's assume the purchase and download takes place on iTunes. Once downloaded, the episode could be viewed from a computer, iPhone, ITV, iPod, or burned onto a disc and viewed from a home theater system. So the choices are to watch it from a TV, computer, DVD player, HDV, handheld media player, or mobile phone. When you consider the variety of ways that digital media can be delivered, licensing Song A for Movie X with time may in fact end up covering cover all bases. As mentioned earlier, it's now common to find licensing agreements whose language accommodates the flexibility of digital media through the use of broad media rights clauses.

All-In Digital Licensing

All-in music licensing agreements have become the prevailing licensing model employed in recent years. Granting a broader scope of rights permits flexibility as digital media technology continues on its course of evolution. It closes potential loopholes that might otherwise require paying additional licensing fees in the future as new digital media formats and devices become available in the years ahead. These revisions have established a new precedent that favors the interests of the licensee. This is offset to some extent by the scope of potential outlets for those who license digital media content, which has also grown exponentially.

End-User Licenses

Although the technical details of music licensing aren't familiar to everyone, other types of licensing agreements that are linked with digital media are probably quite familiar, including *end-user* licensing agreements. These agreements present a set of terms and conditions that must first be agreed upon and accepted, prior to a consumer's being allowed to install software programs or updates onto his computer. Another common user licensing agreement must be entered into before you may post or upload your own digital content onto a hosting website or network. These licensing agreements have become a normal part of working on a computer, updating programs, and accessing or providing content on the Internet. As you strike the "I agree" or "I accept" buttons, it unlocks a door and implies that you've read, understood, and accepted the terms and conditions required.

How many people actually take the time to read the fine print? It's impossible to say, but it doesn't appear to me that most do. As it is for any license, the core concept is granting permission to some activity with a set of agreed-upon rules and conditions. It's important to understand what actions are permissible with the digital content you might download from another party's website or what rules might be applied to yours upon uploading digital media to a hosting website. Tucked within the fine print of these licensing agreements are terms that should be read. Who owns and controls the content? Who else can have access to it? How long does this agreement remain in effect?

Games, Loops, Ringtones, Internet Radio, and Podcasts

The constantly evolving digital world brings new licensing opportunities to musicians by the day. Here's a look at some of the more viable and lucrative options that might match your particular set of skills and interests.

Games People Play

The gaming industry is king of the entertainment business. Period. Its dominance now dwarfs the music, film, and pornography industries. What can be concluded is that people truly enjoy playing games as a lifestyle and culture. Publishing and marketing companies that market music for TV and film are well aware of this shifting market. Pitching songs to gaming companies has been incorporated into their repertoire of outlets to hunt down. If you have no representation, you can pursue outlets and opportunities in gaming on your own. Contact game developers or those directly associated with game production companies. Pursue opportunities with companies that market games whose music is stylistically similar to your own. For example, a company that specializes in games marketed to kids ages five to nine years old probably isn't an outlet for music that's clearly better suited to an older audience.

> You need to understand that it is very much like the movie business. Game developers are looking for music that is going to complement their game in every way possible. They are looking for music that works creatively with the game. Don't think that because a game is called "Phone" and you have a song about phones, it's a lock for the game. These games are incredibly cinematic these days and the music needs to complement the picture, not the other way around.
>
> DAVE PETTIGREW, Senior Vice President, Strategic Marketing, and Head of Advertising and Games, Warner/Chappell Music

The process of licensing music for video games is similar to licensing music for film. Songs can be licensed individually, or one or more composers are hired to write music that's custom-tailored to suit the game's environment. The better paying gigs tend to be offered on a work-for-hire basis. In this case, the gaming company owns whatever music was produced during the term of employment and as such this original score becomes a permanent fixture associated with the game it was written for. The gaming industry brings with it a potentially wide range of musical demands:

- Songs and instrumental music of virtually any style; from light and fluffy to dark and demonic. Music that establishes a mood; action, drama, struggle, war, chase, science fiction, comedic, orchestral, cinematic, surreal, sound effects/textures/design, musical collage, rock, hip-hop, country, world, etc.

- Musical content associated with a historic period, place, event, ethnicity, or culture.

Preparing your song for possible inclusion in a video game may require that you have access to the song file/instrumental parts. For your run-of-the-mill rock band arrangement, you'll probably be asked to deliver several submix versions of the song. Not being able to readily provide a gaming company with alternate mix versions of a song on request can be a deal breaker, despite their liking your music. The best time to prepare these specialized files, even if there seems to be no immediate need or reason to, is when you wrap up a song mix. All of the parts are right before you, loaded into a mix, and up and running. It will take five minutes to solo/render individual instrumental submixes. Years after doing the original mix, it may take you a full day to do it if you can't quite remember where you stored the files, or there are software update bugs and plug-in conflicts, or if you're now using a different computer. Doing all of these mixes initially saves you time and also makes them handy if needed.

If you want to pursue gaming outlets, it's helpful to attend some gaming or digital media conferences. As with music conferences, these tend to be good networking opportunities, and fun. Have CDs and business cards in hand and if you can, talk shop with the people who are involved in the music selection process. Some of the most popular are:

- Game Developers Conference (www.gdconf.com)
- Video Game Expo (www.videogame.net)
- Electronic Entertainment Expo (www.e3expo.com)

Tomorrow's game developers may include students who are currently enrolled in computer science, electrical engineering, and digital and visual arts courses. Read gaming magazines and video game publications (such as *Game Developer*—www.gdmag.com); that is a good way to find out about games, projects, or forums in development. Information about gaming production companies are often found on product packaging. You can also check their websites for more info.

Loops—Licensing Audio Content

The emphasis of this book has been licensing songs, but another closely related area that might have appeal to some is licensing digital audio content. One example involves *audio loops*. These are often short, repeatable, musical sound clips. They're in familiar categories including drumbeats, guitar and bass riffs, piano vamps, and synthesizer patterns and textures. Of course, a loop can feature a single solo instrument, or could be a combination of different instruments. Loops also include information related to a piece of music's original key and tempo (bpm—beats per minute), and duration (four beats, eight beats, etc.).

Loops are made available in different digital media formats. They are sold on DVDs and CDs, are sometimes given away as part of promotional CDs, or can be purchased and downloaded online. As with production music CDs, loops tend to be packaged and sold in collections. Usually, a stylistic theme unifies a given CD/DVD of loops, maybe highlighting a solo instrument or combinations of instruments. Many websites, including www.loops.net and www.platinumloops.com, are dedicated to selling, sharing, or hosting these micro masterpieces.

A loop is surprisingly easy to make and can be done using pretty much any audio program that's currently sold on the market. For loop-based audio production, I prefer SONY's Sound Forge and ACID Pro. If you want to create or license your own custom loops, or pitch an entire collection to a company that might consider doing it for you such as SONY, Cakewalk, or Big Fish Audio, the goal will be to create a collection that is sonically interesting, perhaps a little unusual or unique, well recorded, and has the ability to appeal or appears as being useful to loop fanatics. The money that is earned from selling a single loop or an entire collection is in essence a licensing fee. In other words, what's being covered by the sale is actually twofold—covering not only the physical or digital copy of the content itself, but also an end-user licensing agreement that's embedded within and gives the customer the unrestricted or partial right to use this content as part of their own.

Licensing restrictions sometimes accompany the purchase of digital media content (again, always read the fine print!). In such cases, the end-user agreement makes a distinction between "noncommercial use" and "commercial use." If the license specifies "royalty-free" use, the party who is purchasing the content is free to pretty much use it in any way their heart might desire, so long as they don't turn a profit in the process—well, sort of. If the customer uses the loops to produce a song that ends up becoming a commercially viable recording, they most likely will still be allowed to profit from the recording that includes these "with restrictions" loops, as long as they a) notify the content owner/licensor of the loops, b) pay them an additional "all-in" licensing fee, or c) agree to pay them a royalty on all earnings generated by the song in question.

The way for a customer to avoid this potential hassle is to only use royalty-free loops. The initial purchase provides what is in effect an "all-in" license. When you send music to a publisher or marketing company, hoping they'll market your songs, they'll often grill you on this point. You'll be asked to sign an affidavit verifying that your songs are free of any illegal samples and any loops that might appear as part of the recording are both royalty free and without further restrictions and/or obligations.

Why do strict requirements about sample-free songs and royalty-free loops continue to prevail? Restricted content can present a hassle for a legitimate customer who uses it to produce a song with commercial appeal. Looking at it from the opposite point of view, if a song includes a strings-attached digital loop file and becomes a commercial success, it's certainly not a bad thing for the one who owns the loop. What if this person were you? It's interesting to consider that the digital sound clips you create and sell, or even give away, could end up as part of hundreds of song projects being produced by fellow music makers around the world. Whether you provide this content in a non-commercial use or royalty-free capacity is your choice. Clarify it at the time of purchase. If you have the ability or interest to create compelling loops, and can corner a niche market that's not saturated, it's worth pursuing. Licensing this content may generate exponentially more revenue than selling digital downloads of songs from a CD.

Ringtones

Every time you're in line at the supermarket and you hear someone's funky (or not-so-funky) ringtone go off, it most likely represents another digital music licensing opportunity fully exploited.

To sell or license your song as a ringtone, you can prepare the music file by more than one means. In the simplest sense, a ringtone is a designated MP3 song file that has been stored on a mobile device's hard drive, and is then assigned to start playing from the beginning when the mobile phone/handheld device receives a phone call, text message, or e-mail. The playback eventually stops (although not always soon enough) when the receiving party either acknowledges the announcement or a voice mail is activated.

Two fancier methods of ringtone preparation allow for more control in terms of what part of a song plays, and for how long, and how many times. This requires some extra steps and some basic audio editing know-how. The first, and more straightforward of the two, involves editing a digital song file that lasts for only a certain time duration (say ten to thirty seconds). Here, the objective is to produce an edit that will loop seamlessly upon repeated playback. This typically involves homing in on the main hook, chorus, or idea of the song. A number of specialized software programs address ringtone preparation of this nature, and can be purchased relatively inexpensively (just google "ringtone software" to find products and reviews). These software packages often come with the additional perk of providing their customers with access and membership to an online website that makes these ringtones available to the public for sale and/or free download. They include Ringtone Media Studio by Avanquest and Xingtone by Roxio.

Ringtones uploaded, purchased, or sold in this capacity are usually nothing more than short MP3 clips. As such, in addition to playback from a mobile phone sound card, ringtones can in theory play on any digital MP3 player device. Alternatively, you can skip buying specialized software altogether and use whatever audio recording and editing program is at your disposal that can accommodate both digital music editing and MP3 rendering. You could also download a free program from the Web such as Audacity for the purpose of getting the job done.

Yet another approach to ringtone production involves playback of a MIDI file from a mobile device's internal sound card. These might be classified as those ringtones that sound preprogrammed, robotic, or synthesizer-like, and what is heard is clearly not the result of a live studio recording. When someone's phone rings, and what follows is a playback of an electronic-sounding Beethoven symphony, you're not hearing a recorded orchestra, but rather a digital approximation conveyed as a MIDI file. Of course, the ringtone that is triggered could just as easily be a MIDI file of your own song. The catch is that preparing a song in a MIDI file format requires knowledge in one or more of the following areas: sequencing and programming of MIDI data, digital manuscript software production, the ability to read and write music, or the ability to accurately transcribe audio recordings and turn them into MIDI recordings. These musical skills are all more specialized and require some practice or training. The benefit or incentive for converting a song that was originally in an audio format to MIDI format is that the latter is extremely flexible and small (in terms of actual file size, relatively speaking). MIDI files can play back from a mobile phone, website media player, computer, musical birthday card, toy, and game player or just about anything digital that has a chip and sound card. MIDI files can easily be turned into audio files; however the reverse is often less often the case. For more on MIDI files, and free downloads, check out www.mididb.com or www.externalharddrive.com/midi/midi.html.

Because ringtones involve the download and possible sale of a product, profits occur in the form of a mechanical royalty. The third-party website that decides to sell or host your ringtones will in essence be acquiring a digital mechanical license to your product, thus allowing the company permission to sell, manufacture, and/or distribute whatever digital content you've provided for an agreed-upon commission rate per units that are sold. Business models and profit sharing varies for online digital content retailers, so be sure to do some homework first.

Internet Radio

Internet radio is to radio what websites like YouTube are to television. The entry-level barriers for getting into the digital media streaming game are either substantially lower or, in some cases, nonexistent.

The question to then consider is how this can help you. As with conventional radio, two major perks offered via Internet radio are product promotion and the possibility of earning performance royalties for the use of sound recordings protected by copyright and digitally transmitted.

To take advantage of the promotional aspect of radio, at least in the monetary sense, requires that your music be readily available for purchase online prior to digital streaming, either through your website or via any number of established music retailers (see table on page 231). This way as people hear your song, and happen to like it enough to purchase a copy, there's a means for satisfying the impulse. Having your songs play on Internet radio could also help promote an upcoming tour or performance. Regardless of sales or royalties, being on the radio will provide you with exposure as long as there is somebody, somewhere else, who is listening.

There are many Internet radio station outlets. Here are but a few:

- new.music.yahoo.com
- music.aol.com/radioguide/bb
- www.pandora.com
- www.live365.com
- www.shoutcast.com

SOUND EXCHANGE Most independent musicians now own their own master recordings by virtue of having both paid for and produced them without the assistance of a record label. We've discussed performing rights organizations that represent songwriters and publishers, but what about record companies, or *you*, in the event that you own your recordings or are in effect operating as your own record label? Radio and record companies have a long-standing symbiotic relationship. But what about indie record labels and Internet radio?

Before 1995, those who owned master recordings didn't earn performance royalties on the basis of public performance. So if you had a song play on the radio or TV, it would generate performance royalties if you happened to be the songwriter or publisher, but no such luck if you owned the recordings (record company). For a record company, royalties required cause and effect—the broadcast had to compel people to go out and buy the CD. Two important laws took effect in the 1990s with regard to sound recordings: The Digital Performance Right in Sound Recordings Act of 1995 and The Digital Millennium Copyright Act of 1998. It was good news for record labels or anyone else who owned the copyrights for valuable sound recordings. These acts opened the doors for new sources of revenue by mandating that sound recording owners must also get paid for public performances with regard to certain types of digital transmission. At the time, it must have felt like hitting the jackpot for some. Ironically, the second of these legal victories was signed into law just as Napster was arriving on the scene.

Sound Exchange is an independent nonprofit performing rights organization designated by the U.S. copyright owner to collect and distribute *digital performance royalties* on behalf of recording artists and those who own copyrights for *sound recordings*. In short, it is a performing rights organization that protects the interests of those who own master recordings that are performed in a digital capacity, and is different from ASCAP, BMI, and SESAC, which represent songwriters, composers, and publishers. If you own your own recordings, and are planning on pursuing digital outlets (as of 2009 this now includes all radio, TV, and the Internet), become a member. You can find Sound Exchange at www.soundexchange.com.

Podcasts

Podcasts offer yet another opportunity for you to license your music in a digital format. Podcast producers often look for opening themes, bumper cues, and closing themes to enhance their programs, as well as any cuts that might enhance their product throughout its duration. Podcast music actually involves a number of licensing issues that incorporate many of the concepts we've already discussed. For an overview of the considerations the use of music as part of podcast can entail, let's consider the case of "Joe Podcaster," who intends to use lots of different styles of music for his latest podcast series. For this discussion, let's assume:

- Joe plans on using music by some artists who are well known, and others who are "underground."
- Joe isn't interested in using public domain works and knows that the way he intends to use music in his podcast won't qualify as fair use.
- Joe loves music, and despite his impressive air guitar skills, he isn't a musician, and hasn't the talent or patience to try and record his own cover versions of any of these songs for the sake of cutting corners.

Joe P. is operating his podcast a bit like an independent radio talk show. I make the comparison because many radio talk shows use a wide variety of music in a similar capacity. A number of licenses will have to be addressed if Joe P. is going to follow through with his plan of using music in ways that mimics his favorite national talk-show host. Joe P. is your average hard-working guy, who will on occasion sneak off to the basement to vent and record podcast rants when insomnia gets the better of him. Money is a bit tight these days. On the other hand, sponsors and advertisers fund the types of radio stations Joe wants to emulate via podcasting, and part of this funding is used to cover the annual cost of maintaining a number of music licenses.

Let's consider what happens at various stages as pieces of music are imported into one of Joe's podcast episodes. By virtue of importing songs into the podcast, a copy of each song gets made (requiring a license for each or a *blanket license* that covers them all). More copies are subsequently made as Joe's growing audience acquires their own copies. Sharing this podcast with others will involve making it available for others to download, and this is a form of distribution (doing this requires a license). Covering the two bases requires obtaining a license for reproduction and distribution of musical works, and this will be administered by the Harry Fox Agency.

Streaming the podcast on an Internet radio station or by any other means that makes the podcast available for public exhibition is considered a performance—not only of the podcast itself, but of any music embedded within it (this requires one or more licenses for public performance of a musical work). Joe will have to contact and obtain these blanket licenses from ASCAP, BMI, and SESAC.

Just as Joe is about to press RECORD and vent the day's frustration, he breaks into a sweat as he realizes he's not only using *songs*, but also *recordings* of the songs. Podcasts are digital audio transmissions, and as such will likely require contacting the record companies that own these recordings to obtain licenses for reproduction, distribution, and public performance of sound recordings. (See also Sound Exchange.)

As always, Joe P. is thinking ahead and has been toying with the idea of spicing up his presentation by creating videocasts—podcasts set to images—in the future. He feels a bit faint and lightheaded realizing that this brilliant marketing plan requires licenses for the use of music set to images (creating an audiovisual work). This alternate plan may require that Joe proceed like a filmmaker and pursue a synch/master or videogram license for each song he intends to use. As we know, these licenses are the workhorse contracts that have been used for years to provide music clearance for TV and film, and originally were not intended to address the Internet or podcasts. However, they certainly can work for Joe P., so long as the media rights granted as part of the agreements being used focus on Internet rights. A person or party having the ability to provide "one-stop licensing" could in effect offer Joe what amounts to a podcast license. This could be similar in concept to a film festival rights agreement, providing the clearances required for the purpose of podcasting, but restricting other forms of use, media formats, and methods of distribution.

Peer to Peer Music Networks

A *peer to peer (p2p) network* allows group members to share and exchange digital content through a matrix of computers and network servers. BitTorrent protocol is a type of p2p networking that allows large, uncompressed digital files to be shared and exchanged by side-stepping the limitations of available bandwidth that can be afforded through standard Internet hosting. File and data exchange of this nature has been a hot-button topic for some time now, and p2p networks such as the old Napster.com were among the significant contributing factors that set the wheels of the "indie music revolution" into motion during the late 1990s.

At the core of the debate, at least in terms of digital music file sharing, reside two opposing ideologies. The major record labels have aggressively pursued legal action on the grounds that p2p file sharing amounts to stealing or illegally downloading digital music files that have not been purchased, and are protected by copyright. On the other hand, those who participate in exchanging music files (or other digital content) with others who belong to the same p2p network regard their actions differently, seeing it simply as a form of back-and-forth sharing and exchange—akin to some friends swapping CDs or DVDs with one another.

Some p2p networks require new members to sign up, fill out online forms, and pay recurring fees. In contrast, a true BitTorrent is more akin to a modern-day secret society, where membership is free, lacks any paper trail, and is granted through invitation only. Some BitTorrents involve much more sophisticated ways of exchanging and storing data. The advancement and constant evolution of digital networking and communication protocols has opened a Pandora's box of complex issues related to the rights, privileges, and protection afforded through copyright as we know it. The challenge, and one that applies to any and all forms of digital media, is addressing how copyright can be enforced in the future. Is the answer *digital rights management* (see page 230) or revising copyright law to better suit the digital world? There is lots of debate and understandable concern surrounding the issue, but no clear answer as to the best solution as of yet.

Giving Away Music Free Online

There are compelling arguments as to why it can be advantageous for an artist to allow some amount of their own original music to be given away or freely exchanged over various p2p networks, and thus willingly forfeit the monetary incentive of mechanical licensing deals and royalties. The decision to allow this to happen is an artist's right, as long as the copyright owner for both the song(s) and recording(s) in question takes no issue with this decision. The theory is that circumventing the "prohibitive constraint" of an otherwise mandatory mechanical royalty payment for customers can benefit the artist in several ways, including word-of-mouth promotion, referrals, and any viral marketing that happens as a result.

So why just give your music away? Sharing your music files over a p2p network can amount to a reasonably effective and relatively inexpensive promotional strategy where the incentive and justification, at least initially, might be to "spread the word" about your band and some songs. Creating a buzz over a p2p network can ultimately serve to facilitate a larger fan base, higher concert attendance, and better sales for music releases down the road. With any luck, doing so can help some artists establish a cult following. Again, the greatest expense associated with releasing a new album or movie (with label or studio backing) is most often associated with the out-of-pocket costs that go along with advertising its release, and paying for its publicity and promotion; breaking even or profiting may require surpassing a formidable threshold in terms of the number of units that must first get sold. In such cases, the incentive from the artist's standpoint isn't so much cashing in on digital download sales, but rather the possibility of generating valuable self-promotion without paying a fortune (publicity that isn't free is often very pricey).

So how can you give a song away? Upon uploading the song to a website (either your own or on some third-party website), refer to the settings in the media player being used to stream music. For example, on MySpace, you can either allow or prevent the songs you've uploaded to your profile to be downloaded by others.

Are such marketing ploys ultimately just pie-in-the-sky optimism, or is there any potential for this to actually work? Arguably the best example of this approach succeeding for an artist can be credited to the band Radiohead, who in October 2007 released its seventh album, *In Rainbows*. What immediately drew attention was the asking price for the album's digital download; fans were allowed to pay whatever they wanted (or could afford) to pay, including nothing. Despite the option to pay nothing and download the digital version for free, this album still managed to sell at least three million copies, and by the end of 2007 topped the end-of-the-year "best list" in most of the major music publications.

Protections

As we've now established, licensing content involves acquiring permission by means of a written contract and/or purchasing such rights from the copyright owner(s) of the content. On the other side of the spectrum resides what could be thought of as the opposite of the licensing process—illegal digital downloads, pirated software, or any other use of intellectual property that transpires without having received permission or paying for its use. The amazing flexibility afforded through digitized media is also what makes it so vulnerable and susceptible to this sort of abuse. For better or worse, history shows us that technology develops at an exponentially faster rate than our ability to manage the rules of its use, or foresee all of the unintended consequences.

The complications, problems, and highly publicized lawsuits linked with p2p networks involve sharing or downloading digital music content from network servers without having permission from its copyright owners. Regardless of the opinions related to the topic, it is clear that the penalties leveled at those individuals who are prosecuted and ultimately found guilty are rather severe. Consider the well-publicized case of Jammie Thomas-Rasset, who in June of 2009 was found guilty of illegally downloading twenty-four songs from the p2p network Kazaa. At the conclusion of her second trial (the first was ruled a mistrial), Thomas-Rasset was hit with a whopping $1.92 million fine—or $80,000 for each MP3 song file that had been illegally downloaded to her hard drive.

Digital Rights Management (DRM)

Digital Rights Management (DRM) is one of the strategies that has been employed to help combat the proliferation of illegal music downloads and p2p file sharing. In its broadest sense, DRM refers to any system that limits access to digital content, so as to control its usage. A common form of this technology in the music industry is for a record label to produce CDs containing bits of information that confuse pirating software.

As a combative measure, the DRM solution has been dropped by some music retailers, although others still use it. The implementation of DRM came with an unintended consequence; it punishes legitimate customers by restricting the types of media players and computers that can be used to play back music files purchased from different online music retailers. Furthermore, layering a digital music file with DRM restrictions doesn't deter or prevent someone with the means, knowledge, or desire to make or distribute illegal copies from doing so.

Buying and Selling Songs Online

You enter a digital licensing agreement by virtue of allowing your songs to be sold and distributed through a third-party online music retailer.

When you upload your digital content to a third-party network server for the purpose of selling, downloading, distributing, and even a possibility of manufacturing or shipping hard copies, you must first enter into a digital mechanical licensing agreement with the licensee (website owner). Take the time to read the fine points of this online agreement (which you enter into when you click "I accept"). It enables you to license the right for someone else to sell copies of your song, collect and process payments, earn a commission, and forward any mechanical royalties that result as units are sold.

There is no "entry-level barrier" for this type of licensing deal; anyone can upload and sell their music. The retailer provides the means and infrastructure that enable your songs to be sold worldwide. However, there are no advances or up-front money for promoting such sales from the online retailer; that becomes your responsibility. For this type of licensing deal to eventually generate royalties you must bring the product to the attention of others. This is why viral marketing through the social networking sites can be so beneficial.

There are many options for selling your own music online. The business model, profit-sharing structure, and royalty distribution timetables vary from one retailer to another, and as such, may influence your choice in terms of which ones to utilize. Keep in mind that most people will be inclined to purchase your music online from those stores/retailers whose name and reputation ring a tone of familiarity, seem trustworthy, and make the process of shopping online relatively hassle-free. Music can be sold via social networking websites, and of course, through your own. There are a host of dedicated online music retailers. Here is a breakdown of some of the most popular, along with information on pricing, encoding, and DRM.

ONLINE MUSIC PRICING

ONLINE MUSIC STORES	PRICING (PER SONG)	USER REQUIREMENTS	DRM-FREE?
iTUNES	$0.99–$1.29	Purchases require shopping through Apple's iTunes software	Not by default. However, if you opt to purchase song files from iTunes in ACC file format (advanced audio codec), your purchase will be DRM-free.
AMAZON MP3 STORE	$0.79–$0.99		Yes; 256-kbps MP3 files.
eMUSIC (emusic.com)	As low as $0.25	Requires a subscription; offers various plans and social networking	Yes; 192-kbps MP3 files.
NAPSTER (napster.com)	Around $0.99	Requires downloading/ installing Napster software	Some files are DRM-free, while others are not; most MP3s are offered at a variable-bit-rate of 256 kbps, although some are as low as 128 kbps.
RHAPSODY (rhapsody.com)	$0.99 and around $10 for an entire album	Offers various service plans	MP3s purchased that are not part of Rhapsody's subscription service are DRM-free.
ZUNE (zune.net)	Around $0.99 using Microsoft's point currency	Requires Microsoft's Zune marketplace software	Some files are DRM-free, while others are not. Music is encoded at 256 kbps for major-label artists and 320 kbps for indie artists. Nice!

Key Points to Remember

When someone contacts you online with a proposition to license your music, ask the potential licensee to forward you either a request proposal or actual licensing agreement (if available). This puts you in a better position in terms of negotiation, and saves you the hassle of being the party having to provide the preliminary paperwork. At the very least, whatever tentative agreement is brought to the table establishes a benchmark for moving forward, or opting out. The first issue will be clarifying the type(s) of streaming media that will include your song. For example, webseries, individual episodes, visual advertisements, or any other form of streaming audiovisual media content will require that either you or a representative have the authority to provide clearance for both the recording of the song as well as the composition itself. Thus, the licensing process is conceptually similar to clearing a song for use in a TV series or film.

Other considerations include:

- Are the provisions of the license limited to Web-based (only) streaming, or does it cover and/or include additional media formats that will extend beyond the scope of the Web (e.g., DVD releases, downloads for various media players)?
- Are the fees being offered "all-in" (that is, limited to a one-time-only lump-sum payment) or is there any possibility of also receiving a royalty percentage in the future based on download sales? The former is to the licensee's advantage, while the latter provision favors the licensor's position (assuming future sales actually occur).
- Will terms of the agreement expire or last in perpetuity?

|||||||||||||||||||||||||||||||||||||||||||||||||||||||||||||||||||||||||||||||||||||||||||||||||||||||||||||||||||||||||||||||||||

CHAPTER 16

Getting Music Licensed in Less Obvious Markets

For many of us, the mere mention of TV or film triggers an immediate association with Hollywood or the Big Apple. Although these cities are still regarded as the primary hubs for film and television production in the U.S., they certainly aren't the only places to land licensing deals. It's best not to limit your sights on a few locations. There are video production companies all throughout the country and the world. People need musical content for a variety of types of projects everywhere.

Exploring less obvious markets for licensing music can start by simply considering what's available in your own backyard or within reasonable proximity. It's possible that there are opportunities within arm's reach that you might not be aware of, so don't forget to think locally, such as stores or other businesses that advertise on local radio or TV, local theaters and playhouses, community event centers, educational facilities, or people in your community involved with media production (amateur or professional). Many smaller licensing outlets can provide you with something beneficial, including practice and self-confidence. It can simply be a satisfying experience or a project that's involved with a good cause, such as a charity event or fund-raiser. The value of experience often extends beyond money.

The World Outside of TV, Film, and the Internet

Determining the best markets for your product is arguably the most important step in figuring out which events, presentations, or less conventional licensing opportunities to explore. This is a potentially vast list, and includes any entity that prioritizes entertainment as it produces media content, or organizes presentations, live shows, private parties, or corporate events.

It's sometimes hard to get past your own emotional attachment to your music, but it's necessary if you are going to figure out what niche it can fill in the licensing marketplace. When you're in doubt about the best markets for your music, brainstorm with others. Don't limit your scope to just your friends or fellow artists. Try approaching people you know from the business world, too. Business types might not respond to your music by saying it's "loud, hip, cool, and those drums! How many microphones did you use while recording them?" but they're likely to give you pragmatic advice. Remember, in this part of the licensing universe, all that matters is if your music can *sell* or effectively *market* someone's product to that product's target audience.

Brainstorming with people outside of the music world can lead you to licensing possibilities you've never thought of before. For example, say your music sounds powerful and energetic. It might be worth looking into what car shows are scheduled to take place in your area. Start with a Web search, and continue to narrow down the search result listings to find event locations and types of cars that seem best suited for the type of music you write and record; a classic car show may not be quite right, but a sports car show might be an excellent fit. If your music is more ethereal or meditative, perhaps a company that offers healing and/or spirituality oriented products is the right direction. If your music is highly dynamic and full of energy, you might look for licensing opportunities in the booming gymnastics world — competitive gymnastics programs and individual competitors often license music for floor routines. Similar opportunities exist in figure skating, at both the competitive and exhibition level. Also, there's a burgeoning market for music that can be embedded in museum audio tours and downloaded from home.

> We've licensed music for large-scale video installations and art projects, fashion shows, ringtones, and hold music (music used when a company puts you on hold on the phone).
>
> DRAZEN BOSNJAK, Q Department

Not all music publishers or other players in the industry who pitch music are thinking this way yet. Their focus is on the markets they already know. However, the world of music licensing is a bit like the Wild West; you can opt to head in any given direction because they are all available and many are unexplored. Any one that you choose brings along with it the potential for both new opportunities and challenges.

Getting to the Right Person

Whether you're trying to get your music licensed in a mainstream outlet, an emerging market, or an unconventional venue, the same basic rule holds true: You'll need to find and make contact with the person or party in charge of screening, selecting, deciding, and with any luck agreeing to license your music. In the case of pitching music for licensing deals in TV and film, the decision makers are obvious (music supervisors, producers, directors, and the like). However, knowing where and whom you'll need to turn to when pursuing opportunities outside of film and TV can be less readily apparent. When dealing with a company that has many employees and lines of command, it's important to correspond with the person who has the authority and ability to enter into a licensing agreement on behalf of the company.

When you target a specific company, look for the name of the person who organizes the event or program you think your music would be right for and take note of her contact information. This information might appear on the company or event website, or in program notes, a catalog, a brochure, a CD or DVD card insert, or a corporate directory.

Take some time to organize your thoughts and come up with a plan. Why would they want to license your music? Maybe the notion of licensing music is completely foreign to them at this point, and as such, would be a process that seems intimidating or cost-prohibitive. These are legitimate concerns— ones you will need to deal with once you make contact. If there is a trick, it's to come across already knowing a little about your customer and then offer them something that's interesting, affordable, entertaining, and fun.

Keep in mind that many companies employ one or more publicists to plug new products or event coordinators who organize conferences or presentations. If you envision your music being used as part of a live or digital media presentation, publicists and event coordinators can be good starting points of contact. Prior to e-mailing or calling the company you've targeted, it will really help your cause to research the company in the following ways:

- What's the company's upcoming events schedule? Know the date(s), location(s), and overarching purpose. What, if any, form of entertainment will be offered as part of the event? If none, how can your music be used to make the event or presentation more entertaining, interesting, or memorable? If you can answer this question beforehand, you're heading in the right direction toward sparking some interest.
- Who is the primary target audience for the products and services offered through the company? Does the demographic targeted, generally speaking, listen to the type of music you are able to provide as part of a licensing arrangement? If the answer is no, the concept becomes a tougher sell, and perhaps isn't the best outlet to pursue.
- Can you identify the company as one whose product and services you personally believe in or purchase/use on a regular basis? If so, your sales pitch will seem more genuine, and although this in itself provides no guarantees, more often than not it will work in your favor.

Having some basic information at your fingertips about the company (related to its products, business philosophy, or recent announcements) before contacting them will help guide your introduction, and be very useful as you prepare a pitch or, at the very least, plant seeds that one day may blossom into a licensing opportunity, even if there doesn't appear to be one right now. Of course, the other important consideration is how can your music become part of an event or presentation? This is a question worth reconciling before attempting to make contact. It's safe to assume that licensing music isn't a procedure or process that most folks are going to be familiar with. However, many companies whose business falls somewhere beyond the scope of the entertainment world may be familiar with licensing other types of content, such as software, intellectual properties, trademarks, or the right to manufacture, produce, or sell third-party products.

Now let's explore some specific opportunities outside the worlds of TV, film, and the Internet.

Licensing Music in Colleges and Universities

If you are a student, schools may be the best place to begin exploring the unexplored. Try to meet students in the dance and theater departments. Post a flyer on the department bulletin board. Consider what programs are offered, and of those, the ones that are most likely to need music, including the departments of journalism, media studies, and of course, the film school if there is one. Many college professors have pet projects in the works that need music. Schools also make educational and training videos or documentaries about a specific field that require the use of music.

Most arts programs require that students complete a graduation or thesis project. This not only represents a chance to explore new outlets for your original music, but can also end up being a collaboration that becomes a project with considerable artistic merit. This can generate high praise or good reviews in the student or local press. If writing or performing original music is your focus, team up with students in other departments and propose a joint collaboration. Most performing arts programs love these types of arrangements, and upon reviewing your plan, might offer the school's full support in order to bring the project to fruition. When in doubt, referring to the pretentious-sounding phrase "interdepartmental collaboration" may prove useful for the purpose of winning approval from an academic committee in order to proceed with a team-based collaboration.

Academic institutions are required to file and renew annual licenses with the performing rights organizations. If you write original music that's included as part of a live performance at a school and are a member of a performing rights organization, you can register the score titles. This may qualify you to receive performance royalties. A copy of the program will need to be submitted to the PRO. The theater's stage manager will most likely address this. When in doubt, you can always submit a copy of the program to your performing rights organization.

Some PROs have separate departments to address performance royalties that fall into the category of "serious music," such as musical theater, plays, concerts, and recitals, as distinct from "popular music," which includes TV, film, and radio. Make sure any program that your music is included in has your name and the titles of the songs or compositions that were included as part of the show. In addition to live performances, some colleges have their own TV stations, and televise school performances on regional public broadcast stations. It's a start.

Licensing Music for Live Performances

The licensing process for live stage performances—including theater, choreographed dance performances, slide shows, and visual presentations on public exhibit (planetariums, art shows, circuses, and museums)—can involve steps that are rarely if ever encountered in music licensing situations for TV and film. However, the same legal obligation associated with licensing music for TV, film, and advertising also applies to the use of someone else's music as part of a public performance or other type of live entertainment.

Like movies, staged productions can be complex and massive undertakings. The up-front costs or financial risks that accompany most productions at the onset are often accepted and endured for the sake and possibility of *profiting* in the end. In the case of a staged performance, ticket sales, merchandise, selling recordings, and/or DVDs of the performances create profits. Music often adds substantial marketing and entertainment value, and when it's effective, can increase a presentation's appeal and ability to generate its own profits.

The types of live performances that warrant having their own soundtrack continue to grow. The notion of traditional "live performance" now expands beyond stage performances to include presentations involving video clips, large projection screens, and/or those beginning or ending with a keynote speaker. If a presentation can be accompanied by music, it's potentially a new or unexplored music licensing opportunity. This flexibility is why the practice of music licensing continues to prevail while other facets of the music industry that are predicated on less flexible business models or markets face a struggle.

Licensing Music for the Theater
The use of music as part of staged theatrical performances (plays, musicals, and operas) requires obtaining a license from the publisher of the musical

and/or owner of the score's copyright. The fees in these situations can depend on multiple variables, including the number of performances that are scheduled to take place, the theater's seating capacity and type of venue (educational institution, playhouse, etc.), its location, and the intended arrangement (piano/voice, small ensemble, big band, or full orchestra). Upon contacting a publisher, the licensee may be asked to provide these details in request form for review.

Having your music licensed for inclusion in a theatrical performance will likely require pitching your songs to a stage director, playwright, and executive producers (those who are providing the project's financial backers).

If you're trying to license your work for use in the production of a non-musical or "straight" play that will include *incidental* music (highlighting dramatic tension, or perhaps to fill the moments between scenes), you will need to match the tone, spirit, and perhaps the setting of the play itself. Your music must help achieve the director's dramatic vision for the particular sections in which the music will be used.

For musicals, a song you wish to license for a stage performance must entertain, but it also must complement the timeline of the plot, bring attention to an event, or assist in character development. In musical theater, a song with lyrics isn't treated as "background texture" as it might be in film and television licensing—the *message within the song* and the *story* are often one and the same. Any misalignment that might exist between the story and a preexisting song makes the prospect of licensing the song far less promising.

If an up-and-coming playwright or musical director admires your work, it may be easier to simply agree to write songs for a show while it's in development, especially one that could debut in a local or regional theater. The musical arrangements can be simple enough (piano/voice) to make it feasible. In some cases, teaming up with a playwright could warrant having a musical commissioned. You would need to carefully examine whether the producing entity that is commissioning your music is truly licensing your work, or if you are entering a work-for-hire relationship, wherein the producer will own the copyright to your finished product.

To get your preexisting song licensed for a staged production, you may need to modify it (slightly or considerably) in the event that *it's close, but not quite close enough* to matching the details of a plot. As the song's copyright owner, you have the right to grant or deny permission to others for its use within the context of a theatrical work—one that will be performed or exhibited in public for an audience that pays for admission. Performing a song, play, or musical or reproducing another work of art that isn't your own as part of a publicly performed *theatrical* or *dramatic exhibition* requires obtaining permission from the appropriate copyright owners beforehand. If it's an original musical that you scored, no clearance is necessary. Depending on the situation, you're justified in asking for a reasonable commission from ticket sales for each performance (or ask to be paid a flat rate regardless of how many tickets are sold). This can be thought of as licensing the stage rights for the use of your music during each performance.

In a best-case scenario, writing the music, lyrics, and/or libretto for a musical has the potential to be lucrative for a long time to come. In most cases, these shows start out small, and might premiere at a local or regional theater, school, or playhouse. A staged production may go on to experience mainstream success as the result of glowing reviews and press early on, a healthy box office, an amazing cast, strong industry connections, controversy stirred up by the subject matter, or the fact that it's just really good. Commercial success is further validated when *other* theater companies then decide to acquire the stage rights to perform this musical in their own venue(s), and use their own cast and crew. The musical acquires "hit" status as this process repeats itself for years to come.

Every time other theater companies want to perform the musical, they have to license the stage performances rights (fees are usually charged on a per-performance basis). These licensing fees are then split between the musical's publisher/agent, composer, and playwright. Other revenue streams, including soundtracks, printed sheet music, and broadcast royalties, may occur as the result of televised performances or radio broadcasts of the show.

In contemporary theater, musicals are often created out of preexisting song catalogs. Recent examples include *Movin' Out* (based on the music of Billy Joel), *Mama Mia!* (Abba), and *Jersey Boys* (Frankie Valli and The Four Seasons). However, because of the enormous production cost and investment capital that is necessary for publicity, advertisements, and getting the production stage-ready, these larger scale productions may require or all but demand that the song catalog under consideration be widely known.

Fair Use

Staged performances and live-audience productions do not incorporate music *accidentally*; many mistakenly believe that music used as part of staged performances, especially in small local theaters, falls under the umbrella of a special categorization known as *fair use*. Fair use, goes the argument, would provide an exemption from the otherwise legal obligation to obtain a license for the use of this copyrighted material.

The flaw in arguing that fair use is the proper label for these situations is that the performances are in fact *staged*, and whatever music appears as part of the performance was predetermined and deliberately selected with intention. To clarify this point, an example that illustrates fair use might involve live news coverage of a breaking story. Let's say that during this coverage a car just happens to drive down the same street with its windows rolled down and the radio cranked. Of course, the sound emanating from the loud car stereo leaks into the journalist's microphone for a time, and in doing so, becomes part of the overall presentation that is broadcast. It could be argued that the use of the music in this case is a form of fair use, because it wasn't used intentionally or under a controllable set of circumstances.

Licensing Music for Corporate Training Videos

Corporate videos use a lot of music. There are plenty of opportunities for licensing music for use in corporate videos, yet few people actually know about them. They're usually produced for a company or corporation, most often for in-house use. Their purpose can include:

- training new employees or highlighting important company policies or procedures
- providing a prospective employee or one who was recently hired with an overview of the company's history, business philosophy, products, and goals in the marketplace
- assisting in technical training purposes
- adding to an annual event, presentation, morale booster, or celebration

Corporate videos can help target a select consumer group. These niche target-audience videos may be packaged as part of a product or service that a company is selling. For example, you'll often find company-related video clips included on a software disc in the extras subfolder. These provide the viewer with information about the product itself, or promote other products that may be of interest.

Providing the music for corporate or educational videos usually involves payment, although the budgets are often less robust on a per-song basis compared to licensing fees paid by a network television series or commercial advertiser. The norm is a one-time flat-fee payment that is nonexclusive. Often the videographer hired to produce the video project assumes the responsibility for the musical requirements and will turn to production music CDs or a library collection that's already covered by a blanket license. Yet, many videographers I know find relying on these sources limiting. They say that most of what's available sounds like stock or generic music. While they might prefer working with more hip music selections, they're often constrained by a limited budget and deadline.

> We tend to use music libraries and blanket licensing agreements with our projects, go to the usual suspects, and browse for the right piece. Most of this is now being done online. In addition to library music, there are times when I would love to also include original songs, but for the most part, our client doesn't want to step-up and "pay-to-play." This in turn narrows the scope of our music search. There is no ideal method, but through working with people like Darren, we can go past the "gray area" and straight to black-and-white. In our ever-changing world of music and video technology and content licensing we need direction.
>
> GRANT MONREAN, Videographer, Editor, Producer, and Owner, Monrean Multimedia

Videographers know that stepping outside the safety zone of a blanket license could potentially result in inefficiency if there's a problem or the music provider can't suggest solutions that are more compelling than what's already available. Most will consider other sources, so long as these other options will keep their clients happy. As a musician, it's best to be able to offer a videographer a blanket license that covers a better choice than what's already available. The challenge is to have a catalog of your own that's diverse enough to cover the spectrum of scenarios in the video and, when necessary, can provide background support for video content with heavy dialogue.

If you don't have access to a back catalog large enough to merit a blanket license, you could simply write, record, and produce whatever music is needed. For some, a challenge of this nature will appear as an exciting opportunity—just realize that situations like these can end up being a considerable amount of work compressed into a small amount of time. In contrast to a thirty-second TV commercial, a corporate video might be twenty minutes or longer. If it becomes your sole responsibility to address all the music requirements for a project, it will most likely require providing multiple music cues. Five, ten, or fifteen music clips may be necessary. The budget for covering all that's required will most likely be capped. Since these videos are seen or presented in an in-house capacity, they won't end up on television later. So there's no possibility of generating future performance royalties.

These situations can give you valuable, hands-on experience writing new music and/or editing preexisting music files that will work within the context of whatever video content is provided. You may be asked to do more than simply license your music; the project could become an interactive multimedia production experience that exposes you to working with a number of different media formats while fine-tuning your production skills. These gigs are also good preparation for those interested in pursuing film scoring work, where the marriage between music and visual imagery tends to become more micromanaged due to a larger budget, higher expectations, or more flexibility in a production schedule to allow for some experimentation.

Licensing Music for Music Compilations

Licensing your music for inclusion on a third-party music compilation CD most often happens as the result of pitching the song(s) to the company that will be releasing the compilation. In the event that it's accepted for inclusion on the compilation's track list, the deal is finalized when you enter into a mechanical license with the company overseeing the CD's release. At this point, some record companies may pay you an advance (money paid to you against future royalties), while others may not.

Niche Category Music Compilations

These discs are sold in stores that will typically highlight or feature a specific musical genre. This audio content evokes a suitable mood or ambience during an activity or event.

The producers of specialized niche category compilation music CDs target their products to people who might enjoy music as background accompaniment while participating in a hobby, activity, or as part of living a lifestyle event (exercise and fitness, meditation, yoga, or dining music). They are often sold in home improvement stores, hotel/resort gift shops, fitness centers, spas, and coffee shops, as well as superstores like Wal-Mart and Target. The niche category music compilation discs share certain attributes in common with *production music CDs* (the kind that are frequently used by video producers—although these are not often sold in stores; see below). One similarity is that both tend to be quite specific in terms of the style of music featured on the CD and the intended use (*Jazz for Fine Dining, Music for Cycling Vol. 3, Holiday Music for the Kazoo*).

If you're interested in this area, start researching niche category CDs that have already been commercially released and are currently available in stores (these can be found through online music retailers or boutique record companies, or you can find physical copies in many department stores). Try to home in on companies that have released compilations that overlap with your own music specialty or are in close approximation. The preliminary contact information for the company that has released the disc is most likely available somewhere within the fine print of the J-card insert, or tucked away on the label's website. Again, collections of this nature tend to be very specific when it comes to whom they market their products, and where they distribute new releases, and thus you should be very specific when describing the type of content you have available for consideration. What you're able to provide needs to align with the kind of product they are known to deliver. Follow directions when music submission policies are stated; if there are no instructions, send a short note explaining who you are and what you have, and asking if it's okay to forward your music for future consideration.

EXAMPLE In 2003 I had a couple of songs licensed for inclusion on a cycling/fitness CD. The tempo of the songs may have contributed to their selection. The producers required that the tempo of each song on the CD would have to increase in increments of ten bpm up until the two-thirds mark, at which point the tracks gradually slowed back down. This was necessary to match the pacing of a workout program. Details that might otherwise get taken for granted can turn out to be important when it comes to selecting tracks for specialized music compilation discs.

Production Music CDs

These are specialized CDs that are marketed (mostly) to film and video professionals. These discs are highly specific in terms of their audio content. A given disc typically contains a single musical genre and might highlight certain instrumentation. These CDs are formatted to accommodate common editing situations with ease (there can be multiple edits/versions of each composition). These CDs are not sold in stores, but rather are forwarded directly to a video production company by the licensor (a music publisher, music production company, composer, or producer). This may be done as part of a new or preexisting blanket license agreement or by request.

Licensing Music for Restaurants

According to the National Restaurant Association (www.restaurant.org), there are more than 870,000 restaurants in the United States that do over $400 billion in sales a year.

To stay competitive, restaurant owners constantly look for ways to create a more appealing dining experience for their clientele. Music that complements a restaurant's style of cuisine can be a key to that quest—opening up a host of possibilities for you to license mood, genre, or ethnic music to individual restaurants as well as chains.

Restaurants often use royalty-free compilations of public domain music, or pay licensing fees to the PROs for music that is protected by copyright. So it will be up to you to research the corporate structure of major chains, or approach the owner of your favorite local *trattoria*, and prove why your music can give their establishment an edge over the rest. Licensing fees will depend upon the size of the restaurant, its entertainment budget, the frequency with which it plans on playing your music, and, for chains, the number of sites involved.

Licensing Music for Massage Therapy Centers

For the most part, massage therapists go out of their way to create a tranquil and relaxing environment. In addition to the soothing sounds of the little rock waterfall, fragrant smells, and low lighting, many will play mood music that they've purchased. To play that music in a professional setting, they must pay a licensing fee to one of the PROs.

Many massage therapists turn to compilation CDs they find online, only to discover that the content is repetitive or doesn't provide them with enough variety to meet the needs of their varied clientele. That's where your unique take on this soothing subgenre can create licensing opportunities for you.

If you're new to this area, try booking a massage and, while you're enjoying it, pay attention to the music you hear. Ask the massage therapist about her criteria for choosing music. Compare what you have in your own music library with what you're hearing in the field. While massage is a very eclectic art, your research into the musical needs of therapists will likely reveal some overarching rules, such as: Go easy on the nature sounds; avoid trying to license music with religious overtones; avoid music with lyrics or sing-alongs.

The massage practioners you license your music to might, in turn, help you sell CDs to their clientele. For a listing of more than 52,000 licensed massage therapists in 27 countries, go to www.amtamassage.org

Licensing Music for Resorts and Hotels

When you visit a resort or luxury hotel, you will often hear music throughout the property—be it in the lobby, poolside, in the gym and fitness center, in outdoor cabanas, or in the spa. The establishment cannot play that music without paying a licensing fee to one of the PROs. That music could be yours, if you find a way to match your style to the specific needs of the resort and manage to strike a licensing deal.

The best way to start your research is to do some legwork. Explore the more prominent hotels in your area. When you get there, walk around the property and listen. Make notes about the music you hear. Pay close attention to how the volume and style of music changes as the day moves into night. Hotels, like retail outlets, restaurants, and other mood-music-playing places, often change their playlist at certain times of the day to reflect the mood and music its clients want to be in and hear. Then, determine which places are silent. These might be good locations where your background music could eventually play.

The licensing fees that hotels and resorts must pay for the use of music vary, depending on the size of the facility and how much music is used. These businesses have arrangements with BMI and ASCAP, which regularly collect set fees.

To pursue this route, contact the manager of the specific hotel you'd like to do business with, or, in the case of a large chain or franchise, start with the brand's central corporate headquarters.

Licensing Music for Educational Purposes

Let's assume that you've written and recorded a conventional pop-sounding song that features lead vocals, some background vocals, two guitars, bass, and live drums. A few keyboard parts were also recorded, but at the last minute you decided to mute them during the song's final mix-down. Let's assume you have direct access to all of the individual parts (or "takes") that were recorded either at home or in a studio.

If there are any educational institutions or trade schools nearby that offer audio production or sound engineering courses, you might look into licensing one or more of these songs to the school's music department for a semester, offering it in "project format." This would give students who are learning the art of digital mixing, processing, or editing the chance to gain direct access to a real song and its individual instrumental and vocal parts (sometimes referred to as *stems*). They will use the song to fine-tune their mixing and editing skills. While this sounds simple, it can be a challenge for students who are relatively new to the world of audio production to locate decent songs and recordings that are available in this format. In this situation you could offer a blanket license that covers any educational, on-premises use, but doesn't include permission, without the student obtaining your written consent, to sell or distribute any of the variations or alternate mixes that he creates using your music as a foundation.

> *I have noticed that educational companies are using a ton of music. We are working with content aggregators who allow teachers and students the ability to use photos, film, and music to create multimedia as a teaching tool or as homework assignments. It's amazing to see the progression of education with all of this new media.*
>
> LARRY MILLS, Vice President, Marketing
> and Partnerships, Pump Audio

Licensing Music for DJ Remixes

The content delivered in the licensing situation described above is similar to what would also be delivered to a DJ for the purpose of producing a remix. Many DJs love the idea of having access to a song's raw data—unhindered individual parts allow for the greatest flexibility and creativity when producing a remix. Furthermore, a remix that's produced with your consent circumvents all of the problems that can go along with the use of illegal samples.

DJ and remixing agreements are most often approached as a licensing agreement, where you, the songwriter and/or copyright owner, grant permission to the DJ to modify, enhance, and/or alter the original song for the purpose of producing what becomes a derivative master recording ("DJ mix" of the song). The approach to tackling the issue of licensing fees in such cases can be addressed in more than one way—it all depends on what works for both parties.

In one scenario, you would charge nothing for licensing the song in this capacity. The time and production required for producing the remix is the DJ's responsibility. Furthermore, should it yield a very catchy remix and the DJ has agreed to play it at future club dates, doing so will be excellent promotion for your song and/or band, and best of all, it's done at no cost to you. The remix will create a new master recording of the song, and arrangements are often worked out so that royalties earned in relation to this *new* master recording (only) are shared. This arrangement has no bearing on the song itself or the original recording.

In another scenario, you would charge a licensing fee for the use of a small portion of a song's original song mix (legal sample) or perhaps one or more of its individual vocal or instrument parts (stems). The distinction is that what is produced in this case will be a new song that can be thought of as a *musical collage*. Charging a licensing fee in this situation is justified, because what comes about as a result is technically a new song—the "songwriter" just happens to have included some of your licensed content. This is conceptually similar to a movie director owning her own film, despite the fact that she licensed one of your songs for use in the soundtrack. Because the use of content was aboveboard and confirmed with a license, the director retains ownership of the movie's copyright.

On the other hand, if one opts to forego receiving any up-front licensing fee payment, doing so often happens with the contractual understanding that you become a cowriter of the new song by virtue of donating your content to the cause. The end result not only includes sampled material from whatever song you've licensed, but will more than likely include additional vocal or instrumental parts unrelated to your song, or are the result of using other samples that were licensed elsewhere from other recordings. The fee rates can vary dramatically—they might be as little as a few hundred dollars or much more. This depends on the "star power" of the players who are involved, and the value assigned to the recording.

When well-known DJs legally sample well-known songs, it isn't uncommon for record companies to charge a licensing fee that, for all intents and purposes, would be the same for licensing the entire song. So if the DJ uses a sample that is four seconds, twenty seconds, or two minutes, the same licensing fee will be charged.

Licensing an Idea

There is yet another licensing opportunity worth mentioning, and could appeal to the tech- or gear-savvy musician, as well as anyone else who has stumbled upon some novel way of improving a product design that's already in existence or has come up with an idea for a new product invention altogether. In these situations, you don't protect your idea by registering it for a copyright; rather, you file for a patent.

Over the past couple of years, I've designed and built prototypes for a number of music-based gadgets in the area of audio production. Applying for a patent is a more complicated and time-consuming process than filing a copyright registration. Being granted a patent depends on your ability to demonstrate that your idea, design, and/or invention is in fact new or unique in some way. Once this is confirmed, and you're granted a patent, you can sell your idea to a manufacturer in a buyout capacity, or should you choose, build and sell it yourself. Or, you can *license* your idea to a company that is willing and able to manufacture and distribute your product to retailers. As the product's inventor and patent owner, you are entitled to earn a commission for every unit that is then sold.

For more information on licensing ideas, visit the United States Patent and Trademark Office (www.uspto.gov).

Capitalizing on the Unexplored

When exploring uncharted territory, you're likely to deal with people with no experience addressing issues related to music clearance. Once someone expresses serious interest in using your music for a project, explain that it's advisable to draft a simple licensing agreement and that this document is merely a means of guiding the process for everyone's protection.

As you look for alternative licensing opportunities, focus your energy on situations that are the most likely candidates. When you approach the appropriate contact person, appear organized and professional. Stick to the key selling point: if they license your music, they will be purchasing a new way to expand their own marketing horizons and broaden their potential customer base. Until someone approaches them with this suggestion, it may not occur to them as an option.

It's really important to have in place a clear sense of the types of products, services, situations, customers, or concepts that are in alignment with your area of musical expertise. Some styles of music, including those that spotlight unique instruments, naturally lend themselves to specific lifestyles, cultures, and geographic locations, and can evoke mental images or learned associations. For example, if you write music for the ukulele, you might consider forming alliances with travel agencies, or stores that cater to surfing, beach clothing, or Hawaiian culture and lifestyle. Use your greatest musical strengths to your advantage by aligning with people, products, and services that will fit with your music in ways that don't sound contrived. This makes the process more inspiring. If you explore uncharted territory and create something with artistic merit in the process, you may carve out a niche of your own and corner a new market.

|||||||||||||||||||||||||||||||||||||||||||||||||||||||||||||||||||||||||||||||||||||||||||||||||||||||||||||||||||||||||||||||

CHAPTER 17

Making Money Internationally

If you've had the opportunity to travel abroad, you're probably already aware that different parts of the world have different tastes in music. A genre or style that might be considered obscure, exotic, or even out-of-date in one corner of the world can have immense popularity elsewhere. It's possible for an artist to remain relatively unknown or unappreciated in their own country, but experience a fair amount of success in other countries where their music is broadcast or publicly performed. When this happens, it generates foreign royalties, and the collection process is more complex. In this chapter, I'll discuss some issues related to licensing music internationally.

Foreign Royalties

Songwriting royalties in international markets are often a lot bigger than those paid in the U.S. There are many opportunities for licensing music for use in TV commercials, games, and many media outlets. Europe and Japan can be reasonably accessible if you put in the work. Publishers who see value in your music are likely to give you a larger advance for representing your songs since songwriting royalties can be worth a lot more overseas than in the U.S. If your song gets onto a soundtrack album in foreign markets, royalties are based on sales as opposed to a flat rate. If the album sells, you'd get a percentage of the retail price, which is usually higher than royalties in the U.S. Performance royalties are also much better in these markets than in the U.S. In many countries, your music is prohibited from being used if you don't get a fee for the synchronization license. So the market for songs in foreign markets is much more lucrative!

Many TV shows go into syndication. When this happens, exclusive broadcast rights in a given territory expire, and the ability to license broadcast rights become available. Any subsequent re-airings that occur, domestically or internationally, generate additional performance royalties for use of the musical content. As a point of distinction, international broadcasts generate foreign royalties. Depending on the exact terms of the original music licensing agreement that was used, syndication may also require payment of additional licensing fees to cover what will become an expansion of territories, options, or any other rights relevant to the situation.

International royalties are in a class of their own. In the case of performing rights organizations, they're distributed independently from domestic royalties. A partial explanation for treating domestic and foreign royalty payments independent of one another is that the process of collecting, compiling, and tabulating the required data that's used to calculate foreign royalty payments is more complicated. Each country has its own performing rights organizations (see below). There is an established system for compiling this data, which involves a network of performing rights organizations. Each country has its own rates and standards. That's why having a publishing administrator who knows foreign markets can be especially helpful in keeping track of money you're owed if you get your music licensed.

International Performing Rights Organization Affiliates

When composers, songwriters, or publishers have their music performed in a foreign country, whether on TV, radio, in a commercial, or a video game, their lack of citizenship makes claiming the royalties they're entitled to prohibitive—at least on their own. Therefore it's helpful to have support for gathering detailed information about how your music was used in royalty-earning situations so you can collect royalties for documented public performances of your music. Copyright protection makes your royalty demands enforceable. However, the extent of the protection that is afforded or acknowledged in one country versus another sometimes varies. Each country has its own individual standards and royalty rates.

In addition to the three major performing rights organizations that operate in the U.S. (ASCAP, BMI, and SESAC), there are many other performing rights organizations that represent writers and publishers who reside in other countries from around the world. They include:

Argentina (SADAIC)
Australia (APRA)
Austria (AKM)
Belgium (SABAM)
Brazil (UBC)
Britain (PRS)
Bulgaria
(MUSICAUTHOR)
Canada (SOCAN)
Chile (SCD)
Colombia (SAYCO)
Croatia (HDS)
Czech Republic (OSA)
Denmark (KODA)
Estonia (EAU)
Finland (TEOSTO)
France (SACEM)
Georgia (SAS)

Germany (GEMA)
Greece (AEPI)
Hong Kong (CASH)
Hungary (ARTISJUS)
Ireland (IMRO)
Israel (ACUM)
Italy (SIAE)
Japan (JASRAC)
Korea (KOMCA)
Lithuania (LATGA-A)
Malaysia (MACP)
Mexico (SACM)
Netherlands (BUMA)
Norway (TONO)
Panama (SPAC)
Peru (APDAYC)
Philippines (FILSCAP)
Poland (ZAIKS)

Romania (UCMR)
Russia (RAO)
Serbia (SOKOJ)
Singapore (COMPASS)
Slovakia (SOZA)
South Africa (SAMRO)
Spain (SGAE)
Sweden (STIM)
Switzerland (SUISA)
Taiwan (MUST)
Thailand (MCT)
Trinidad & Tobago
(COTT)
Ukraine (UACRR)
Uruguay (AGADU)
Venezuela (SACVEN)

A performing rights organization for any given country is the entity that pursues and collects annual licensing fees from any business establishment within its own borders. Their business involves the use of music that's written or published by either their own members or those who belong to affiliate performing rights organizations. The licensing fees are collected from television networks, radio stations, clubs, restaurants, and down the line. They are all deposited in a trust account. A portion of this money is used to keep the PRO operational and is allocated to pay domestic royalties that are distributed to its members. In addition, a percentage of this royalty pool is forwarded to foreign PROs. They all have preexisting agreements established for the purpose of working together as partners or affiliates.

Cue sheet submissions and radio playlist data are used to verify and determine the amount that each affiliate's members have earned in royalty credits over the course of a given payment period. Once it's calculated, the net sum is forwarded to any credited affiliate PRO. Upon receiving these payments, the affiliate PRO in turn distributes this money to their own writers and publishers under the definition of international performance royalties. Affiliate performing rights organizations reciprocate the courtesy. They do accounting for any payments that are owed to songwriters belonging to affiliates in other countries and perform similar administrative duties related to allocating the appropriate percentages of licensing fees collected in their country for uses of music by these foreign songwriters.

How Royalties Get Collected

The ability of a performing rights organization to successfully collect licensing fees depends on its political clout, the number of members it represents, the legislative support it gets, the political climate of the country, and its reverence for copyright laws. All of these factors, in addition to their tax structures, influence the actual dollar amount you'll be paid for any royalties earned in a foreign country annually. No two PROs in different countries address all of these factors the same and some allocate higher royalty rates than others.

The system of data sharing, licensing fee exchange, and subsequent royalty distribution that transpires between performing rights organizations is what allows an American composer to earn performance royalties if his music is used for a movie and ends up being broadcast on television networks or shown in theaters abroad. Any songwriter that belongs to one of the affiliates that cooperate to pay each other's members can earn royalties from having their licensed music aired in any of these markets.

> *Collecting foreign royalties can definitely be a challenge for a composer. It is difficult enough keeping track of domestic royalties let alone figuring out if you have been paid correctly for royalties generated outside of the U.S. An administrator can most certainly help with this. As with domestic societies, administrators develop relationships with key contacts at all foreign societies or establish relationships with other publishers (subpublishers) in foreign territories to help administer copyrights on their behalf. These are very important relationships that are key in dealing with language*

barriers and differences in system procedures at the various foreign PROs. An administrator gathers and submits placement information to its foreign partners and orchestrates collection and back-claiming of royalties that can otherwise go uncollected.

MEGAN HALDEMAN, Copyright Management/
Royalty Accounting, pigFACTORY

A music licensing agreement can include some restrictions about which territories the agreement covers. It might indicate that it's only for North America or Australia, or the world except for specified territories. In the latter case, additional synchronization and/or master fee payments will be required if the scope of territories covered by the agreement increases. For a production company to take advantage of syndication opportunities for a series or TV film in parts of the world not included in the original agreement, they must renegotiate with you for those territories.

As you might imagine, keeping close tabs on each use of a piece of music on an international basis is a formidable undertaking. Inefficiency or inadvertent miscommunication that comes as a result of language barriers or other cultural issues paves the way for a process that some feel is prone to error and lends itself to the kind of oversight that isn't necessarily obvious, easily identifiable, or simple to correct retroactively. Odds are that an uncontested oversight or credit omission will slip under the radar.

I am truly amazed and impressed with the services that performing rights organizations provide. There is little doubt that the vast majority of artists and music publishers would be at a loss without them. I've found that should an occasional mistake or omission happen, performing rights organizations are usually more than willing to assist in the process of correcting it. However, getting these situations straightened out does require a certain burden of proof. It's to your advantage to have your paperwork prepared before notifying your PRO. That includes a rundown of the film, series, episode, airdates, production company, and any other specifics about the project. If the issue stems from a cue sheet that never was forwarded, you will have to provide that information.

Unless you primarily operate as a music publisher, as an artist, it's advisable to allow your PRO and their international affiliates to handle and address the issues of foreign royalty collections. It's simply too complicated to pursue on your own. The cost of doing all that's necessary isn't the best use of your time. If you have a significant amount of music that's getting performed internationally as a result of licensing agreements for TV shows or films that are now in international syndication, you may need help collecting and administrating your foreign income. At that point it's worth considering working with a company that specializes in providing its clients with international administration services. Some publishing companies offer this service as an additional option. As I said in Chapter 2, there are publishing administrators that review deals, file registrations, address paperwork, forward notices, collect fees, and perform other administrative tasks. Handling the foreign administration of your licensing business is most often done by one or more of the following:

- the songwriter's performing rights organization (PRO) and affiliates
- a songwriter's publisher
- publishing administrators

By agreeing to let a publishing company handle foreign administration for you, you assign them the right to pursue international royalty and licensing fees on your behalf. In this capacity, administration service providers and performing rights organizations perform similar functions. They pursue, collect, and allocate domestic or international royalty payments to their clients/members. Each deducts an agreed-upon commission rate for whatever fees they collect. In addition, both administration services and PROs rely on the participation and back-and-forth cooperation of an established network of international affiliates and partner companies.

The incentive and claim that administration companies typically give for why you should use one is that they have a more effective ability to perform these services and duties on your behalf than you'd get from relying solely on your PRO. Administrators represent far fewer clients and have closer and more personal ties with their international affiliates, which they say results in higher annual international royalty payments to their clients compared to that from a PRO on an annual basis. Because administrators work on a commission, they have an added incentive to leave no stone unturned.

This being said, administrative service providers are more prone to work with clients who've already had their music licensed and therefore have enough international performances that have either already occurred, or will occur in the near future, to make this responsibility worth their while. They may not be as beneficial to someone who isn't bringing in a lot of royalties.

Many music publishers work with a network of *subpublishers*. These are foreign publishing affiliates who provide representation and administration for a music publisher within a specific region/territory. Publishers assign to them administration rights and privileges within that territory/nation. Subpublishers address issues related to negotiating licensing deals, collecting payments, and performing administration duties for the song catalogs they represent within the territory assigned. The incentive and assumption behind these arrangements is that a subpublisher is better equipped and can more effectively perform the role of a publisher in a country where they speak the language fluently, and understand the culture, rules, and proper codes of conduct for doing business. Relatively speaking, they are on location and more accessible for the purpose of negotiating contractual terms or following up on loose ends for deals that are already in the works. Logically, since they work in the foreign country, they know where to look for money and whom to speak with regarding any issues related to your royalties.

> Get in touch with a publishing company that has experience licensing music and collecting the royalties that will be generated by the use. You can ask questions and they will be able to estimate what kind of royalties might be outstanding and collectible.
>
> MEGAN HALDEMAN, Copyright Management/
> Royalty Accounting, pigFACTORY

The rules, standards, and conditions that generate domestic performance royalties compared to those that apply for international performance royalties are not necessarily the same. Depending on the circumstances, these subtle distinctions may not be trivial. For example, an American film composer isn't entitled to royalties for domestic theatrical performances (cinema). However, a number of foreign PROs pay royalties for cinema performances. International royalties are paid based on all song titles that are included in an *annual report*. This is a breakdown of the performance location, methods of public performance, and royalty amount that is being credited. The types of performances are addressed separately (radio, TV, TV film/series, and, in some cases, cinema). The time lapse from the actual performance date to the day when a royalty statement based on this credit is forwarded can be one to two years or longer.

International Royalties for Performing Artists

Most of this discussion about PROs and royalty allocations is related to publishers and songwriters. However, in some foreign markets, artists who are featured on a recording, even if they weren't contributing songwriters, are recognized for their contribution, too. Many artists perform songs (whether for a live show or to create a studio recording) they haven't actually written. This is important to be aware of, because there's a classification system that provides lines of distinction when it comes to entitlement, rights, and royalties paid. Young bands or demo singers frequently overlook these details until the last minute, particularly if they haven't had some prior experience with getting paid royalties for different types of public musical performances and broadcasts.

In some cases, participating in a recording can entitle the performer, in addition to the writer and publisher, to receive royalty payments, for a song that features them as the artist, once that song is regularly broadcast or performed publicly in other countries. This is partially why the process of registering song titles with a performing rights organization includes providing the names of the performers. However, in order to be credited as a performer due royalty payments, you're required to document that one or more public performances or broadcasts occurred in the foreign nations that acknowledge allocating royalties to performing artists in addition to writers and publishers. The performing artist must be a member of a performing rights organization and might need to work with an administrator that has both solid ties to established affiliates in those countries and the ability to collect on any outstanding royalties.

If you're a singer who regularly does work-for-hire demo gigs, always request that your name be included in the credits as a performing artist for any song you sing on. That includes all or partial portions of the performances that you recorded as part of the agreement. Should the song eventually be broadcast in foreign countries with PROs that pay royalties to performing artists, the process of verifying your participation will be easier if your name shows up in the credits. If you know the recordings are in other countries, contact the performing rights organizations in your country and explain your situation. Tell them the countries that either have, or are most likely going to publicly perform/broadcast recordings that feature you as a performing artist. Do some research and join the PRO that seems best qualified to address the specifics of your circumstances or consider getting administration services from a company with well-established affiliates in the countries/territories that specifically apply to your situation.

Pursuing royalty credits retroactively can be done, but, for you to be credited for a performance, you need to go after your royalties within a certain window of time from the date when the first international broadcast occurred. Making the case requires having some information at your fingertips and getting this together in a way that's organized and supports your claim will most likely require doing some homework. The more accurate and detailed the information that you're able to provide when first contacting your PRO, the better your chances will be of successfully resolving issues that stem from oversight, credit omission, or administrative error.

Tapping into Foreign Licensing Opportunities

Some people find a publisher in a foreign market to help them license songs. But this isn't any easier than finding a label deal. Unless you have songs that have been used in ways that they recognize, cold calling will be tedious. But people in international markets can be more accessible. If you're polite and persistent, your music has a chance of being listened to and considered for representation. If you make any contacts overseas, ask if they can refer you to someone else. Since most European countries are small, people in the song business tend to know each other. If you can create some sort of buzz around your music, there's a better chance that a publisher will pay attention.

Foreign markets boast a variety of publishers and companies that represent songs for licensing opportunities. The Internet makes it much easier to tap into them. Someone in Europe can access your MySpace page or website just as easily as someone in the U.S. or Canada. So many of the ways I recommended for approaching people for domestic licensing also apply to companies in other countries. Some of the directories mentioned in Chapter 9 also list some publishers in other countries. There are also directories for overseas markets. You can search online for publishers or companies that offer licensing services.

A great, but expensive way to make contacts is to attend one of the big international music business conferences—MIDEM and Popkomm (more below). SXSW (South By Southwest), a conference held in Austin, Texas, every March, attracts a lot of people from other countries. It's huge and can be hard to find people but the networking possibilities can be rewarding. If you attend, see if there are showcases for bands from other countries and go to them. You can make some good contacts! As you network, ask everyone you meet if they have any advice for reaching people who represent music for licensing purposes. If you meet artists from other countries, tap into their resources, too. Try to connect with songwriters who live in overseas markets on social networking sites. Bebo (www.bebo.com) and hi5 (www.hi5.com) are good ones for the European market and other foreign countries. Orkut (www.orkut.com) targets the South American and Indian market. Search for others that are specific to the countries you'd like to pursue opportunities in.

When you call or e-mail a potential publisher or representative, be polite and professional. Be aware of the time difference in other countries before you call. Keep your communication short. People tend to be more polite in foreign markets so you might at least get a reply or someone might talk to you. If you have any, give a brief overview of your credits. Success in the U.S. can make someone check your music out. Any ammo you can offer can pique their interest in hearing your music. If you're an indie artist, a publisher might also want to work with you if you show potential to attract a record label to license your album for release in that territory.

International Showcase: The Music Business Guide is considered the bible by some for finding the contacts for international professionals in the music industry. It covers England, and parts of Europe, South America, South Africa, Australia, and Japan. Besides listing record companies, artist managers, producers, venues, promoters, booking agents, tour support services, recording studios, festival organizers, and other kinds of professionals, it also includes music publishers. It's expensive, but if you plan to pursue international markets, it can be a good investment. It can be ordered through the Music Business Registry (www.musicregistry.com).

All countries have licensing opportunities for TV, film, video games, advertising, and everything else that I've discussed in other chapters. Sometimes they may find you on MySpace, CDBaby (www.cdbaby.com), or sites like Ricall or Pump Audio. Developing relationships can be key to opening doors to more opportunities. You can search for companies online. There are also a lot of music libraries that need music. They work similarly to the ones discussed in Chapter 1. If you do a search on music libraries and put in specific countries, you'll find many to pitch your music to. If you do get a deal, make sure you have a good entertainment attorney—one who is very familiar with international markets—handle the negotiations and review the agreements.

MIDEM and Popkomm

MIDEM (www.MIDEM.com) is an international music conference held every year at the end of January in Cannes, France. It's considered the largest gathering of music industry professionals from around the world. Often the top brass from companies are there—prepared to deal with other participants who do serious business. The registration fee is much higher than any other conference. Cannes is one of the most expensive cities in the world to stay in. Getting there is more expensive than flying to a major city and the trip from the airport is a long, expensive ride. But if the cost doesn't discourage you, this conference will give you the potential to network with many of the eight to nine thousand movers and shakers from the music industry that attend. They come from all countries in all areas of the music industry.

Attending MIDEM can be extremely overwhelming. There's an exhibit hall that has so many booths it can take days to get through them all. All sorts of music-related companies have one. There are also panels on a variety of very current topics. If you go to one related to licensing, you might make some good contacts in the audience alone. People come to MIDEM to do serious business. The main event takes place in the Palais, but many of the meetings are held in other places. Wherever you look in hotel lobbies, restaurants, and outdoors, people are sitting and talking business. They know it's an opportunity to meet with major players from all over the world so it's best to take full advantage. At night there are bars for schmoozing and clubs for hearing live music and more networking.

If you go to MIDEM, the best way not to waste your money is to make a plan of attack months before. Going on the fly is a bad idea. Appointments for the days of MIDEM are booked weeks or months before it starts. Register in the fall, before the early-bird rate ends so you pay as little as possible. Book your hotel then, too, so you can get into one of the cheaper rooms if your budget is tight. Once you register, you get access to their online directory. Since many of the big companies register early, their info will be in the MIDEM directory. The earlier you contact people, the better your chance of getting appointments. Be very professional when you do. Ask if you can set up a meeting. Say as little as possible, unless they ask what it's about. The online database allows you to search for people in a variety of ways—by the company type, genre, country–and any combination thereof. When you arrive you'll get a huge book with all the contacts at the conference. With eight thousand to nine thousand contacts, this directory is very valuable to have when you get home.

Given the time difference, it can take a bit to regain your equilibrium. Be prepared. Rent an international cell phone to use during MIDEM since you'll be running around all day. Calling is the best way to hook up with people, especially when you're meeting someone you've never seen before for an appointment and it's packed. People come home from MIDEM with enough business cards to keep them busy with follow-ups for months, if not longer. Bring lots of business cards and samples of your music. Have a link on your card where people can go to access it online. People walk around with portable playback equipment and listen on the spot. If you ship anything over, do it way in advance and put a very small value on it or you'll pay high taxes to receive it.

Popkomm (www.popkomm.de) takes place in Berlin, Germany, in September. While MIDEM has a very businesslike atmosphere, Popkomm is a more casual alternative. While there's a conference with lots of business going on, there's a bigger emphasis on the actual music. There are a number of panels on a variety of topics related to the music business and technology. The film and game industries also participate, so it's a great opportunity to make contacts for licensing in those areas. But there's also a great club festival. Music is played in all the venues and in outdoor settings. Popkomm allows you to make many international contacts and learn more about the music industry in other countries. It's cheaper then going to MIDEM and known to be a lot more fun because of the emphasis on live music. Whereas at MIDEM people are dressed in more corporate attire, at Popkomm people dress down. Your approach to Popkomm should be similar to how you prepare for MIDEM. Just remember, above all: try to make appointments beforehand!

||||||||||||||||||||||||||||||||||||||||||||||||||||||||||||||||||||||||||||||||||||||||||||||||||||||||||||||||||||||||||||||||||||

CHAPTER 18

Frequently Asked Questions

The vast and complicated fields of licensing, songwriting, and marketing raise a ton of questions for the average musician. In my travels and teaching, I've found that the same concerns constantly pop up. I've gathered together some of the questions I've been asked the most, many of which emphasize some of the points I've discussed earlier in this book.

Q: Should I join a PRO before or after my songs are getting broadcast or performed?

I would suggest taking care of this beforehand. This way, when your songs are first licensed, information about them, entitled parties, and PRO affiliations are all identified and included as part of the initial clearance paperwork. The advantage is that clarifying all this information from the very beginning increases the likelihood that this same information will end up appearing on cue sheets and playlists in the future.

Q: Haven't they found a better way to track performances?

There's a new tracking technology called *digital fingerprinting* that will overhaul this entire process in the near future. It's just a matter of when. All digital audio files (in theory) have what is in essence their own unique signature or digital fingerprint. Signals that are transmitted from TV networks, cable stations, radio stations, and Internet broadcasts will be monitored and scanned in order to identify the music content. This technology is now advanced enough to identify a music cue that's used in either a foreground or background capacity. Furthermore, it can identify song titles by scanning short excerpts or the entire file. In theory, this technology should greatly reduce the number of inaccurate royalty statements that are the result of cue sheets containing mistakes due to human error.

Q: Does a "poor man's copyright" protect my song?

Many musicians believe that sending a copy of their own work to themselves, which is sometimes referred to as a "poor man's copyright," will protect their songs. It's assumed that if they don't open it when it arrives, the postmark is the proof that they had the song at least by that date. But there's no provision in copyright law that offers this kind of protection, so it's not a substitute for registration. The legitimacy and scope of protection offered by the poor man's copyright can't compare to the more legitimate protection offered by actually registering songs and/or recordings with the Library of Congress.

In the event that two parties are in a dispute involving copyright ownership of a song, the law tends to favor and show partiality to whoever registered the copyright first. The ability to enforce copyright protection has its greatest potential when any such claim or defense can be supported and substantiated by an official document that's on public record and has been stamped with the date it was received. While copyright begins the moment of origination and continues throughout the process of creation, filing copyright registration creates an official public record that, when in doubt, serves as proof that a copy of the song existed at least since the date of registration. A poor man's copyright won't do that.

Q: How much can I legally sample from another record? I've heard that it's legal if it's twenty seconds or less.

This is one of the most commonly asked questions by artists who do hip-hop, techno, or urban music. Since sampling has been so prevalent, many think it's okay to just use a little. But it's not. When you lift something off of someone else's copyrighted sound recording—as little as just a single note—it's still copyright infringement if someone can prove it came from his or her recording. Of course, people do get away with it. But technology keeps getting more sophisticated. You can be sued by the person who owns the master recording and also have to pay money to the publisher of the song you're using in yours.

It's become an urban myth that you can use a certain amount of seconds from another recording legally. When hip-hop first became popular, there was a bit more courtesy involved and people got permission, or were excused, for sampling. No more! Since it's a source of money for the record label, they no longer let illegal sampling slide. Be very careful. Sampling can be a very expensive risk. Plus, as I explained earlier, if a music supervisor even suspects that you have an illegal sample, your music will not be used for licensing purposes.

Q: If I have no publishing company behind my music, how do I collect the "publisher's shares" when my songs earn them?

You should open your own publishing company. Forming a publishing company for the sake of overseeing administration chores and responsibilities as they apply to your own copyrights is fairly straightforward. If you're self-published and have music being licensed for broadcast, becoming a member of a performing rights organization as a publisher, which is separate from a songwriter membership, allows you to collect the publisher's share of any performance royalties that are generated from song placements on television, radio, etc. You can open one through whichever performing rights organization you belong to. Each one has different procedures but it begins with finding a name that isn't being used. ASCAP, BMI, or SESAC will help you check.

Once you have a name, apply as a publisher. After you're approved, register any songs you control and your PRO will take care of collecting the royalties on your behalf. You should register your publishing company as a business so you can open a bank account once you start getting checks. They won't pay those royalties to an individual songwriter. You can form a corporation or *d/b/a* ("doing business as" a sole proprietor) certificate from your local county clerk's office and then open a dedicated business banking account for the publishing company.

Q: How is it possible that some television networks don't pay up-front synch/master licensing fees, yet may still turn out to be profitable for an artist?

There are a few networks that mostly offer what are known as *gratis use blanket licenses*. This arrangement is used to clear the bulk of music that winds up appearing in the programming. It's the equivalent of entering a synch/master licensing agreement where you agree to waive any up-front payments in exchange for granting the license. As already mentioned, and because this gratis license pertains to a television show, the door that still remains open for a potential revenue stream comes in the form of performance royalties rather than licensing fees. If your song is included on a show that airs repeatedly or ends up broadcasting internationally for a period of time, the performance royalty earning potential is often what justifies waiving what would likely be nominal up-front fees to begin with.

The key distinction in this case is that the gratis license being issued here involves TV transmission and/or a broadcast, and it qualifies it for a secondary revenue steam (back-end profits). The royalties are independent of whatever licensing fees are paid or, in this case, waived on the front end. In contrast, granting a gratis license for a project that will only be shown in some movie theaters is equivalent to allowing your music to be used for free, as no performance royalties will be involved.

Q: What is MTV's protocol in regard to notifying you when they use/place your song?

There isn't any protocol. Occasionally, you might receive a courtesy notification, depending on your relationship with a show's music supervisor and their schedule. For the most part, MTV primarily uses music from an assortment of collections, all of which is precleared via blanket licensing agreements the network has with music publishers and record companies. When you consider the amount of music that is used in their programming, it is easy to imagine the time requirements and inefficiency that would result from notifying everybody when their song is used. The blanket license has already provided them with the necessary preclearance and permission to use and include the song while the episode is being edited and assembled, and by design, agreements of this type don't usually require or mandate that prior notification be given when a song gets placed. However, when the show airs, all the relevant information is logged onto a cue sheet, and copies are eventually forwarded to the entitled party's performing rights organization. When you're dealing with blanket license situations, receiving confirmations or being notified as to when, where, and how your music was placed, especially prior to airdate, is a courtesy, not a requirement.

Q: Will I ever know before an airdate that my song will appear in a TV show?

In the case of a single song that requires synch/master licensing agreements, then in theory, yes. These licenses are used in situations that involve placing a single song in a single episode of a network television series. This deal might be brokered by you directly, or a rep to whom you've granted the right to pitch your songs will be notified. Contact involves a brief conversation with the show's music supervisor, who will a) reconfirm that any necessary clearance rights are indeed still available, b) outline what options need to be included as part of the licensing agreement, and c) accept, negotiate, or decline the proposed licensing fees. Assuming that a marketing company is the party involved with these direct discussions, once a tentative verbal agreement is reached with the show's supervisor, the marketing company often contacts the artist to get the final go-ahead and the agreement to the licensing fee that's been offered. When the artist accepts the offer, the marketing company gives a final confirmation to the music supervisor. From there, contracts are faxed and signed and payments are forwarded accordingly.

Q: In the case of a blanket license that covers the use of my music for a number of different shows, will I be provided with a copy of a cue sheet for songs they've used and what TV show it went in?

Receiving a copy of a cue sheet probably won't happen on its own in these situations, unless specifically mandated by your licensing agreement. If you need a copy, you can contact the TV network or the show's production company and one will probably be forwarded to you without too much fuss, assuming it's already available. Cue sheets are ultimately prepared for the performing rights organizations.

Q: Surely we're not obligated to watch every TV show that uses a ton of blanket licensed music in the hopes of catching one of our songs to know if it's used?

Of course not! I've been amazed at how many times I discovered something I'd written featured on a television show, by accident. It's happened while I've flipped through stations, or a friend has told me about it, or months later, the information appeared on an ASCAP statement. A bummer with giving a blanket is that notification about exactly how or where your music gets used probably won't be communicated to you with any urgency. Of course, you can ask for a clause in the agreement that requires such notification, but pushing too hard may become a hassle for some. It's done this way out of necessity.

Consider the time it would take to notify an artist each time a song is slated for inclusion on a TV show. If you had to send thirty e-mails on a busy workday, it's unlikely you'd want to.

Q: When and why is modifying a preexisting song a useful option?

The ability to remix, modify, or enhance a preexisting audio track is useful in instances where a certain piece of music from our collection renders the right feel for a given scene or possibly the project at large. Should this happen, it is possible to produce additional variations and alternate mixes of the original track, and these variations and alternate mixes can make for some very useful cues elsewhere in the project. The incentive behind all of this is to establish a recurring musical device, and has been a historically effective method for establishing a global sense of continuity for a movie project.

Q: What type of music did they use in shows like *The Sopranos*? I'm talking about the composed music, not the occasional song with lyrics that they throw in every once in a while.

I was quite a *Sopranos* fan. A few years ago, I bought all the DVDs of the show and watched four or five episodes at a time. In doing so I made a few observations about the use of music. The theme song is very distinctive, and at this point, conjures imagery that is one and the same with the show itself. This may explain why it's so commonly referenced as a benchmark in music requests that are in search of a soundalike theme song for some new series that has a similar character. I think what makes this theme song so effective is its vibe. It has gritty vocals and a distinctly memorable lyric—"You woke up this morning/Got yourself a gun." That says it all. People remember it.

There's very little underscore in this series. This is one of the few shows I can think of that embraces a very powerful sonic device—silence! The audio portion of many scenes features long stretches of nothing but conversation and environmental ambience that comfortably intersperses moments of silence in between. It renders an almost 1970s-like vibe in this regard. When music is used in a scene, it really stands out. Typical applications include a) bar rock in strip clubs, b) traditional Italian songs/arias in restaurants, or c) a closing feature song that usually uses music that's considered a classic (early Rod Stewart for example).

Q: Why are some music requests vague?

There are instances when it's clear that music will be needed to provide some magic or excitement for a particular TV spot or advertisement clip. But when the request goes out, it still isn't clear exactly what the right musical direction will eventually be. Perhaps the visual imagery involved easily lends itself to a wide range of musical styles, or any music that has already been suggested and/or tested isn't working. The selection process in these instances is usually guided by some trial and error. A group of people debate until they reach a final decision. The power of suggestion can have considerable influence on the selection process. Different members of the team may have different opinions. So they wait to see what comes in and stands out as an option that could work.

||||||||||||||||||||||||||||||||||||||||||||||||||||||||||||||||||||||||||||||||||||||||||||||||||||||||||||||||||||||||||||||||||

CHAPTER 19

Advice from the Pros

These days, licensing music is a process that gets you in the game. In doing so, you become a participant in the fabric of a larger community, and contribute to that vast network that is the entertainment industry. When you try to license your music, you will explore and pursue viable opportunities that—should you land deals—can enable you *to keep making music*. I have always felt that the greatest satisfaction in music isn't reaching a career apex where you can say, "I've made it," but rather, to have the luxury and desire to continue doing it.

I've asked many of the pros who have shared their wisdom throughout this book to give their best advice for this chapter. Here's what they had to say.

> *As a musician, your job is to play music. As a successful musician your job is to play music and be a good businessperson. There are many musicians who hole themselves up in a studio somewhere or play gigs to small crowds and hardly anyone ever gets to hear their songs. There needs to be a balance between writing, playing, and performing music and self-promotion, networking, and searching for new opportunities to showcase your songs. All music supervisors need to continually find fresh new music to present to their projects. They are generally friendly and willing to check your stuff out. If possible, try to get them to go to your MySpace site or other Web place where they can instantly listen to something of yours right then and there while you're on the phone with them so as to not get forgotten after they hang up.*
>
> BRENT KIDWELL, Freelance Music Supervisor
> (MTV Networks, E! True Hollywood Story,
> numerous other TV series and feature films)

Always be driven by your passion to create music. Create as much as possible. A quality body of work that has range will never work against you.

BARRY COLE, Music Supervisor on over
seventy films, SPOT

Know as many people as you possibly can. It's usually more about the people you know than about the music you create. Get a publisher who's going to work for you, who's going to be a fan and promote your music.

DAVE PETTIGREW, Senior Vice President, Strategic Marketing,
and Head of Advertising and Games, Warner/Chappell Music

The most important thing about getting music licensed is being in the right place at the right time. That doesn't mean dumb luck, however, it means you need to hustle! You need to meet people and get out to where professionals are. Find out what movies are in production and find out who is working on them. Find a name and find an e-mail. Make a call. Go to sets. Knock on doors. Do gumshoe detective work. You have nothing to lose by badgering people. Don't be shy. Also, get honest feedback from your friends about your music. Is it good enough to license? What kind of production would be interested in it?

RAMSAY ADAMS, Music Supervisor for film
and television

I think that musicians need to think outside the "boom-box" and be willing to take some chances when writing and recording their riffs, lyrics, and melodies so that whatever they come up with sounds like it's their own.

GRANT MONREAN, Videographer, Editor, Producer,
and Owner, Monrean Multimedia

Be prepared to do it yourself. Even if you work with a third party, do it yourself. It's hard work. You have to buckle down and do it yourself.

MICHAEL AIKEN, Managing Director,
Spring, LLC, a music marketing company

If you'd like to have your music used for pay, the Internet has created a market never seen before in the history of intellectual properties be it for music, art, photos, or video. Anyone can build a site and upload their content that they would like to sell in an easily navigated fashion on a professional website. But then—it's all about the marketing of the site, just like any other product. Your website, which is loaded with content for sale, has to be brought to the attention of the users of that element. You can't sell the world's best mousetrap if nobody knows about it, so do marketing, marketing, marketing. Take out ads in production periodicals and on websites. Sending out personalized letters to studios and producers listed in various places on the Internet is how music has been brought to my attention by savvy guerilla marketing music producers. Network, give it away for free, cold call—after you've produced it. It's all about selling it, and to sell it you have to find the users of your product/service just like any other salesperson. You can make it, but can you sell it?

DAVE DEMAIO, Director, Editor, and
Videographer, Full Speed TV Productions

Get it out to music supervisors and young filmmakers! These days, there are so many online venues to reach filmmakers directly that there's no excuse for sitting on your music. Set up accounts with MySpace, Facebook, and the myriad of other services and reach out. Other useful resources are the preproduction listings at Variety, Hollywood Reporter, *and* IMDB. *Some of them even list the production office addresses!*

SEAN FERNALD, Producer/Music Supervisor,
3Mac Studios

Here are the paths that an artist should consider. Start by assessing the landscape of supervisors and music production companies and choose the best fit. Sending music directly to a supervisor means you've reached a gatekeeper, but your music is also stacked among dozens of other submissions from that week alone. Sending music to a licensing house means you'll have an ally in the industry, but understand that each broker will have penetration into different markets; generally speaking, Los Angeles–based brokers are heavier on television shows while New York City–based brokers are heavier on advertising work. Once you've found good people that you would enjoy working with, you'll need to sign a basic contract—ask for nonexclusivity so that you can work with different people in different markets, but if you sign over exclusive rights make sure you're comfortable with the finder's fee/percentage and that you'll be a priority for them. As you continue, take an active role in the promotion of your music and update your new partners with news, tour dates, and any other noteworthy information that will help them in your shared cause. Most of all, keep your expectations in check—finding that perfect fit for your music could take a lifetime.

ALEX MOULTON, Founder and creative
force behind Expansion Team

The advice I give to all musicians is to get your music as many places as possible, and be as proactive as possible. This is true with hitting the road and playing shows, as much as it is for submitting your music to radio stations, online services, and licensors. It's your career and waiting around to get discovered doesn't work. Just having a MySpace page won't necessarily get your music in Grey's Anatomy. Companies like Pump Audio are great outlets, and all you have to do is submit. It only takes a minute and even if it takes awhile to get paid or placed, so what. As a friend of mine likes to say, "You're not paying for parking." Just ask the artists who submitted to Pump Audio six or seven years ago when we were putting ads in music magazines. Some of them are making over $100,000 a year.

LARRY MILLS, Vice President, Marketing
and Partnerships, Pump Audio

The first step is the most obvious, and the most difficult: make certain that the music you are offering is unique, special, an artistic statement in its own right, and that it is well produced and recorded. Because of the Web (thank you, MySpace!), literally thousands of musicians and composers have emerged from the shadows to share their music with the world. Only the best will be really heard.

LYLE GREENFIELD, Founder and President,
Bang Music

You've got to be patient and true to yourself. If you don't know who you are, why would someone else want to work with you? A lot of people, unfortunately, will not have the success that they think they deserve and their music is worthy of. Out of desperation, they reach out to film and TV, saying that it's good for a TV show. Step back and really listen to yourself and your music to see if you really have a shot.

ED RAZZANO, Vice President, Business
Development (North America), Ricall

Successful composers and songwriters have the same qualities as any successful businessperson: persistence, the ability to play the field (i.e., by not making exclusive arrangements with publishers on one-off license opportunities), and, in the case of songwriters, the skill to carefully choose cowriters who themselves have their own resources—whether as producers or via relationships with artists or other producers. Doubling up on the odds is never a bad thing.

PETER M. THALL, Esq., author of *What They'll
Never Tell You About the Music Business, Revised
and Updated Edition* (Billboard Books)

Keep working on your music as hard as you can and don't be shy about performing or handing it out. Don't necessarily just play one format or style and always follow up with different types of music to show a range. It is incredibly important to never ignore college-area performances and college radio because that represents the cutting edge in discovering new music, new fans, new audiences, new filmmakers. In the same way, I think that concerns about budget and fees are irrelevant. Get your music seen; get it up on the screen.

CARLTON BUSH JR., Filmmaker

The best advice I can give is to network and to try to develop relationships and to have an understanding of how those opportunities are created.

RANDY GRIMMETT, Senior Vice President,
Domestic Membership, ASCAP

Learn about what's involved in licensing a song. Understand that there are two licenses to clear, the song (writing/publishing) and the master (the recording), and if you control "both sides" (your independent CD of all original material) you are more attractive to a music supervisor. Research who you are pitching to, so that you are pitching your material to the right supervisor (don't waste your time or theirs) and be clear on what you control. If you control both sides, promote that fact in your cover letter! Music supervisors are looking for easy-to-clear songs. Be prepared. Have a lawyer or licensing agent on call to help you negotiate terms when you get called for a placement. You must be able to come to terms ASAP, as there is no time to waste! There are several very good independent licensing companies that actively look for independent situations like I've described above (self-owned) and there are more opportunities for independent artists than ever. Self-owned product is used very often in placements because they are less expensive, and often will fill the bill. But they must be easy to clear.

LINDA LORENCE CRITELLI, Vice President,
Writer/Publisher Relations, SESAC

Activate your music in culture—when people license music they are also tapping into authenticity for their brand.

Q Department, a music and
sound design initiative

Look for music licensing companies that do nonexclusive agreements. This way you're not tied to one company. You can have many companies pitching your songs at the same time.

MIKE ELL, Director of TV/Film Licensing,
Song and Film

Be sure the production quality you send out is top-notch. Look into joining up with a music library to increase your exposure. Build a working list of music supervisors and follow up with them on current projects.

ADAM SWART, Music Supervisor,
35Sound

Acknowledgments

Thank you to everyone who provided me with their moral support, time, advice, and encouragement throughout the process of writing this book. I wouldn't have been able to do it without you. And thank you to all of the people who have provided me with inspiration and positive guidance, and have generously shared their vast knowledge over the years. I love you all. These include my family, friends, teachers, bandmates, fellow musicians, coworkers, and business partners.

Special thanks to my beautiful wife, Susan, and our sons, Rocco and Oliver, for all of their unwavering support and understanding throughout this project. Also, thanks to my brother, Dr. Jared Wilsey; my mother, Chris Wilsey; my sisters, Elissa and Jennica Wilsey; Shane and Melissa Stineford; Dean Dufresne; Scott Merlino (1971–2009); Peter Schorr; Rob Lipari; Tim Budney; Mike Gray; Dev Napoli; Eric J. Logan; Dave Cole; Keven Atteniese; Phil Vassil; Steve Bonacio; Dave Diamond; Patrick Klein; Giovanni Fusco; Frank Walsh; Dr. Alex Pevsner; Tin Pan Alley Studios; MTV; Keatly and Megan Haldeman; Steve Secci; Mike Ell; Sam "Bodi" Bodenheimer; friends, staff, and/ or former teachers at University of California at Irvine, IVC, the Manhattan School of Music, the Juilliard School, Hunter College, and Oneonta High School; Alan Terricciano; Chris Dobrian; Bernard Gilmore; Dennis and Kristina Turechek; Jim Adams; Alan Herrington; Doug Decker; Fred and Ruth Cleveland; Janet Nepkie; Jim and Carol Ross; Bob, Mindy, and Casey Stineford; Terry and Kevin Molinari; Rocco and A.P. Molinari and family; Bill, Cord, and Clay Pereira and family; Herb and Irma West; Bill and Patty Wilsey and family; Sarah Mattea; Susan MacEachron; Engine Entertainment; Thurston Smith; Todd Wade; Linda Palmer; Tony Gimble; Peggy O'Brien; Michelle Bayer; Rich Hardesty; Julissa Aguirre; Claudia Johnson; Andrew Herrington;

Dave Rosenberg; Mitch Axene; Matt Nichols; and all the other musicians I've worked with over the years. Special thanks to Gary Sunshine, Amy Vinchesi, Robert Wolff, Crown Publishing Group, and you!!

Another very special thanks goes to the people who work in music licensing and contributed their input to the book. For your reference as you read their advice, I've included them in alphabetical order, with a little about who each one is. Thanks to all of them for their gracious input!

Ramsay Adams is a film and television music supervisor and cofounder of the Music Supervisors, a music supervision services company. He's worked as a music supervisor for Fox News Channel and many award-winning films including *Heights, Justice,* and *A Jihad for Love.* He coauthored *Music Supervision: The Complete Guide to Selecting Music for Movies, TV, Games, and New Media* (Schirmer).

Patrick Arn is president of Gotham Records and Gotham Music Placement.

Michelle Bayer, with Shelly Bay Music, does artist representation and pitching songs.

Drazen Bosnjak heads the team at Q Department. They call themselves "a thrill-seeking Original Music, Sound Design and Music Supervision initiative dedicated to stealth adaptation of technology and information to perform noteworthy missions through entertainment."

Carlton Bush Jr. has been in the filmmaking business since 1981. Two feature films for his company entered production in 2009.

Barry Cole founded SPOT music supervision and has been music supervisor on over seventy features, including *Sling Blade, Beauty Shop, American Psycho, Drumline,* and *Talk To Me.* He has been nominated for a Best Soundtrack Grammy for "Brown Sugar." He also manages Blue Mountain Music Publishing North America, founded by Chris Blackwell (Island Records founder), which is the publishing home for artists such as Bob Marley, Free, Third World, Justice, and The Plasticines.

Linda Lorence Critelli is vice president of writer/publisher relations at SESAC.

Dave DeMaio is a producer, director, editor, and videographer with Full Speed TV Productions. His projects have aired on ABC, NBC, CBS, Discovery, A&E, and many cable stations. He's also produced over twenty direct-to-DVD releases that sell around the world (sports/extreme sports).

Mike Ell, director of TV/film licensing at Song and Film, does music clearance and song placements.

Sean Fernald is a music supervisor with 3Mac Studios. He has fifteen years of major record label experience with MCA Records, Virgin Records, Capitol Records, and Sony Music, specializing in visual marketing, music video production, and promotion and music licensing for film.

Lyle Greenfield is founder and president of Bang Music, which celebrated its twentieth anniversary in 2009. He began his career as a copywriter and creative director at major ad agencies (JWT, Saatchi) and has been president of the National Board of the Association of Music Producers (AMP).

Randy Grimmett is senior vice president of domestic membership at ASCAP. He oversees all of ASCAP's domestic membership operations for film/TV, rhythm and soul, pop, and Latin music. He's worked at ASCAP since 1994 and is also a licensed attorney.

Keatly Haldeman is CEO for pigFACTORY, an international music publishing and licensing company.

Megan Haldeman is the copyright administrator for pigFACTORY, doing copyright management and royalty accounting.

Brent Kidwell, freelance music supervisor, has done music supervision on many series for MTV/VH1 including *Making the Band*, *Road Rules*, *Meet the Barkers*, *Celebrity Fit Club*, and *Driven*, on other network series including *E! True Hollywood Story*, Fox's *Love Cruise*, A&E's *The Two Coreys*, TLC's *Miami Ink*, Bravo's *Rachel Zoe Project*, and numerous others. He's also done music supervision for many films.

Patrick Klein is a musician and producer with Mighty Music.

Larry Mills is vice president of marketing and partnerships for Pump Audio, an online service for music licensing. He also started two independent record labels (one acquired by a major label), a management company, and a sports marketing company.

Grant Monrean, owner of Monrean Multimedia, is a videographer, editor, and producer. He is a 2000 LA Emmy Award Winner for Television News.

Alex Moulton is the founder and creative force behind Expansion Team, as well as being a musician, remixer, director, and media guru. He has supervised and scored music for hundreds of campaigns and brands, scored Rosario Dawson's film *Descent*, executive-produced a dozen releases for Expansion Team Records, and recently released his solo debut, *Exodus*.

Peggy O'Brien, Esq., is a licensing consultant with Sound Advisors, Inc., and does licensing and clearance for film, television, and theater, as well as talent representation.

Reginald Osborne is senior vice president and director of multicultural marketing at Arnold Worldwide, an international advertising agency.

Cord Pereira, Chairman and Executive Producer, BrandEntertain, handles branded entertainment media platform development.

Dave Pettigrew, senior vice president of Strategic Marketing and head of advertising and games at Warner/Chappell Music. He's been in the ad/games business for more than twelve years and has licensed music to almost every product and every game developer out there.

Ed Razzano is vice president of business development (North America) for Ricall, an online music licensing marketplace. He's the former senior director of BMG Music Publishing and has worked in the music end of TV and advertising for many years.

Robert Rosenblatt is a New York–based entertainment and media attorney, who represents TV producers, media companies, creative talent, and rights holders of music, music footage archives, and literary property in traditional and new media.

Steve Sechi composes and produces sample CDs for Big Fish Audio and production music for two music libraries that he co-owns. He also does freelance production.

Adam Swart is a music supervisor with 35Sound who has worked on films including *Tall, The Great Debaters, Let's Go to Prison, Dawn of the Dead, The Brothers Solomon, The Bronx Is Burning,* and *Flash of Genius.*

Peter M. Thall is an attorney who specializes in music law and is the author of *What They'll Never Tell You About the Music Business: The Myths, the Secrets, the Lies (and a Few Truths), Revised and Updated Edition* (Billboard Books).

Index

About the Authors

DARREN WILSEY is an award-winning composer, songwriter, and music producer. He has written and licensed songs and scores for numerous independent films, soundtracks, best-selling DVDs, and network and cable television, including *Third Watch* (NBC), *Ghost Whisperer* (CBS), *The Hills* (MTV), *Sex and the City* (HBO), *Dane Cook's Tourgasm* (HBO), *Punk'd* (MTV), *Queer As Folk* (Showtime), *Ice Wars* (CBS), *Beverly Hills 90210–The Complete First Season* (Paramount Entertainment), *Melrose Place–The Complete First Season* (Paramount Entertainment), and *Teeth* (2007 Sundance Film Festival).

Songs from Wilsey's music catalog have also appeared in TV commercials and have been licensed for use in various sporting and entertainment events and video games. Music from Wilsey's compilation series *X-treme Drama (Volumes 1 & 2)* has been extensively licensed by film and television production companies around the world.

Wilsey holds a B.M. from the Manhattan School of Music, studied piano and music composition at the Juilliard School of Music, and received an M.F.A. in music composition and technology from the University of California at Irvine. His website can be found at www.DarrenWilseyMusic.com.

DAYLLE DEANNA SCHWARTZ is a music-industry consultant, self-empowerment counselor, and successful author of many books, including *Start & Run Your Own Record Label* and *I Don't Need a Record Deal!* She lives in New York City.